D1784632

The Integration of Internet of Toys in Early Childhood Education

This book offers a fresh look at recent developments in policy, curricula and pedagogical discourse around children's play with Internet of Toys (IoToys). By expanding the notion of digital and smart play perspectives in early childhood education, the authors critique and develop the broader subject area of IoToys play to better serve its end users.

The book brings together research from across three different countries: Australia, Norway and England. It offers tangible examples of how one can use IoToys to build children's social skills, emotional intelligence, sense of achievement, collaboration and aspects of STEM and design play thinking processes. The learning stories of children's IoToys play will deliver a comprehensive review of how practitioners and parents can come together to build communities of practice for (re)enhancing children's learning and growth using evolving technology-based play and engage in paradigmatic debates. Readers as a result will better appreciate the growth in pragmatic applications of technologies together with theoretical perspectives.

The book will be a valuable resource for any academic or practitioner just beginning to understand the complexities and success stories of integrating IoToys for children's playful learning.

Sarika Kewalramani is a senior lecturer at Swinburne University of Technology, Department of Education, Australia. Sarika's research expertise resides in conceptualising kindergarten teachers' understanding of the nexus between inclusive STEM-based play and technology (IoToys/Robotics) integration practices in ways that promote "All" children's learning and development.

Ioanna Palaiologou is working in the School of Education (Psychology in Education) at University of Bristol, UK. Her research interests are in digital technologies (with an emphasis on haptic technologies) and implications for children's cognitive, social and emotional development and play and participatory methods and ethics in research with young children.

Maria Dardanou is an associate professor of pedagogy in early childhood teacher education at UiT The Arctic University of Norway. Her research interests are in digital technology in the early years, with a special focus on the use of IoToys and touchscreen technology in relation to pedagogical perspectives.

Evolving Families
Series Editor: Sivanes Phillipson

This series focuses on issues, challenges and empirical best practices surrounding evolving families that impact upon their survival, development and outcomes. The aim of this series is twofold: (1) to showcase the diversity of evolving families and the multiple factors that make up the function of families and their evolution across time, systems and cultures; (2) to build on preventative, interventionist, engagement and recovery methods for the promotion of healthy and successful evolving families across generations, social and political contexts and cultures.

Policification of Early Childhood Education and Care
Early Childhood Education in the 21st Century Volume III
Edited by Sivanes Phillipson and Susanne Garvis

Growing Children's Social and Emotional Skills
Using the TOGETHER Programme
Joanna Grace Phillips, Sivanes Phillipson and Gaye Tyler-Merrick

Parental Engagement and Early Childhood Education Around the World
*Edited by Susanne Garvis, Sivanes Phillipson,
Heidi Harju-Luukkainen and Alicja Renata Sadownik*

Identities, Practices and Education of Evolving Multicultural Families in Asia-Pacific
Edited by Jan Gube, Fang Gao and Miron Bhowmik

The Integration of Internet of Toys in Early Childhood Education
Research from Australia, England, and Norway
Sarika Kewalramani, Ioanna Palaiologou and Maria Dardanou

For more information about this series, please visit: https://www.routledge.com/Evolving-Families/book-series/EF

The Integration of Internet of Toys in Early Childhood Education

Research from Australia, England, and Norway

Sarika Kewalramani,
Ioanna Palaiologou and
Maria Dardanou

LONDON AND NEW YORK

First published 2023
by Routledge
4 Park Square, Milton Park, Abingdon, Oxon OX14 4RN

and by Routledge
605 Third Avenue, New York, NY 10158

Routledge is an imprint of the Taylor & Francis Group, an informa business

© 2023 Sarika Kewalramani, Ioanna Palaiologou and Maria Dardanou

The right of Sarika Kewalramani, Ioanna Palaiologou and Maria Dardanou to be identified as authors of this work has been asserted in accordance with sections 77 and 78 of the Copyright, Designs and Patents Act 1988.

All rights reserved. No part of this book may be reprinted or reproduced or utilised in any form or by any electronic, mechanical, or other means, now known or hereafter invented, including photocopying and recording, or in any information storage or retrieval system, without permission in writing from the publishers.

Trademark notice: Product or corporate names may be trademarks or registered trademarks, and are used only for identification and explanation without intent to infringe.

British Library Cataloguing-in-Publication Data
A catalogue record for this book is available from the British Library

Library of Congress Cataloging-in-Publication Data
Names: Kewalramani, Sarika, author. | Palaiologou, Ioanna, author. | Dardanou, Maria, author.
Title: The integration of Internet of Toys in early childhood education : research from Australia, England, and Norway / Sarika Kewalramani, Ioanna Palaiologou and Maria Dardanou.
Description: First Edition. | New York : Routledge, 2023. | Series: Evolving families | Includes bibliographical references and index.
Identifiers: LCCN 2022048578 (print) | LCCN 2022048579 (ebook) | ISBN 9781032029245 (Hardback) | ISBN 9781032029252 (Paperback) | ISBN 9781003185840 (eBook)
Subjects: LCSH: Early childhood education--Case studies. | Internet of things--Research. | Play--Technological innovations. | Internet and children. | Electronic toys. | Information technology--Social aspects.
Classification: LCC LB1139.23 .K49 2023 (print) | LCC LB1139.23 (ebook) | DDC 371.33/7--dc23/eng/20230113
LC record available at https://lccn.loc.gov/2022048578
LC ebook record available at https://lccn.loc.gov/2022048579

ISBN: 978-1-032-02924-5 (hbk)
ISBN: 978-1-032-02925-2 (pbk)
ISBN: 978-1-003-18584-0 (ebk)

DOI: 10.4324/9781003185840

Typeset in ITC Galliard Std
by KnowledgeWorks Global Ltd.

List of figures

1.1	Alpha Mini robot	8
1.2	Coji robot	8
1.3	Qobo the snail	8
1.4	LegoBoost Bot	8
1.5	Osmo Monster Mo	9
1.6	Osmo Coding Awbie	9
1.7	Dash – Coding Robot	9
1.8	Blue-Bot robot	10
1.9	Botley the Coding Robot Activity Set	10
1.10	COSMO	10
1.11	TTS wireless Digiscope	10
1.12	Beast of Balance	11
1.13	Vai Kai	11
1.14	Robot Mouse	11
1.15	Spin Master Code-A-Pillar	11
1.16	Learning Resources Zoomy Handheld Digital Microscope	12
4.1	Conceptual framework for children's STREAM literacy development	56
4.2	Teacher's explicit scaffolding and modelling how Sphero changes colours	65
4.3	Children constructing palace obstacle course during Sphero play	66
4.4	Children taking turns to code Sphero to enter into the palace	67
4.5	Children's numeracy skills development using visual cards during coding Botley	68
4.6	Children play with Qobo's QR operational visual cards	71
5.1	The creative learning spiral	80
5.2	Andrew programming Blue-bot	88
5.3	Testing the Bluetooth	89
5.4	Blue-bot on iPad	90
5.5	Monster Mo	91
5.6	Sivert takes photo of Markus	92
5.7	Photo of Markus' drawing of the table during Monster Mo play	92

6.1	The interplay of social-emotional development and robotic technology	104
6.2	Milan feeding Sam, the cat with some fish to make the cat feel happy	109
6.3	Milan's inventory with shapes and real-world objects as visuals	110
6.4	Argus codes Coji to display a surprised face	111
6.5	Argus codes Coji to have an angry face during imaginative destruction play with Iron Man toy	112
7.1	Harry pretends he is a soldier	131
7.2	Harry pretends he has died	131
7.3	Children collaborating in Osmo Monster play	132
7.4	Myra as a digital tactician while coding of spy bot	137
7.5	Riya-Niya's coding with AI robot, Alpha Mini	139
7.6	Children as digital explorers	140

Contents

List of figures   vii
List of tables   ix
List of abbreviations   x
Series Editor Note   xi
Acknowledgements   xii
Foreword   xiii
Preface   xvi

1 Introduction: Setting the scene: *"New" toys – "new"*
   learningscapes?   1

2 Curricula landscapes for (re)culturing children's
   learning in the 21st century   22

3 Technological landscapes at home, but do they
   really play? A case study from English homes   37

4 Is there a space for "A" and "R" in early childhood
   STEM education? Building a case for AI robotic
   technologies integration in Australia   51

5 The technological landscapes with IoToys in early
   childhood education in Norway   78

6 IoToys and social-emotional literacies   98

7 Children's agency: Mentally linked and digitally
   connected, but are they heard?   125

8 Conclusions: The changing playscapes of early
   childhood education   147

   Index   152

List of tables

1.1	IoToys used in the research	8
2.1	Components of analyses and proposed questions used for the analysis	26
3.1	Overview of the participants and IoToys used in the households	39
3.2	Examples of play styles and descriptions	42
3.3	Characteristics associated with play when children engage with IoToys	43
4.1	STREAM-based play observational protocol and pedagogical steps for robotic integration	58
5.1	Overview of periods, participants, IoToys integrated and data	86
6.1	All-inclusive teaching and learning framework to integrate IoToys/robots in children's play	106
7.1	Overview of children's data reported in this chapter from Australia, Norway and England	128

List of abbreviations

AI	Artificial Intelligence
ECE	Early Childhood Education
ECEC	Early Childhood Education and Care
EYFS	Early Years Foundation Stage
EYLF	Early Years Learning Framework
IoT	Internet of Things
IoToys	Internet of Toys
NESH	The National Committee for Research Ethics in the Social Sciences and the Humanities
OECD	Organisation for Economic Co-operation and Development
STEM	Science, Technology, Engineering and Mathematics
STEAM	Science, Technology, Engineering Arts and Mathematics
STREAM	Science, Technology, Robotics, Engineering, AI and Mathematics
UNICEF	United Nations International Children's Emergency Fund
EECERA	European Early Childhood Education Research Association

Series Editor Note

I am delighted to have this book added to the Evolving Families Series. This series, to date, has published a range of quality publications that showcase diverse and global families and their narratives that speak to the aim of this series. The collection in this series has a focus on curricula design, pedagogical development and legislative and socio-political paradigm shifts that have enriched knowledge in the field and inspired further thinking and research on evolving families of the past, present and future.

The Integration of Internet of Toys in Early Childhood Education takes this series one step further by situating families and their role in early childhood education and children's play with Internet of Toys (IoToys). I am particularly intrigued by the notion of IoToys as a platform for both childhood play and learning that speaks of the rising zeitgeist for early childhood education. The critical stance that the authors, Kewalramani, Palaiologou and Dardanou, have taken throughout this book incites readers to engage in thoughtful reading of their research work and learning stories across three countries that have successful early childhood education. The comparative nature of this book invites readers to come to their own practical conclusions on the submissions made by the authors and how these conclusions align to their own contexts.

If you are a parent or a teacher who has embraced technology as part and parcel of your lives, you will find this book useful in diversifying children's play with IoToys. For those who are yet to see the usefulness of technology in children's learning, I implore you to read this book to be convinced of the pragmatic application of IoToys in children's development and learning.

Enjoy the book!

Sivanes Phillipson

Acknowledgements

This book could have not been completed without the help of the children, their families, teachers and early childhood education settings that participated in our research projects in the three countries of Australia, England and Norway.

Our sincere gratitude goes to those who participated in this study despite the COVID-19 pandemic where we reverted to online modes of data collection: the preschools, educators, parents, children and esteemed colleagues – Dr. Gerarda Richards, Blake Cutler, Caroline Robinson and Andrea Ng who were the research assistants for the Australian data collection. We thank you, and we are grateful for being so cooperative in this research. We also wish to express our gratitude to Mr. Karthik Kameswaran, the Director of STEM Incubators, a not-for-profit organisation, in supporting the Australian data collection from families and home-based settings during the COVID-19 2020–2021 lockdown periods. The children and parents have been pivotal in allowing this research to continue despite the pandemic.

We would also like to thank the European Early Childhood Education Research Association (EECERA) and in particular Dr. Lorna Arnott, one of the co-convenors of the SIG "Digital Childhoods," as she has been influential to the birth of this book. We also acknowledge our heartfelt thanks to Professor John Siraj Blatch-ford for his critical feedback on the early conceptions of this book's introduction chapter and suggestions on incorporating forms of play, particularly pedagogical understanding of free-flow play and digital play affordances.

Last, but not least, we would like to thank our families for their support, encouragement, patience and understanding when this book was being developed.

Foreword

The problem with technologies in early childhood education and care (ECEC) is that not everyone agrees they are suitable, relevant or useful for young children, their learning and development. This problem is in contrast to the near universal acceptance in ECEC of children's play as a basis for or even a context in which young children explore their worlds, make meaning and build social connections with others as a mode of cultural participation (Johnson et al., 2019). In ECEC, the inherent tensions between technologies and play have been manifested for many years and explored by some scholars in terms of technologies as tools for play (Johnston, 2019), technologies as pedagogically distinct from play (Edwards, 2013), technologies as explorable via play (Fleer, 2016) and within notions of digital play – an attempt to integrate the technological with children's play as a mode of learning (Sakr, 2019). All of these contributions have proved valuable, providing philosophical and theoretical mechanisms for thinking about and understanding how and why very young children engage with technologies and what such engagements signify for children as learners and educators as teachers for young children in ECEC settings. As such discussions have unfolded, digitalisation, in which the practices comprising society have become increasingly networked with the technological and social, has continued to unfold (Feenberg, 2017), with young children today born into a largely digital world. A caveat for such a claim is, however, always necessary, as digitalisation, like many a social practice, is unevenly experienced and accessed by children, with those growing up in the Global South, or those experiencing social, economic or cultural vulnerabilities not always as enabled in their access to technologies as others (Livingstone & Bulger, 2014).

Digitalisation presumes access to information, communication and content. However, such access does not contain an assumed universal value, as access implies children are located within the network of digital activity in which information, communication and content are distributed. Therefore, there are both benefits and limitations to digitalisation for young children, including enhanced opportunities for learning through, about and with digital content and engaging with others (Lewis Ellison, & Solomon, 2018), and justifiable concerns regarding young children's online safety, datafication and learning and developmental trajectories relative to the digital (Sprung, Froschl,

& Gropper, 2020). As the authors of the book rightly point out, these benefits and limitations incur a chorus of research and discussion concerning the pros and cons of technology use by young children. However, their adroit reframing of the pros and cons debate suggests that the solution per se to any perceived issues concerning technology use by young children lies within the problem itself. Namely, instead of trying to separate children from technologies, and technologies from children and their play, all aspects may be viewed as the one and the same dynamic interaction. Thus, as children engage with technologies, especially toys connected with the internet (Internet of Toys (IoToys)) (Holloway & Green, 2016), understanding how children are situated within a technological network means that attention can be directed towards determining what communication, sociality, problem-solving and creativity look like within the nexus of the child and the digital, and the expression of this nexus in the many multimodal forms of communication bringing the human into relationship with the technological enables.

The IoToys provide an analytical focus of activity in this book, directed towards highlighting how multimodality is essentially activated between children and the digital as they play, explore, experience and interact with technologies – either at home or within their ECEC settings. Conducted across several countries, including Australia, England and Norway, this book provides timely insight into how young children touch technologies, hear with and through technologies, see and engage with the digital and experience movement and gesture via the technological. Opportunities for developing these multimodal interactions with technologies as a process of cultural meaning making and participation are increasingly necessary, but not always pedagogically interpreted in ECEC (Mertala, 2019). The authors are sensitive to the range of issues compromising the interpretation of multimodality for children's learning in these situations. They note that educators require access to professional learning opportunities concerning the digital; that there remains an unequal distribution of digital resources and available technologies in ECEC settings for children and educators alike; and that increased attention should be directed towards helping educators understand how and why to assess for young children's digital learning. Establishing the multimodality via the IoToys in relation to ECEC pedagogy means that the authors of this book are able to propose that educators and policymakers consider the landscape of learning experienced by children at home and in their ECEC services. Landscapes encompass various degrees of digitality, defined and shaped by technological access and understandings of what young children require in terms of digital capacities, capabilities and competencies to live within a largely digitalised world. Readers of this book will enjoy an engaging journey, learning more about the IoToys and being offered a pathway to traverse in their own thinking about young children, technologies and ECEC.

Professor Suzy Edwards
Australian Catholic University, Australia.

References

Edwards, S. (2013). Digital play in the early years: A contextual response to the problem of integrating technologies and play-based pedagogies in the early childhood curriculum. *European Early Childhood Education Research Journal, 21*(2), 199–212.

Feenberg, A. (2017) *Technosystem*. Cambridge, MA: Harvard University Press.

Fleer, M. (2016). Theorising digital play: A cultural-historical conceptualisation of children's engagement in imaginary digital situations. *International Research in Early Childhood Education, 7*(2), 75–90.

Holloway, D., & Green, L. (2016) The internet of toys. *Communication Research and Practice, 2*(4): 506–519. DOI: 10.1080/22041451.2016.1266124.

Johnson, J. E., Sevimli-Celik, S., Al-Mansour, M. A., Tunçdemir, T. B. A., & Dong, P. I. (2019). Play in early childhood education. In O. N. Saracho (Ed.), *Handbook of research on the education of young children* (pp. 165–175). London: Routledge.

Johnston, K. (2019). Digital technology as a tool to support children and educators as co-learners. *Global Studies of Childhood, 9*(4), 306–317.

Lewis Ellison, T., & Solomon, M. (2018). Digital play as purposeful productive literacies in African American boys. *The Reading Teacher, 71*(4), 495–500.

Livingstone, S., & Bulger, M. (2014) A global research agenda for children's rights in the digital age. *Journal of Children and Media, 8*(4), 317–335. DOI: 10.1080/17482798.2014.961496.

Mertala, P. (2019). Teachers' beliefs about technology integration in early childhood education: A meta-ethnographical synthesis of qualitative research. *Computers in Human Behavior, 101*, 334–349.

Sakr, M. (2019). *Digital play in early childhood: What's the problem?* London: Sage.

Sprung, B., Froschl, M., & Gropper, N. (2020) *Cybersafe young children: Teaching internet safety and responsibility, K-3*. New York, NY: Teachers College Press.

Preface

Children playing with digital technologies, such as the Internet of Toys (IoToys), iPad apps and tech toys, have become an important concern for early childhood education researchers and practitioners (Danby et al., 2018; Stephen & Edwards, 2018). Teaching children ethical and safe use of technologies, including artificial intelligence (AI) tech toys, should become an area of scrutiny for educational policy, curriculum and practice. As will be shown in this book, research has offered examples of effectively integrating technology in early childhood education, but these attempts are still sporadic and there often remains resistance to the adoption of digital play practices. However, a quick look at international comparisons of educational accomplishment reveals that, with few exceptions, top-performing jurisdictions such as in the Scandinavian contexts have introduced digital play and education in early childhood.

Teaching and learning age-appropriate and educationally sound pedagogical practices for the integration of technologies in early childhood settings is not easy for policymakers, curriculum designers, educational leaders, teachers or learners. It requires intensive research and developing grounded knowledge of pedagogical and technological knowledge creation, as well as development of teachers' abilities and autonomy. Although previous research (e.g. Arnott, Palaiologou, & Gray, 2019; Mascheroni & Holloway, 2019) describes the pros and cons related to the integration of technology in early childhood education and the subsequent influences on children's cognitive learning and affective engagement with their everyday world, early childhood teachers need more guidance in relation to what high-quality pedagogies with technologies may look like. This guidance needs to align closely with the founding principles of early childhood education – linked to play and child centredness – to ensure technologies such as IoToys, robotic toys and the like become complementary resources, rather than competing artefacts which, some consider, may threaten early childhood ways of *being, becoming and belonging*.

Sarika Kewalramani, Ioanna Palaiologou
and Maria Dardanou

References

Arnott, L., Palaiologou, I., & Gray, C. (2019). Internet of Toys across home and early childhood education: Understanding the ecology of the child's social world. *Technology, Pedagogy and Education, 28*(4). DOI:10.1080/14759 39X.2019.1656667.

Danby, S., Fleer, M., Davidson, C., & Hatzigianni, M. (2018). *Digital childhood. Technologies and children's everyday lives.* Amsterdam: Springer.

Mascheroni, G., & Holloway, D. (2019). Introducing the Internet of Toys. In G. Mascheroni & D. Holloway (Eds.), *The Internet of Toys: Practices, affordances and political economy of children's smart toys* (pp. 1–22). Cham: Palgrave MacMillan.

Stephen, C., & Edwards, S. (2018). *Young children playing and learning in a digital age: A cultural and critical perspective.* London: Routledge.

1 Introduction

Setting the scene:
"New" toys – "new" learningscapes?

Introduction

The emerging types of information technologies, video games, technology toys and gadgets inevitably being introduced into the lives of children are becoming a part of their daily contexts (Stephen & Edwards, 2018; Mascheroni & Holloway, 2019). Due to this, the child's play activity has become different and its role as a leading activity in early childhood education (ECE) has acquired new features. Yes, these changing natures of children's play both in and home contexts are much less studied than the traditional types of children's games (rule play, role-play, dramatic play, etc.). Thus, in this book we intend, through our research findings, to further understanding about the role of technologies in children's lives, focusing on the Internet of Toys (IoToys).

This introductory chapter sets the scene relating to the terminology to be used throughout the book and provides an overview for understanding multimodality, identifying where we were and where are we now. We present on how we (re)define IoToys and multimodality and the role it plays to afford polymodes (tactile, visual, virtual and physical) of playful learning. By looking at the role of hybrid learning spaces, such as makerspace learning, we consider play with IoToys fits in well with such fast-paced technology use in the ecology of children's everyday play spaces. We position the redefined role of IoToys as a polypronged and transfunctional to use them as a pedagogical tool in ECE. In doing so, the chapter also explores the characteristics of IoToys and the programmable functions that were integrated and piloted in our research studies in age-appropriate ways, ensuring safe and ethical use.

The *"new"* era of playful learning:
The case for multimodality

In previous times discussions on the digital lives of children, especially in the inter-multi-disciplinary field of ECE, have been a reaction to the deficits on both an empirical and theoretical level (e.g. Edwards et al. 2016; Marsh et al., 2016). The dominant discourse in ECE promotes the view of child's and teacher/practitioner's agency, differentiating the notion of play as child-centred-initiated

DOI: 10.4324/9781003185840-1

pedagogy and children's engagement of digital interactions (Edwards & Bird, 2017). Similarly, empirical research is divided debating the dominant question whether we need "new concepts of play" (Edwards, 2015) or reconceptualising playful encounters of children, with some proposing "new types of digital play" (Marsh et al., 2016). Other research investigated teachers' agency – their beliefs, capabilities and capacity – to conceptualise how digital devices can be integrated in play-based pedagogy, exploring the dispositions which cause teachers to see the use of digital devices as static and controlling and not part of children's playful encounters (Nikolopoulou & Gialamas, 2015; Aldhafeeri, Palaiologou, & Folorunsho, 2016; Palaiologou, 2016a, 2016b).

Research is now emerging, however, which examines how and why children use digital devices and how the nature of these interactions/encounters counts as play (Arnott, 2016; Huh, 2017; Lawrence, 2018; Palaiologou, Kewalramani, & Dardanou, 2021). These debates have transcended what constitutes playful learning and to what extent technology can facilitate this.

Discussions have been also taken place on the landscapes in which young children's learning takes place. It has been argued that when learning or inter-acting goes beyond one mode (e.g. printed text), it becomes multimodal. Yelland (2018) defines multimodal learning as the application of more than one mode for learning that offers rich learning experiences for young children. For example, multimodalities can include linguistic (text-based), visual, haptic (digital touch), aural and spatial movement (both physical and digital). Children make sense of their real world and everyday phenomena available in their natural environments through such multimodal ways. Further, when children use technology for play, they make sense of their natural learning environments by blending the real world and their imagination via digital experiences (Arnott et al., 2020; Arnott & Yelland, 2020). As technologies continue to evolve and emerge, multimodal ways of learning, when used together with two- and three-dimensional (2D and 3D) materials, can provide children with multiple forms for meaning making. As such, the child's meaning making of the phenomena at hand is facilitated because of the multimodal ways of interactions afforded by the technology being played with. For example, a robot's codable characteristics, such as prompting (e.g. talking [speech and language], movement and digital touch), provide an interesting stimulant for children to engage in multimodal playscapes (Palaiologou, Kewalramani, & Dardanou, 2021) and inquiry (Kewalramani, Kidman, & Palaiologou, 2021). Such research has shown that children's curiosity motivates them to learn how to code the robot to perform a set of actions, which can then aid in meaning making when children are engaged in inquiring about a particular phenomenon under investigation with their peers and adults.

When educators provide children with the opportunity to manipulate digital objects and experience their textures, this can often demonstrate implicit knowledge which they may not be able to yet verbalise (Flewitt, Messer, & Kucirkova, 2015). Multimodal research on haptic modes and design has opened new ways to consider how touch operates in, for example, interactive cardboard books as well as on digital touchscreens (Neumann & Neumann, 2013; Rowsell, 2013).

By stroking furry, rough or smooth textures in baby board books, children figure out what it means to coordinate gazing at visuals, physically touch the textures and learn to associate speech to the feeling of touch and language with various textures. As a bonus, or an add-on, to that learning experience that can go beyond the print version of texture books, however, children not only get to feel (the haptic experience) but also see that by tapping on touchscreens and monitor user actions to regulate the pressure used, e.g. to determine the thickness of a brush stroke in paint programs, or to adjust the speed and duration or abruptness of contact that discriminates between a drag and a swipe, an exploratory hover and a confirming tap (Rowe, Miller, & Pacheco, 2014).

More recently, studies have picked up on researching multimodal learning as a methodological approach employing interaction analysis as an approach that enables an illumination of the diverse array of communicative, social and material resources that children can draw upon (Wilmes & Siry, 2021). While engaging with technological play, for example, multimodal interactions begin with children's embodied engagement with the imaginary play situation created by the robotic toy, which is the central character in children's role-play (Kewalramani et al., 2020). The embodied engagement gets coupled with children's and the adults' (e.g. teachers) written and spoken engagement that can provide exemplars of children's understandings of the real-world phenomenon being imagined or role-played with their peers. Using examples of children's understandings of science phenomena, Wilmes and Siry (2021) demonstrated explicitly the multimodal interactions between the spoken, gesture, body language and written (drawings) aspects of children's engagement in science learning practices. Furthering the concept of multimodal interactions and related learning, Wu, Kim, and Markauskaite's (2020) study showed how game-based apps provided a multiplier effect platform for children's engagement with the social-emotional aspects of learning.

Such studies demonstrate there is a need for a shift in the discourse analysis of multimodal learning and the ways technology can expand the arena for children's play-based learning. While we know that there is an emerging concern that modern technology-saturated environments, particularly digital games and apps, are inhibiting the development of children's empathic behaviour and social skills, this book highlights that the solution is embedded in the problem. When educators and parents design and integrate hybrid learning opportunities for children right from their early years, we can provide multimodal learning that blends real-life social interpersonal interactions with digital representations (Wu, Kim, & Markauskaite, 2020). Research has shown us, for example, that when children use social robotic toys they have opportunities to perceive empathy-worthy cues in various scenes to further their perspective-taking and to associate emotions with social contexts (Ge et al., 2010; Huijnen et al., 2016; Huijnen, Lexis, & de Witte, 2017). The robot creates an environment that capitalises on multimodal learning opportunities by utilising the strengths of a *hybrid design* within which children's embodied literacies become visible and interactive. The robot's human-like features and digitally operated characteristics provide a flexible medium for activating children's vocalisation of imagined ideas, thus increasing children's opportunities to grow their repertoire of play-based learning, which becomes multimodal and goes beyond the text and/or spoken words, from 2D to 4D learning practices in ECE. As will be argued in this book, based on the findings of our research, as technologies rapidly develop, there is a need, however, to (re)examine the multimodal playscapes of learning. It is important to provide definitions of the terms that will be used throughout the book prior to any discussions about the context of this research and its aims.

Setting the scene

Definitions

In this book, we use the term "digital technologies" as "a collective term for all equipment that contains a computer or microcontroller and to which adults and children might have access, a list which now includes toys, games consoles, digital cameras, media players and smartphones as well as handheld, laptop or desktop computers" (Palaiologou, 2016a, p. 1). The most common devices are as follows:

- Touch screens
- (Smart)phones;
- Game consoles;
- Digital cameras;
- Media players;
- Netbooks;
- In-car *sat-nav*;
- Handheld computers.

Recently, advancements in technology have seen the increase of haptic technology as part of digital technologies. "Haptic technology" is used to refer to the experience of touch by applying force, vibrations or motions by the user (Biswas & Visell, 2019). These technologies can be used to create virtual objects in a computer simulation and to control virtual objects. For example, through haptic technology (digital touch) digital games can be controlled in a virtual environment. Part of this type of technology are artificial intelligence (AI), the Internet of Things (IoT) and IoToys which is the focus of this book.

Although AI is not a new technology, it is a rapidly developing and gaining popularity in daily life. AI has the ability to operate tasks that normally require human intelligence, such as thinking and acting (e.g. spam filters on emails, the Google search, manufacturing robots or smart assistants such as Siri or Alexa). AI has now been used in toys for young children (e.g. robots). Moreover, the rise of the interface paradigm has introduced in the market the robotic user interface (RUI). RUIs are advanced AI toys where, in contrast to other technological toys (remote-controlled toys), "the interface [is not] to a robot which then executes a certain action, but the robot being the interface to another system" (Bartneck & Okada, 2001, p. 131). "Such toys either look like tools or animals or are anthropomorphic, enabling the child user the opportunity to programme the interface to create interactive projects" (Kewalramani, Kidman, & Palaiologou, 2021, p. 652). These robots can perform tasks such as face/voice recognition, talk back or be coded by the user to achieve certain tasks. Their physical appearance and the interactions that now can be achieved make them attractive to the children (Kewalramani et al., 2021).

For example, in an earlier study, Anzalone et al. (2015) found that the humanoid robot Nao can generate empathy because its shape is cute, resembles a child and is easy to anthropomorphise. Educational experiments with the Nao robot showed that the robot's artificially intelligent behaviours (ability to talk, smile and move) and children's interactions with such *robotic beings* can produce a dramatic and emotive paradigm, which can help improve children's empathic performances. The mere closeness between the robotic beings and the children, together with the other adults in the learning environment, is an emerging area of scrutiny for researchers studying digital childhoods (Danby et al., 2018; Arnott, Palaiologou, & Gray, 2019; Arnott et al., 2020; Kewalramani, Kidman, & Palaiologou, 2021; Palaiologou, Kewalramani, & Dardanou, 2021).

Part of the AI family are the IoT and the IoToys. The term IoT is referring to physical devices that are digitally enabled and allow the collection and manipulation of data (Kopetz, 2011). IoT comperes with touch screen technology and offers opportunities "in which digital and physical entities can be linked, by means of appropriate information and communication technologies, to enable a whole new class of applications and services" (Miorandi et al., 2012, p. 1497; Ling et al., 2021). The IoT is now widely used and linked to smartphone apps that remotely can, for example, control home-based objects from distant locations, as well as wearable technology measuring owners' sleep patterns, heart rate and exercise regimes (Sung, Chang, & Liu, 2016).

As this technology is advancing, it is also entering the world of children's toys, by introducing the IoToys. These toys are internet connected and build on technological successes of IoT. They operate with apps and also need Bluetooth or Wi-Fi connections. Such toys include Hello Barbie and Smart Toy Bear, which use voice and/or image recognition, connecting to the internet to analyse, process and respond to children's conversations and images. Other examples are app-enabled toys such as drones, toy cars and robots (Star Wars, BB-8 Droid); toys-to-life, which connects action figures to video games (Skylanders, Amiibo); puzzle and building games (Osmo, Lego Fusion); and children's technology wearables such as smart watches and fitness trackers. IoToys are designed with intended pre-programmed functions and typically are either anthropomorphised characters, such as robots, or imaginary animals. In our research, we argued that "whilst with the touchscreen technological toys the children have less control over the device, these haptic IoToys devices offer opportunities for programming the interface to create interactive projects and actions" (Palaiologou, Kewalramani, & Dardanou, 2021, p. 2101). Research with the integrations of

IoToys in young children's lives is still emerging, and more explorations are needed in this area, making us determined to make sure this book will offer insights of how this technology can be used.

As IoToys are increasing in popularity, research is emerging and examining on how they can be used in learning. Learning with robotics toys (referred to as r-learning in recent literature; see Bers et al., 2014; Sullivan & Bers, 2016; Lahiri, 2020) is now a *new generation* of technological artefact that needs scrutiny. For example, how young children engage with these or what skills are used to code them, the types of computer programming languages needed and can be developed are still unresearched in ECE (Bers et al., 2014; Relkin et al., 2020; Ling et al., 2021; Palaiologou, Kewalramani, & Dardanou, 2021).

In this technological era, research is now beginning to show that children's digital competence goes beyond mere mastery or control of digital tools and tinkering. It is about children learning to be creative in combining digital and traditional activities and tools (Ilomäki et al., 2016). Digital competence includes children's ability to apply technologies in meaningful ways and as appropriate tools for creativity and inquiry. Learning the basics with IoToys (e.g. robotic toys) at an early age fosters positive learning experiences and boosts children's motivation and creative imaginative abilities to grasp abstract concepts (Arnott, Palaiologou, & Gray, 2019; Fleer, 2019; Arnott et al., 2020; Palaiologou, Kewalramani, & Dardanou, 2021). However, not all children enjoy easy access to high-speed internet technology at home as there is an apparent digital divide that cuts through along the lines of socioeconomic class, gender and race (Folorunsho & Palaiologou, 2019), with this divide becomingmore apparent during the pandemic. Hence, it becomes crucial for ECE settings to be used as *hubs of techno-learning* when it comes to children's play *with* IoToys and be given equal opportunities to become digitally literate citizens.

Our research

This book is based on our research on how IoToys are integrated in children's lives in our three countries: Australia, England and Norway. The research was based on our previous research on touch screen technology (e.g. Palaiologou, 2016a, 2016b, 2017) and aimed to examine how IoToys are used by children and to what extent and how children use them at home and in ECE settings. Some of this research has been reported previously (Arnott, Palaiologou, & Gray, 2019; Kewalramani et al., 2020; Kewalramani, Kidman, & Palaiologou, 2021; Palaiologou, Kewalramani, & Dardanou, 2021); so in this book we aim to discuss the data collectively and reflect back in order to examine:

- How children use IoToys at home and the patterns of behaviours they engage with when they are using them and whether these constitute play (Chapter 3);
- How IoToys can be used within ECE settings to promote learning (Chapters 4 and 5);

- How IoToys can support children's social and emotional literacies (Chapter 6);
- How children's agency is enacted when they use IoToys (Chapter 7).

Central to this research was to gain an understanding of the role of new technologies, such as the IoToys in children's lives. Understanding how play *looks like, feels like and tastes like* will allow us to effectively integrate them in children's playful learning environments.

This project is not a cross-cultural examination or comparison on how IoToys are used in children's lives at home or ECE. Neither was it in our intention to unify our research in such a way. On the contrary we intended to collect data through diverse methods in each country to offer us rich data. Thus, we did not have a unified methodology as will be seen in each chapter where the methods, participants and analytical lenses employed in each country will be discussed. The approach of examining examples of effective integration in three different ECE systems which have cultural, pedagogical and curricula ideological differences will allow us to move beyond the moral panic often exhibited around the understanding of use of technologies in ECE, particularly IoToys.

Ethical dilemmas around data protection, safety and consumerism of technologies by children, both in formal ECE and informal home-based learning settings, will be covered. Based on our theoretical conceptualisation of our previous research, we (re)define IoToys and the different types of emerging classes and sub-classes of IoToys we establish through the research reported in this book.

The IoToys used in the research will be explained in each chapter, but collectively Table 1.1 is listing all the ones that were used in all three countries and offers a brief explanation of each one.

The main methods used in this project were observations, videos and photographs. As will be shown, the timelines of the project differ in each country. For example, the research in Australia was disturbed by the Covid pandemic, with data collection being carried out remotely via Zoom calls. In England and Norway, however, data was suspended because of the continuing lockdowns.

Theoretical conceptualisation: *Beyond multimodal learningscapes: The case for transplay learningscapes*

As discussed above, within the research examining technologies, there is a consensus that digital devices can "support" or "sustain" children's play to build on the playful learning (e.g. Aladé et al., 2016; Huber et al., 2016). However, there are still voices that caution about the balance in children's play between digital and non-digital activities as damaging for children's self-worth and social and emotional growth (AVG, 2015; Kabali et al., 2015; Nathanson, 2015; Radesky et al., 2015). These voices became stronger during the pandemic as we all relied in the digitalisation of the 21st century to "continue" with our disturbed lives and to connect with our loved ones that physically we could not do anymore

Table 1.1 IoToys used in the research

Name	Description
 *Figure 1.1* Alpha Mini robot	A wireless AI robot (with voice and face recognition) that can be coded via an app to perform a variety of actions. For example, it can demonstrate and model play activities such as meditation, mindfulness activities and exercises such as Taichi. It can also demonstrate emotions.
 *Figure 1.2* Coji robot	Coji is controlled wirelessly via an iPad that children can program to move using emoji language and physical actions.
 *Figure 1.3* Qobo the snail	Qobo uses puzzle cards with different meanings that are recognised by a reader when placed under the Qobo robot. These cards allow the robot to move, sing, interact and talk.
 *Figure 1.4* LegoBoost Bot	The LegoBoost Bot introduces basic coding skills to younger children. The robot can create and animate different LEGO constructions, for example a cat or a car that can be coded to move, talk, sing, dance and perform certain tasks.

(Continued)

Table 1.1 IoToys used in the research *(Continued)*

Name	Description
 *Figure 1.5* Osmo Monster Mo	With Osmo Monster children's drawings become part of magical animated activities.
 *Figure 1.6* Osmo Coding Awbie	Uses hands-on physical blocks to control Awbie, a playful character who loves delicious strawberries. Each block is a coding command that directs Awbie on a fun-filled adventure enabling coding and problem-solving.
 *Figure 1.7* Dash – Coding Robot	Kids can give Dash Robot voice commands and explore loops, events, conditions and sequences with the five free apps that come with Dash Robot. The function of the toy not only supports children to learn how to code but also controls the toy to explore their creativity and problem-solving skills and encourage language interactions.

(Continued)

Table 1.1 IoToys used in the research *(Continued)*

Name	Description
	**Educational robot Blue-Bot** is a small mobile robot that can be programmed with a tablet or a computer. Data is transmitted via Bluetooth, to a programming strip or to the Blue-Bot application.

Figure 1.8 Blue-Bot robot

Figure 1.9 Botley the Coding Robot Activity Set

Botley is a colourful robot and remote control combo that teaches kids beginner code. Children can program their Botley coding robot by entering a code on the remote and then ask Botley to "run the code." Kids will learn the basic concepts of coding like algorithms, loops and debugging while playing with Botley.

Figure 1.10 COSMO

This is a wireless robot. It includes a robot and cubic that can be programmed and moved around. It is controlled by a tablet-based app. However, it also can be controlled by touch or voice recognition.

Figure 1.11 TTS wireless Digiscope

A wireless microscope that can be used on its own indoors or outdoors.

(Continued)

Table 1.1 IoToys used in the research *(Continued)*

Name	Description
 *Figure 1.12* Beast of Balance	A construction internet-connected toy. Pieces are provided, and children can construct "beasts" by looking at the app. It includes pieces where children can use to construct.
 *Figure 1.13* Vai Kai	It includes wooden figures that can be connected in an app with a tablet. The figures can be used as children decide to.
 *Figure 1.14* Robot Mouse	Children can code in order to move the mouse around the hurdles of the game.
 *Figure 1.15* Spin Master Code-A-Pillar	Introduces basic coding skills to younger children. Children can construct the caterpillar and move it any way they like.

(Continued)

Table 1.1 IoToys used in the research *(Continued)*

Name	Description
	A digital microscope where children can use indoors or outdoors for observations.

Figure 1.16 Learning Resources Zoomy
Handheld Digital Microscope

because of the lockdowns. We show cases where technology was used for children to "meet" with relatives and friends where physical social spaces were replaced with virtual ones. This causes alarm to some who perceived direct physical interaction, especially direct contact play, as essential to children's development.

Education at all levels relied on technology during this time, however, and played a central role. We argue that it has now become part of our lives as, for example, electricity was in the previous century. Furthermore, it is now accepted that when children are using digital devices they can be supportive of play (Edwards & Bird, 2017). The types of play in this respect are described as creative (Kurcikova, 2017), exploratory, pretend and active (especially with tangible technology as, for example, in the work of Chung, Vanderbilt, & Soares, 2015; Marsh et al., 2016; Sullivan & Bers, 2016; Palaiologou, Kewalramani, & Dardanou, 2021). Thus, differences have been identified between children's play with technology in relation to how it supports children's play (Marsh et al., 2015; Zaman et al., 2016).

The published work on children's use of digital technology mainly happened at home or at school, but research has started examining the types of play in other areas such as libraries (Campbell et al., 2015) or churches (as in the work of Guynn, 2016).

Moreover, examining the existing literature on children's interaction with digital devices under the age of five years, we identified that the children under three (infants/toddlers) have been overlooked and there is relatively little research that examines their interactions in depth, despite the evidence that they are using digital technologies (e.g. Myers et al., 2016; O'Connor & Fotakopoulou, 2016; Palaiologou, 2016a). Most published research works tend to examine types of uses and parental concerns, rather than how infants or toddlers are using digital devices. It was found that there are attempts to classify the children's digital interactions under a form of play, but the majority of the studies agreed that digital devices are used in a social context, either with other family members or peers (siblings and friends) (e.g. Marsh et al., 2015; Plowman, 2015), and focused on how technology can impact on children's social-emotional development (i.e. Coiro 2015; Edwards, 2016; Suskind et al., 2016; Danby et al., 2017a, 2017b). Hesitations about the physicality of the digital devices and children's agency have also been raised, but these are focusing mainly on touch screen technology and pay little account to the tangible technologies of IoToys.

Although research now recognises that when children engage with digital devices, there is evidence of characteristics of playful patterns and children exhibiting different types of play, the digital activities of children are mostly treated and analysed on how adults can support (scaffold) children's interactions with technology (e.g. Parish-Morris et al., 2015; Nikolayev, 2016). Studies have also started looking early childhood (EC) ideology of play (e.g. Edwards et al., 2015; Nuttall et al., 2015) and suggest that the dominant ideology in the field comes from a view of play that is engrossed in children's engagements with "real world" object and "hands on experiences," with this reinforcing the binary views of digital play versus play. Such views have limited attempts to conceptualise the use of technologies in ECE to see what constitutes playful learning with technologies. Although some research outputs are now making the case for multimodal learning, in this book we pose the question as to what extent such lenses take into account the transfunctionality of AI and IoToys technology (which not only bridges physical and virtual spaces but transcends the functions with the user being in control rather than the application).

When embarking in this collaborative research, this led us to examine theoretical underpinnings or frameworks that are suggested for ECE. There was a tendency to frame children's uses of digital devices through social cultural frameworks (i.e. Marsh et al., 2015), digital personalisation (Kurcikova, 2017), critical perspectives (Stephen & Edwards, 2018), eco-culturalism, ecological systems theory (Bronfenbrenner) and social constructivism (Edwards et al., 2015; Arnott, 2016). In some cases, researchers are applying the three Cs (the child, the content and the context) approach (Miller et al., 2017; Paciga & Quest, 2017). Selwyn's (2010) critical perspective has also been used (Edwards et al., 2015) to ECE.

It was the idea of "web mapping" by Edwards (2016) that was the most close, home-grown attempt to theorise digital play and offer a framework to the field. There have also been some attempts to frame children's use of technology under postmodernism paradigm borrowing the work of Bourdieu (social capital and habitus) (Palaiologou, 2016b; Marsh, 2017). All attempts to use a theoretical framing acknowledge that children are part of a complex system influenced by many socioeconomic, political factors and technology, all of which should be utilised to support children to grow, develop, explore and pursue interests in a playful manner. However, a psychological developmental perspective in these attempts to theorise children's interactions with technology has been limited or ignored. Instead the research is focusing on documenting children's engagement with digital devices, focusing mainly on the facilitation of development and playful learning and ignoring relationships to self and whole development.

We argue that this lack of examining the interactions contributes to the well-documented, as shown above, problems orienting young children's interactions with technology in a play-based ideology and consequently in developing suitable pedagogies. This adds to a divisive ideology between play- and digital-based pedagogy. The closest attempts to blend digital and non-digital are the latest suggestions to frame learning under multimodality lenses.

Children in 21st century, however, are growing in an era that is developing rapidly technologically, where the internet and digital environments provide unlimited access to data, information and knowledge. Consequently, we argue that there is a need to examine play and play-based pedagogy in a digital landscape/playscapes. We propose that there is a need for a different understanding of children's engagement with digital devices, as social and collective, which allows for different sensitivities and methodologies and theoretical underpinnings in research on childhood in a digital world. The core argument that we want to push forward is that a relational conception of digital lives in ECE can be one productive reaction to the integration of technology and that we need to reflect on existing understandings of children's digital lives, striving for a different approach towards children's playful engagements with the repertoire of toys available to them and not divide them to digital and non-digital. This perspective builds on and extends beyond predominantly intentional and cognitive understandings of these engagements. We seek instead to understand through children's digital profiles whether there are patterns among play variables that contribute to play activity, how they express their internal world to make sense to the external one to enhance coping strategies and, most of all, how this impacts in their learning.

Consequently, reflecting collectively on our research, we propose that children's digital lives can be seen as a realised, situated and altered capacity, which can be accomplished through the combination of various interconnected "persons" and "things," processes and actions that aim at transformation which uses the Freire's notion of praxis:

> Human activity consists of action and reflection: it is praxis; it is transformation of the world. And as praxis, it requires theory to illuminate it. Human activity is theory and practice; it is reflection and action.

(p. 125)

Such a theoretical position re-examines the common dominant discourses and the binary views that continue to separate play from digital engagements of children. As we will argue in this book, children's engagement with digital devices requires synergy of action, contemplation from action and theory from practice that should be autochthonous to ECE, taking into consideration the social landscapes and communities of the 21st century.

In that sense, although, as mentioned, the research reported here did not have a unified methodological approach, we shared axiologically the same lenses. Our starting point was to define IoToys and their role in playful learning in ECE. Based on the nature of IoToys and their transfunctionality, we propose to position a redefined role of them in children's lives. Instead of seeing them as only technological toys that can facilitate educational purposes, which does not bridge the divide between non-technological and technological toys, we show them as polypronged, transfunctional toys that enable children to engage in playful learning that moves beyond multimodal playscapes (e.g. Arnott & Yelland, 2020; Palaiologou, Kewalramani, & Dardanou, 2021) and becomes translearning that takes place in transplayscapes.

Under these lenses (and as haptic technology offers opportunities to afford polymodes, tactile, visual, virtual, physical and haptic, of playful learning), in our research, we aimed to examine how we create playful learning environments that sychronise with the digital eco-communities we live now by looking at the role of such translearning spaces afforded by IoToys play.

Overview of the book

This research monograph stands on three integral pillars to shine light on the important challenges regarding firstly the understanding of and, secondly, the integration of IoToys within ECE. Following an overview of the origins of technologies and technology-based instruction, the first pillar highlights a crisp exploration of hierarchies of digital technologies as the *third teacher* in a child's learning environment; their characteristics and seminal early childhood contextualised theories are described to paint a holistic picture for children's playful learning. Notably, while we know that curriculum frameworks act as guiding documents for teachers to become creative and aware of technology integration practices, so far curricula frameworks have rarely been scrutinised for such a purpose. While lauding the commitment to sense making of how curricula provide a roadmap for digital learning and competencies frameworks, Chapter 2 of this book identifies examples of alignment and misalignment in how digital learning is defined and reinterpreted. The Australian, Norwegian and England curricula contexts, including culture, policy and early childhood ideologies for children's digital learning and related instructional practices, are discussed.

The second pillar provides the basis for constructing a structure of high-quality evidence-based practices for the integration of IoToys in early childhood and home settings. The authors provide several related examples of alignment and misalignment between the broad intentions for IoToys play and the places and spaces where such meaningful integration occurs for child learning and development.

These examples are highly relevant for early childhood educators and professionals in the three countries, but readers in other countries should not be deterred by this specificity as similar practices can exist elsewhere. Although this book does not explore specific lessons and a particular pedagogical model, it does highlight universal digital technology issues and success stories that impact on what happens in early childhood formal and informal learning environments. This book aims to be pragmatic for practitioners/parents/pre-service teacher educators to use and apply without being drilled down into theories. The exemplars of success stories discussed in each of the four chapters – stories and lessons learnt from Australia, England and Norway – we put here are aimed to support end users to easily use and integrate IoToys in their settings.

The third pillar brings together research on children's voices while playing with IoToys. Studies provide much evidence that practitioners and policymakers can adapt to offer integrated technological learning experiences for young children. However, young children's voices and ideas around what they think about IoToys, such as how robots work and operate, have rarely been heard. This book thus also provides innovative research evidence about how children's understandings, or misunderstandings, can be considered for technology creation and commercial developers. The last chapter provides a summary of meaningful ways to engage the disengaged, how technology as multimodal artefacts complements the interactions that happen in an EC setting, to extend education outside the classroom to enable children to not only engage with digital data but also manipulate the technologies to the best of their creativity and imagination.

In essence, this book takes a strength-based approach and is an amalgamation of emergent knowledge that contributes to the development and implementation of early childhood integrated pedagogies – the complex connection between technology, pedagogy and content – for effective planning, instruction and review of young children's playful learning.

Promoting ways of blending physical and virtual worlds represents a progressionist view of early childhood where technologies are viewed not as a challenge, but rather an inevitable evolution in children's learning landscapes. Thus, a nuanced stance is presented here in terms of how EC educators integrate technology while making instructional decisions for young children's playful learning. Nevertheless, the challenge remains in the selection of unique digital resources that are meaningful and purposeful for children's learning in developmentally appropriate ways, together with building teachers' professional learning repertoire for IoToys integration.

References

Aladé, F., Lauricella, A. R., Beaudoin-Ryan, L., & Wartella, E. (2016). Measuring with Murray: Touchscreen technology and preschoolers' STEM learning. *Computers in Human Behavior, 62*, 433–441. DOI: 10.1016/j.chb.2016.03.080.

Aldhafeeri, F. M., Palaiologou, I., & Folorunsho, A. (2016). Integration of digital technologies in play-based pedagogy in Kuwaiti early childhood education: Teachers' views, attitudes and aptitudes. *International Journal of Early Years Education, 24*(3), 342–360. DOI: 10.1080/09669760.2016.1172477.

Anzalone, S. M., Boucenna, S., Ivaldi, S., & Chetouani, M. (2015). Evaluating the engagement with social robots. *International Journal of Social Robotics, 7*, 465–478. DOI: 10.1007/s12369-015-0298-7.

Arnott, L. (2016). An ecological exploration of young children's digital play: Framing children's social experiences with technologies in early childhood. *Early Years: An International Journal, 36*(3), 271–287.

Arnott, L., Kewalramani, S., Gray, C., & Dardanou, M. (2020). Role play and technologies in early childhood. In Z. Kingdon (Ed.), *A Vygotskian analysis of children's play behaviours: Beyond the home corner*. London: Routledge.

Arnott, L., Palaiologou, I., & Gray, C. (2019). Internet of Toys across home and early childhood education: Understanding the ecology of the child's social world. *Technology, Pedagogy and Education, 28*(4), 401–412. DOI: 10.1080/1475939X.2019.1656667.

Arnott, L., & Yelland, N. (2020). Multimodal lifeworlds: Pedagogies for play inquiries and explorations. *Journal of Early Childhood Education Research, 9*(1), 124–146. https://jecer.org/wp-content/uploads/2020/02/Arnott-Yelland-issue9-1.pdf.

AVG. (2015). *Digital diaries.* Retrieved from http://now.avg.com/wp-content/uploads/2015/06/updated_17.07.15_dd_2015_executive_summary.pdf.

Bartneck, C., & Okada, M. (2001). *Robotic user interfaces.* Retrieved from https://ir.canterbury.ac.nz/bitstream/handle/10092/17873/bartneckHC2001.pdf?sequence=2.

Bers, M. U., Flannery, L., Kazakoff, E. R., & Sullivan, A. (2014). Computational thinking and tinkering: Exploration of an early childhood robotics curriculum. *Computers & Education, 72*, 145–157. DOI: 10.1016/j.compedu.2013.10.020.

Biswas, S., & Visell, Y. (2019). Haptic perception, mechanics, and material technologies for virtual reality. *Advanced Functional Materials*, 31, 39.

Campbell, C., Haines, C., Koester, A., & Stoltz, D. (2015). *Serving youth.* Retrieved from http://www.ala.org/alsc/sites/ala.org.alsc/files/content/2015%20ALSC%20White%20Paper_FINAL.pdf.

Chung, P. J., Vanderbilt, D. L., & Soares, N. S. (2015). Social behaviors and active videogame play in children with *Autism Spectrum Disorder. Games for Health Journal, 4*(3), 225–234. DOI: 10.1089/g4h.2014.0125.

Coiro, J. (2015). The magic of wondering: Building understanding through online inquiry. *The Reading Teacher, 69*(2), 189–193. DOI: 10.1002/trtr.1399.

Danby, S., Davidson, C., Theobald, M., Houen, S., & Thorpe, K. (2017a). Pretend play and technology: Young children making sense of their everyday social worlds. In S. Lynch, D. Pike, & C. Beckett (Eds.), *Multidisciplinary perspectives on play from birth and beyond* (pp. 231–245). Singapore: Springer.

Danby, S., Davidson, C., Theobald, M., Houen, S., & Thorpe, K. (2017b). Playing with technology: Young children making sense of technology as part of their everyday social worlds. In D. Pike, S. Lynch, & C. Beckett (Eds.), *Multidisciplinary perspectives on play: From birth to beyond*. New York: Springer.

Danby, S., Fleer, M., Davidson, C., & Hatzigianni, M. (2018). *Digital childhoods: Technologies and children's everyday lives* (International Perspectives on Early Childhood Education and Development). Singapore: Springer.

Edwards, S. (2016). New concepts of play and the problem of technology, digital media and popular-culture integration with play-based learning in early childhood education. *Technology, Pedagogy and Education, 25*(4), 513–532. DOI: 10.1080/1475939X.2015.1108929.

Edwards, S., & Bird, J. (2017). Observing and assessing young children's digital play in the early years: Using the digital play framework. *Journal of Early Childhood Research, 15*(2), 158–173.

Edwards, S., Nuttall, J., Mantilla, A., Wood, E., & Grieshaber, S. (2015). Digital play: What do early childhood teachers see. In S. Buffin, N. F. Johnson, & C. Bigum (Eds.), *Critical perspectives on early childhood education*. Palgrave Macmillan's Digital Education and Learning Series. New York: Palgrave MacMillan.

Edwards, S., Skouteris, H., Nolan, A., & Henderson, M. (2016). Young children's internet cognition. In S. Gurvis & N. Lemon (Eds.), *Understanding digital technology and young children: An international perspective* (pp. 38–45). London: Routledge.

Falloon, G. (2015). What's the difference? Learning collaboratively using iPads in conventional classrooms. *Computers & Education, 84*, 62–77. DOI: 10.1016/j.compedu.2015.01.010.

Ferguson, C. J. (2015). Clinicians' attitudes toward video games vary as a function of age, gender and negative beliefs about youth: A sociology of media research approach. *Computers in Human Behavior, 52*, 379–386. DOI: 10.1016/j.chb.2015.06.016.

Fleer, M. (2019). Digitally amplified practices: Beyond binaries and towards a profile of multiple digital coadjuvants. *Mind, Culture, and Activity, 26*(3), 207–220. DOI: 10.1080/10749039.2019.1646289.

Flewitt, R., Messer, D., & Kucirkova, N. (2015). New directions for early literacy in a digital age: The iPad. *Journal of Early Childhood Literacy, 15*(3), 289–310.

Folorunsho, A., & Palaiologou, I. (2019). Children's playful encounters with iPads. In C. Gray & I. Palaiologou (Eds.) *Early learning in the digital age* (pp. 3–17). London: SAGE.

Ge, S. S., Li, H., Cabibihan, J.-J., & Tan, Y. K. (Eds.). (2010). Social Robotics Second International Conference on Social Robotics, ICSR 2010 Singapore, November 23–24, p. 30.

Guynn, J. (2016, June 20). Black churches put faith in coding classes. *USA Today*. Retrieved from http://www.usatoday.com/ story/tech/news/2016/06/20/black-churches-put-faith-tech-labs/85939132/.

Howrey, S. (2016). Preparing pre-service teachers to use internet technology for early reading skills: Insights from an action research project. *The Journal of Literacy and Technology, 17*, 80–111. Retrieved from http://www. literacyandtechnology.org/uploads/1/3/6/8/136889/_jlt_sp2016_howrey.pdf.

Huber, B., Tarasuik, J., Antoniou, M. N., Garrett, C., Bowe, S. J., Kaufman, J., & Team, S. B. (2016). Young children's transfer of learning from a touchscreen device. *Computers in Human Behavior, 56*, 56–64. DOI: 10.1016/j.chb.2015.11.010.

Huh, Y. J. (2017). Uncovering young children's transformative digital game play through the exploration of three year old children's cases. *Contemporary Issues in Early Childhood, 18*(2), 179–195.

Huijnen, C. A. G. J., Lexis, M. A. S., & de Witte, L. P. (2017). Robots as new tools in therapy and education for children with autism. *International Journal of Neurorehabilitation*. DOI: 10.4172/2376-0281.1000278.

Huijnen, C. A. G. J., Lexis, M. A. S., Jansens, R., & de Witte, L. P. (2016). Mapping robots to therapy and educational objectives for children with autism spectrum disorder. *Journal of Autism and Developmental Disorders, 46*(6), 2100–2114. DOI: 10.1007/s10803-016-2740-6.

Ihmeideh, F. M. (2015). Assessment of children's digital courseware in light of developmentally appropriate courseware criteria: Assessment of children's educational software. *British Journal of Educational Technology, 46*(3), 649–663. DOI: 10.1111/bjet.12163.

Ilomäki, L., Paavola, S., Lakkala, M., & Kantosalo, A. (2016). "Digital competence– an emergent boundary concept for policy and educational research". *Education and Information Technologies, 21*(3), 655–679. DOI: 10.1007/s10639-014-9346-4.

Jewitt, C., & Kress, G. (Eds.). (2003). *Multimodal literacy.* New York: Peter Lang.

Kabali, H. K., Irigoyen, M. M., Nunez-Davis, R., Budacki, J. G., Mohanty, S. H., Leister, K. P., & Bonner, R. L. (2015). Exposure and use of mobile media devices by young children. *Pediatrics, 136*(6), 1044–1050. DOI: 10.1542/peds.2015-215.

Kewalramani, S., Kidman, G., & Palaiologou, I. (2021). Using artificial intelligence (AI) interfaced robotic toys in early childhood settings: A case for children's inquiry literacy. *European Early Childhood Education Research Journal, 29*(5), 652–668.

Kewalramani, S., Palaiologou, I., Arnott, L., & Dardanou, M. (2020). The integration of the Internet of Toys in early childhood education: A platform for multilayered interactions. *European Early Childhood Education Research Journal, 28*(2), 197–213.DOI: 10.1080/1350293X.2020.1735738.

Kewalramani, S., Palaiologou, I., Dardanou, M., Allen, K. A., & Phillipson, S. (2021). Using robotic toys in early childhood education to support children's social and emotional competencies. *Australasian Journal of Early Childhood.* DOI: 10.1177/18369391211056668.

Kopetz, H. (2011). Internet of things. In *Real-time systems* (pp. 307–323). Boston, MA: Springer. DOI: 10.1007/978-1-4419-8237-7_13.

Kurcikova, N. (2017). *Digital personalisation in early childhood: Impact on childhood.* London: Bloomsbury.

Lahiri, U. (2020). *A computational view of autism: Using virtual reality technologies intervention.* Cham: Springer.

Lawrence, S. M. (2018). Preschool children and iPads: Observations of social interactions during digital play. *Early Education and Development, 29*(2), 207–228.

Ling, L., Yelland, N., Hatzigianni, M., & Dickson-Deane, C. (2021). Toward a conceptualization of the Internet of Toys. Australasian Journal of Early Childhood, 46(3), 249–262.

Marsh, J. A. (2017). Russian Dolls and three forms of capital: Ecological and sociological perspectives on parents' engagement with young Children's tablet use. In C. Burnett, G. Merchant, A. Simpson, & M. Walsh (Eds.), *The case of the iPad: Mobile literacies in education* (pp. 31–47). Singapore: Springer.

Marsh, J., Plowman, L., Yamada-Rice, D., Bishop, J., Lahmar, J., Scott, F. L., … Winter, P. (2015). *Exploring play and creativity in pre-schoolers' use of apps.* Final project report. Retrieved from http://www.techandplay.org/reports/TAP_Final_Report.pdf.

Marsh, J., Plowman, L., Yamada-Rice, D., Bishop, J., & Scott, F. (2016). Digital play: A new classification. *Early Years, 36*(3), 242–253.

Mascheroni, G., & Holloway, D. (Eds.). (2019). *The Internet of Toys: Practices, affordances and the political economy of Children's play.* Cham: Palgrave Macmillan.

Miller, J. L., Paciga, K. A., Danby, S., Beaudoin-Ryan, L., & Kaldor, T. (2017). Looking beyond swiping and tapping: Review of design and methodologies for researching young children's use of digital technologies. *Cyberpsychology: Journal of Psychosocial Research on Cyberspace, 11*(3), article 6.

Miorandi, D., Sicari, S., De Pellegrini, F., & Chlamtac, I. (2012). Internet of things: Vision, applications and research challenges. *Ad Hoc Networks,* 10, 1497–1516. DOI: 10.1016/j.adhoc.2012.02.016.

Myers, L. J., LeWitt, R. B., Gallo, R. E., & Maselli, N. M. (2016). Baby FaceTime: Can toddlers learn from online video chat? *Developmental Science,* 20, e12430. DOI: 10.1111/desc.12430.

Nathanson, A. I. (2015). Media and the family: Reflections and future directions. *Journal of Children and Media*, 9(1), 133–139. DOI: 10.1080/17482798.2015.997145.

Neumann, M. M., & Neumann, D. L. (2013). Touchscreen tablets and emergent literacy. *Early Childhood Education Journal*, 42(4), 231–239.

Nikolayev, M. (2016). *Improving preschoolers' theory of mind skills with digital games: A training study* (Doctoral Dissertation). George Mason University.

Nikolopoulou, K., & Gialamas, V. (2015). ICT and play in preschool: Early childhood teachers' beliefs and confidence. *International Journal of Early Years Education*, 23, 409–425. DOI: 10.1080/09669760.2015.1078727.

Nuttall, J., Edwards, S., Mantilla, A., Grieshaber, S., & Wood, E. (2015). The role of motive objects in early childhood teacher development concerning children's digital play and play-based learning in early childhood curricula. *Professional Development in Education*, 41(2), 222–235.

O'Connor, J., & Fotakopoulou, O. (2016). A threat to childhood innocence or the future of learning? Parents' perspectives on the use of touch-screen technology by 0–3 year-olds in the UK. *Contemporary Issues in Early Childhood*, 17(2), 235–247.

Paciga, K. A., & Quest, M. (2017). It's hard to wait: Effortful control and story understanding in adult-supported e-book reading across the early years. *Journal of Literacy and Technology*, 18(1), 35–79. Retrieved from http://www. literacyand-technology.org/uploads/1/3/6/8/136889/jlt_v18_1_paciga_quest.pdf.

Palaiologou, I. (2016a). Children under five and digital technologies: Implication for early years pedagogy. *The European Early Childhood Research Journal*, 24(1), 5–24. DOI: 10.1080/1350293X.2014.929876.

Palaiologou, I. (2016b). Teachers' dispositions towards the role of digital devices in play-based pedagogy in early childhood education. *Early Years: An International Research Journal*, 36(3), 305–321. DOI: 10.1080/09575146.2016.1174816.

Palaiologou, I. (2017). Digital violence and children under five: The Phantom Menace within digital homes of the 21st century? *Education Sciences and Society*, 8(1), 123–136.

Palaiologou, I., Kewalramani, S., & Dardanou, M. (2021). Make-believe play with the Internet of Toys: A case for multimodal playscapes. *British Journal of Educational Technology* (special issue: Digitalisation in early childhood: approaches, effects and critical views), 52(6), 2100–2117. DOI: 10.1111/1467-8535.13110.

Parish-Morris, J., Hirsh-Pasek, K., Golinkoff, R. M., & Hassinger-Das, B. (2015, June). Parent-preschooler interaction during electronic and traditional book reading. In *Presented at the Digital Literacy for Preschoolers: Maximizing the Benefits of eBooks for Emergent Literacy, Montreal, Canada*. Retrieved from http:// digitalliteracyforpreschoolers.conference.mcgill.ca/.

Plowman, L. (2015). Researching young children's everyday uses of technology in the family home. *Open Access in Interacting*, 27(1), 36–46.

Radesky, J. S., Kistin, C., Eisenberg, S., Zuckerman, B., & Silverstein, M. (2015). Parent views about mobile device use around and by young children: Implications for anticipatory guidance. In *Abstract presented at the Pediatric Academic Societies, San Diego, CA*. Retrieved from www.abstracts2view.com/ pas/view.php? nu=PAS15L1_2195.2.

Relkin, E., Govind, M., Tsiang, J., & Bers, M. (2020). How parents support children's informal learning experiences with robots. *Journal of Research in STEM Education*, 6(1), 39–51. DOI: 10.51355/jstem.2020.87.

Rowe, D. W., Miller, M. E., & Pacheco, M. B. (2014). Preschoolers as digital designers: Composing dual language ebooks using touchscreen computer tablets. In R. S. Anderson & C. Mims (Eds.), *Handbook of research on digital tools for writing instruction in K–12 settings* (pp. 279–306). Hershey, PA: IGI Global.

Rowsell, J. (2013). *Working with multimodality: Rethinking literacy in a digital age.* London: Routledge.

Stephen, C., & Edwards, S. (2018). *Young children playing and learning in a digital age: A cultural and critical perspective.* London: Routledge.

Sullivan, A., & Bers, M. U. (2016). Robotics in the early childhood classroom: Learning outcomes from an 8-week robotics curriculum in pre-kindergarten through second grade. *International Journal of Technology and Design Education, 26*(1), 3–20.

Sung, Y., Chang, K., & Liu, T. (2016). The effects of integrating mobile devices with teaching and learning on students' learning performance: A meta-analysis and research synthesis. *Computers and Education, 94,* 252–275.

Suskind, D. L., Leffel, K. R., Graf, E., Hernandez, M. W., Gunderson, E. A., Sapolich, S. G., & Levine, S. C. (2016). A parent-directed language intervention for children of low socioeconomic status: A randomized controlled pilot study. *Journal of Child Language, 43*(2), 366–406. DOI: 10.1017/S0305000915000033.

Selwyn, N. (2010). Looking beyond learning: Notes towards the critical study of educational technology. *Journal of Computer Assisted Learning, 26,* 65–73.

Wilmes, S., & Siry, C. (2021). Multimodal interaction analysis: A powerful tool for examining plurilingual students' engagement in science practices. *Research in Science Education* **51,** 71–91. DOI: 10.1007/s11165-020-09977-z.

Wu, L., Kim, M., & Markauskaite, L. (2020). Developing young children's empathic perception through digitally mediated interpersonal experience: Principles for a hybrid design of empathy games. *British Journal of Educational Technology,* 51, 1168–1187. DOI: 10.1111/bjet.12918.

Yelland, N. J. (2018). A pedagogy of multiliteracies: Young children and multimodal learning with tablets. *British Journal of Educational Technology, 49*(5), 847–858. DOI: 10.1111/bjet.12635.

Zaman, B., Nouwen, M., Vanattenhoven, J., de Ferrerre, E., & Van Looy, J. (2016). A qualitative inquiry into the contextualized parental mediation practices of young children's digital media use at home. *Journal of Broadcasting and Electronic Media, 60*(1), 1–22. Retrieved from https://lirias.kuleuven.be/handle/123456789/502675.

2 Curricula landscapes for (re) culturing children's learning in the 21st century

Introduction

In the last decade, the shift in our society's growing reliance on technology mandates that young children's educators have started to integrate technology within play-based pedagogical practices to tune into children's playful learning and affective engagement (e.g. Marsh et al., 2019; Kewalramani Kidman, & Palaiologou, 2021). Through the dialogue provided in the introductory chapter, it can be acknowledged that by examining the integration of IoToys, theoretically and pedagogically, we can build a discourse on how children's play and learning are shaped in the multimodal age. We know that children naturally play and love hands-on learning when creating their own artefacts using imagined ideas. At the same time, technology is an important part of our world that has transformed it, with consequent impact on childhood. Additionally, artificial intelligence (AI) is accompanying a whole generation of children to grow up in a rapidly changing digital world, with the proliferation of virtual assistants such as Siri and Google Assistant and many other AI-enabled applications in all sorts of areas such as education, social media, entertainment, edutainment and robotics (Druga et al., 2018; Su & Yang, 2022; Yang, 2022). Hence, moving forward into a multimodal and 21st century age of learning, as researchers and educators, our goal is to help children, parents, practitioners and ECE leaders to develop safe and healthy habits for technology use together with fostering viable learning habits (Danby et al., 2018; Palaiologou, Kewalramani, & Dardanou, 2021). Thus, curating the child's learning environments as healthy habitats for playful learning in this multimodal age can be using both physical and digital artefacts (Arnott & Yelland, 2020; Kewalramani et al., 2020; Kewalramani, Palaiologou, & Dardanou, 2020), in some cases, as polypronged modes of learning (visual, tactile, virtual and physical) (Palaiologou, Kewalramani, & Dardanou, 2021).

Evidence is emerging as to how IoToys can provide a platform for children's engagement during play (Arnott, Palaiologou, & Gray, 2018). For instance, educators within an adult-led learning environment, together with children, interact to create imaginary situations and provide opportunities for children to engage with literacy and numeracy concepts (Huber, Highfield, & Kaufman, 2018), social interactions (Danby et al., 2018), digital games and playing with apps

DOI: 10.4324/9781003185840-2

(Arnott, Palaiologou, & Gray, 2018; Danby et al., 2018). In practice, there are an increasing number of resources and curricula available for primary and secondary students to learn about IoToys, such as using AI-interfaced technologies and robotics to learn, for example, programming-related concepts (Australian Curriculum and Reporting Authority, ACARA, 2020). However, when it comes to younger children, who are increasingly engaging with IoToys and AI-interfaced resources, how the use of these technologies can be used in the curriculum is limited (Organisation for Economic and Collaboration Development [OECD], 2019, 2021; UNICEF, 2021). Research on how to effectively design and implement technologies involving IoToys and AI curriculum that can help young non-programmers is still in its infancy (Su & Yang, 2022). The main reason for this, it seems, is the lack of curricula frameworks, resources and professional development programmes for educators and parents that strategically target on developing children's communication, creativity, critical thinking and collaboration (the "4Cs") (OECD, 2017, 2019) and their digital literacy and judgement (Dardanou & Kofoed, 2019). Consequently, the use of technology, specifically IoToys and AI-powered technologies such as robotics, to serve as a medium for play in educators' pedagogical practices remains scarcely fulfilled (Mascheroni & Holloway, 2019). Moreover, the OECD's 2019 report provides evidence that the cumulative impact of learning experiences, when starting from early childhood and up to the age of 15 and encompassing integrated social and cognitive experiences in school, has resulted in higher outcomes in children's problem-solving literacy and socialisation skills. Yet, there still exist debates around firstly building educators' and parents' sense making and awareness of integration of technologies and, secondly, how children's safe and ethical digital play and learning in early childhood are warranted.

In a comparison of curricular documents and classroom interactions from Finland and Hong Kong, Lehesvuori, Ramnarain and Viiri (2017) argue that although curriculum documents address policies, expected goals, objectives and preferable pedagogies and provide a lens through which educational actions can be evaluated, the curricula link to pedagogy in preschool classrooms and teacher orientations is rarely reported. As Voogt and Roblin (2012) discuss, if the levels of the intended, implemented and attained curriculum are not in equilibrium, change is unlikely to happen in ECE teachers' digital technology integration and related instructional practices. The authors' comparative study of eight 21st century frameworks indicated much alignment between the frameworks about what 21st century competencies are and why they are important (horizontal consistency), but educators' intentions and practices seemed still far apart, indicating a lack of vertical consistency. As such, Voogt and Roblin (2012) have posed a call that national curricula need to change drastically to comply with the competences needed for the 21st century learners. Meanwhile, research is already beginning to show how early childhood digital learning promotes the 4Cs within 21st century competencies (Fleer, 2018; Arnott, Kewalramani, Gray, & Dardanou, 2020; Kewalramani, Palaiologou, & Dardanou, 2020).

To fill this argument about educators' integration of technology, particularly the use of IoToys, this chapter provides an overview of the curricula cultures in Australia, England and Norway. It aims to examine the curricula culture and discuss to what extent it blends, rather than contests, with the traditional play-based practices in ECE settings in the three countries. It also explores how the curricula cultures and policy are seen as the key drivers for ECE educators' practices while implementing IoToys in the classroom. Finally, it debates how the curricula culture supports educators to provide children safe, ethical and inquiry-based opportunities to interact with technologies.

Curricula cultures for children's digital learning

Traditionally, ECE settings are seen as most relevant to developing children's socialisation process before they enter formal schooling, rather than solely the development of cognitive skills. Indeed, communicating, sharing, expressing themselves and observing social rules governing interpersonal interaction (Williams, Sheridan, & Sandberg, 2014) are critical parts in children's developmental learning process.

We problematise, however, the ways in which the early childhood (EC) curricula and pedagogical landscape prepare children to collaborate, cooperate and conceptualise cognitive learning together. The curriculum in ECE is posing difficulties and dilemmas towards technology integration due to peculiarities in provision, primarily because historically curricula cultures have been influenced by different ideologies and theories (e.g. Wood & Hedges, 2016a, 2016b; Palaiologou & Male, 2019). Moreover, since the 1990s in all three countries there were attempts at the policy level to provide curricula framework for ECE and the discourse of what constitutes an appropriate and effective curriculum has raised critical questions about "what" should be taught when it comes to digital learning, leaving alone "how" it should be taught to young children.

In 2004, UNESCO pointed out the difficulty countries have in introducing curricula for ECE and cautioned that a curriculum with emphasis on either development or learning is problematic as it ignores learning patterns of young children that take place via children's voluntary and experiential features (e.g. play). Thus, it proposed a more integrated approach that takes on board children's development, learning but equally well-being and support for their intellectual and social development as well as participation (Williams, Sheridan, & Sandberg, 2014). As will be argued throughout this book, IoToys are one platform to realise such blended learning for young children (Mascheroni & Holloway, 2017; Arnott, Palaiologou, & Gray, 2018).

Additionally, it is well documented that when educators indulge in high-quality interactions with children, this can support, scaffold and extend children's thinking and learning (e.g. Siraj-Blatchford et al., 2017). Earlier work on guided interaction, based on touchscreen technology (Plowman & Stephen, 2007), provided a frame to show how this was possible with technologies. Yet, few studies have carried Plowman and Stephen's work forward with emerging new technologies such as IoToys. Most studies have taken into account play-based practices, but limited research investigates practices that may encompass digital pedagogies (e.g. Bird & Edwards, 2015; Marsh et al., 2016; Hatzigianni et al., 2018). We also know that educators may bring in different perspectives to their sense making of their curriculum, along with different cultural agendas and aspirations for young children's learning and development (Wood & Hedges, 2016a, 2016b). The current study examines the ECE curricula and instructional practices of the three countries and focuses on the types of instruction that are being offered (adult led/child led). We also examine how these instructions might impact on children's developmental and cognitive growth, as well as in their preparation for more formal educational contexts (school).

This has led us to propose curricula cultures which are being described as follows:

> *Developmental Goals Driven*: The focus of the curriculum is on developmental goals/outcomes (e.g. England and Scotland);
> *Learning Goals Driven*: The focus of the curriculum is on learning outcomes (LOs) that are not necessarily driven by children's development only, but from academic subjects as well (e.g. England);
> *Play-based Approach*: The focus of the curriculum places emphasis on children developing and learning via play, and less emphasis is placed on developmental or learning goals, but more on a pedagogy of play that allows children to flourish (e.g. Norway, Reggio and Emilia);
> *Balanced/blended*: The focus is on all the three above in a balanced or blended way (e.g. Australia and New Zealand).

Methods and curricula contexts

As mentioned above, this chapter aims to examine the "what" and "how" the ECE curricula in the three countries act as the key drivers to support educators' sense making of implementing IoToys in EC classrooms. Traditionally, curriculum making has been understood as primarily a nation-state issue (Wood & Hedges, 2016a, 2016b). However, we consider there is a need to understand and strengthen the discussion of research-based developments of curricula in different cultural contexts. National educational policies are guided by curricula, which set the conceptual and philosophical foundation for the education in the country. There are differences in the ECE curricula and practices between countries (Tao, Oliver, & Venville, 2012; Inoue et al., 2017). As curricula are a core means to develop educational practices, the globally emerging needs need to be discussed in these different cultural contexts and comparative studies are needed to open the discourse of what constitutes an effective curriculum. Although digital competency (DC) frameworks are increasingly being used in the European policy frameworks (Norwegian Directorate for Education and Training, 2017; OECD, 2019, 2021; UNICEF, 2021), in ECE research, policy and curricula, it is not yet a standardised concept internationally (Ilomäki et al., 2016).

Table 2.1 Components of analyses and proposed questions used for the analysis

Curriculum component	Proposed questions for the analyses
Rationale and vision	What is the ultimate ideology of the education for digital learning?
	What are the views indicated about the importance of digital LOs?
Aims and objectives	What are the knowledge and skills targeted in teaching and learning?
	Which goals are for children's digital learning?
Contents	How digital learning is presented as learning domains and what are the key technology topics/strands/themes mentioned?
Teacher's role	How is the teacher facilitating learning?

Source: From Van den Akker (2010).

In search of a rigorously conducted curricula analysis, we applied the framework developed by Van den Akker (2003) and document analysis was conducted to examine the curricula texts in each country. Each researcher collected, recorded and documented the texts to study and encoded and analysed the curricula frameworks according to defined criteria and systems to interpret and elicit the meaning, gain understanding and develop empirical knowledge (Bowen, 2009). Van den Akker's curriculum design framework (2010, p. 181) introduces ten components to be analysed from the curricula (see also Marty, Venturini, & Almqvist, 2018). In this study, we have analysed four of the ten main components (see Table 2.1) – rationale and vision, aims and objectives, contents and the teacher's role – in implementing IoToys in ECE classrooms.

ECE curriculum in Australia

In Australia, the first Early Years Learning Framework (EYLF) was released in 2009, which formed the nationwide core curriculum guideline. The current Australian digital technology curriculum (towards pre-primary and up to Grade 2) requires educators to support children building their independence in observing and sharing their discoveries (ACARA, 2020). In line with this, the EYLF proposed that the planning cycle structure supports educators' understanding of the continuity of learning in the use of technologies from kindergarten onwards. The EYLF is based on the rationale that children's (0–5 years old) lives are characterised by *belonging, being and becoming.* As children participate in everyday life, they develop interests and construct their own identities and understandings of the world.

The five LOs for children are that children "have a strong sense of identity"; "are connected with and contribute to their world"; "have a strong sense of wellbeing"; "are confident and involved learners"; and "are effective communicators" (Department of Education and Training [DET], 2019, p. 8). In particular, the EYLF conveys the highest expectations for all children's learning from birth to five years and through the transitions to formal schooling (Prep–Year 12), where there is a mandated Australian digital technologies curriculum, separately for children of age six and above. Educators are expected to draw on a rich repertoire of pedagogical practices to promote children's learning by planning and implementing learning through play and intentional teaching. Although the purposes of digital learning education, the role of information communication technology (ICT) and digital learning have not been made explicit in the EYLF, the development of ICT skills in young children is intertwined in the five LOs.

Despite the purposes of digital learning having not been directly suggested, the EYLF implicitly emphasises within LOs 4 and 5 that children develop dispositions for learning such as curiosity, creativity and imagination and develop a range of skills and processes such as problem-solving, enquiry, experimentation, hypothesising, researching and investigating. The EYLF emphasises that children learn to participate fully and actively in the society. Regarding the content for ICT/digital learning, children use media to access information, investigate ideas and represent their thinking. With respect to children's use of ICT, an exact and clear direction is posed that children use technologies as tools or props for designing, drawing, editing, reflecting and composing and to engage in fun and meaning making.

With respect to "pedagogical directions" for technology use and digital learning, LO 4 mentions that children benefit from many opportunities to generate and discuss ideas, make plans, exercise skills, brainstorm solutions to problems, reflect and give reasons for their choices. They investigate what products and systems can do and how they work. Increasingly (but when it is not clearly mentioned), children begin to use ICT to assist their thinking and to represent what they know and understand. Children teach others and broaden their learning about the world through connecting with people, places, technologies and natural materials. They manipulate objects to investigate, assemble, invent and construct, and they use their own and others' feedback to revise and build on an idea. LO 5 mentions that children use digital technologies and multimedia resources to communicate, play and learn. They create and display their own information in a way that suits different audiences and purposes. It is evident that there is great focus on children's use of ICT as tools and resources for communication of ideas in the EYLF. And consequently, teachers should intentionally plan and use ICT as resources to enhance children's learning experiences. In addition, in the glossary there are definitions of digital and technological environments for development, communication and knowledge creation (EYLF, 2019, p. 19). Digital environments refer to computers (including laptops, tablets and smart boards) and computer games, the internet, television and radio, among others.

ECE curriculum framework in England

In England, the Early Years Foundation Stage (EYFS) curriculum framework was first introduced in September 2008. This applies to all children from birth to five years. The EYFS aims to set standards for children's learning and development, health, safety and well-being. Core to the EYFS is to show a commitment to equality, cultural diversity and partnerships between parents and early childhood settings (Palaiologou & Male, 2021)

The key aims are as follows:

- Quality and consistency in preschool settings, so that every child makes good progress and no child gets left behind;
- A secure foundation through learning and development opportunities which are planned around the needs and interests of each individual child and are assessed and reviewed regularly;
- Partnership working between practitioners and with parents and/or carers;
- Equality of opportunity and anti-discriminatory practice, ensuring that every child is included and supported. (DfE, 2017, p. 5)

Within the EYFS, there is a strong emphasis on "school readiness," where learning and developmental goals are assessed at three points of children's lives. Such heavy emphasis on measuring the progress of children again on these goals has been heavily criticised (e.g. Bradbury & Roberts-Holmes, 2017; Pascal, Bertram, & Rouse, 2019).

The EYFS divides the learning requirements in seven prime areas of learning and development: communication and language; physical development; personal, social and emotional development; literacy; mathematics; understanding the world and finally expressive arts and design. However, these areas are limited, and the EYFS sets specific learning goals for each of them against which children need to be assessed. These learning goals are limited and do not allow space for a holistic approach to ECE that should include other aspects. As a consequence, EYFS

> [...] places value on children in terms of their meeting future goals and standards and their learning outcomes. It assumes that children need to progress to the next stage of development, from lesser child to better child. The terms 'development', 'developmental goals' or 'learning goals' invoke a sense that children are not yet developed (whole/holistic) and thus need developing ('improving'), or that there is an existing, pre-determined place at which a child may arrive (presumably school).
>
> (Palaiologou, 2019, p. 238)

This curriculum framework is very descriptive on what constituted effective learning by specifying that

- Playing and exploring – children investigate and experience things and "have a go";
- Active learning – children concentrate and keep on trying if they encounter difficulties and enjoy achievements;
- Creating and thinking critically – children have and develop their own ideas, make links between ideas and develop strategies for doing things (Palaiologou & Male, 2021, p. 29).

Although within EYFS playing and learning are of great importance, the role of technologies and their integrations in playing and exploring to create active learning environments is not of equal importance as other areas such as mathematics and literacy. There is little mention of how to support young children to develop technological skills or how to support practitioners to integrate technologies, yet relevant research has shown that their integration can enhance learning environments (e.g. Fleer, 2019).

Compared to Australia and Norway, and despite attempts to raise the standards among the ECE workforce in England, the sector is patchy as there are a variety of qualifications still underdeveloped, low qualified, low paid and lacking diversity and a strategy at policy level to raise the standards (Bonetti, 2019; Bury et al., 2020). These challenges make it even more difficult to integrate technologies and develop practices, as well as widening the gap between home where children use technologies and ECE (Arnott, Palaiologou, & Gray, 2019).

ECE curriculum in Norway

Nearly 92 per cent of children between the ages 1 and 5 attend kindergarten, which is not compulsory, but is very common after parents' paternity and maternity leave allowance (Working Environment Act, 2017, Ch. 12). Approximately 93 per cent attend kindergarten before the age of two (Statistics Norway, 2021), so most children will be affected by the pedagogy and practices they encounter in ECE.

The Norwegian framework plan for kindergartens was released in 2006 and reformed the previous framework from 1996. Revised versions came into force in 2009 and 2011. Both mentioned in one sentence the use of digital devices as a way to promote children's play and creativity and that they could be used. The framework plan that came to force in 2017 has its own reference on kindergarten's digital praxis (Norwegian Directorate for Education and Training, 2017), is distinguished in seven interdisciplinary areas and emphasises children's participation in all the processes of their everyday life in the kindergarten. Regarding the use of digital technology, the Norwegian framework for kindergartens states, "digital practices in kindergarten shall encourage the children to play, be creative and learn" (Norwegian Directorate for Education and Training, 2017, p. 44). This requires practitioners in ECE to use digital technologies with children, and most kindergartens have implemented a variety of technological tools for their practice (Fjørtoft, Thun, & Buvik, 2019).

The discourse in Norwegian society is currently contested when it comes to technology being "good" or "bad." (Dardanou et al., 2020). Many parents are anxious about the effects of screen time on their children, while media discourses feature expected and unexpected positive and negative sides of using technology (Bølgan, 2018). Most parents believe that too much time in front of a screen is undesirable/potentially dangerous, but what is considered "too much" varies. In Norway, there seems to be a consensus to limit the time children spend with screens; this does not seem to be the case in many homes (Statistics Norway, 2021). This all contributes to the dominant Norwegian discourses, which vary depending on who, where and when the usage is being discussed.

The Norwegian kindergarten has a strong tradition of using most of the time outdoors (Moser & Martinsen, 2010). This is something that is underlined by the framework plan for the content and tasks of kindergartens (Norwegian Directorate for Education and Training, 2017) where it highlighted the importance of children's outdoor experiences throughout the whole year. Play in outdoor kindergarten settings is central in the Norwegian kindergarten tradition (Gessiou, Dardanou, & Sakellariou, 2018). Therefore, kindergartens' digital praxis is often undermined in relation to, for example, outdoor activities or trips in natural environments. Educators' pedagogical philosophy is affected by the cultural discourses concerning the use of technology and with its associations of promoting passive, sedentary behaviour (Dardanou et al., 2020; Fotakopoulou et al., 2020).

Nevertheless, kindergartens' digital practices have been more addressed in the newest framework plan, and a shift practice of implementing digital technology in children's play and planned activities has been observed (Dardanou, Mossin, & Simensen, 2021).

Conclusion and implications

This chapter provided a brief analysis of Australian, England and Norwegian curricula to map out the similarities and differences in the rationale and vision, aims and objectives, and contents in deducing the role of teachers to use technologies for children's digital learning. The curriculum of each country has several features in common, with the main objective being to support the developmental characteristics of children, to develop their self-care abilities and to prepare them for a higher level of education. This is especially evident in England.

The analysis poses some tensions regarding the ways the LOs have not been precisely mentioned for children's critical thinking, digital competencies and understanding of technologies such as IoToys and AI education in such important years of their life. The EYLF in Australia has specifically outlined five LOs for children, unlike the England and Norwegian curricula, for the development of ICT knowledge; the questioning of safe and ethical use of technologies as a natural phenomenon and the ability to draw conclusions about the use of technologies need to be fostered right from ECE. The EYLF states that from birth, children are highly engaged with their environment and this is the basis for important development of children's digital competencies and multiliteracies. On the contrary, the Norwegian Framework Plan for kindergarten (Norwegian Directorate for Education and Training, 2017) curricula has an upper hand in clearly having digital learning as the core part of ECE as a learning domain, within which children participate in targeted ICT activities. However, such emphases to technology are not made in the EYFS in England. In previous versions of the EYFS, technologies were mentioned, but in the new revised version introduced in 2017 this has been taken out. In England, documentation is the only apparent and essential working approach for practitioners to be able to use technologies for planning, implementing and evaluating children's learning.

Meanwhile, the COVID-19 pandemic has demonstrated the importance of promoting young children's digital competence at a young age as they develop in a connected world (UNICEF, 2019; 2021). More attention needs to be paid to what children do online, the content they encounter and the support networks facilitated by teachers and parents for children to become creative and critical users of technologies such as IoToys and AI technologies. As such, it is critical for researchers and practitioners to identify curriculum elements that can enable teachers' ways of fostering children's DC development. Thus, in this book, we aim to demonstrate examples from research on how technologies have been used at home (England – Chapter 3, at education level; Australia and Norway – Chapters 4 and 5; and support children's emotional literacies – Chapter 6).

We know that educators may bring in different perspectives to their sense making of their curriculum and planning (Wood & Hedges, 2016a, 2016b), along with different cultural agendas to underpin policy frameworks and institutional-driven aspirations for young children's learning and development. Although most studies have considered play-based practices, they are yet to recognise everyday practices that may encompass experiences involving IoToys and AI literacy resources and programmes. Research on how technology can be integrated in ECE curriculum is thus underdeveloped (Mascheroni & Holloway, 2017, 2019; Stephen & Edwards, 2018) and undertheorised, and more evidence is needed to understand the what and how technology can be integrated into pedagogy and curricula as well as home-based practices for the creation of meaningful multimodal learning in digital ecosystems (Fleer, 2018; OECD, 2019; Palaiologou, Kewalramani, & Dardanou, 2021). The curricula analysis presented in this chapter should provide nuanced knowledge and further directions for policymakers to effectively design a DC curriculum, including ideas around AI curriculum and resources that can help educators to teach young non-programmers acquire AI literacy through age-appropriate learning content (Su & Yang, 2022).

Considerations

Based on the discussion in this chapter, we propose that policymakers need to urgently consider key basic questions about curriculum development for young children aged 0–8 years. These questions need to evolve around the why, what and how (Yang, 2022) education for young children should look like, rooted in the cultural practices of each country. In that sense, key considerations should focus on the following:

1   Why is DC education needed for young children?
2   What are the appropriate digital competencies, for example AI education during the early years?
3   What is the subset of key technology ideas and concepts (e.g. IoToys, robotics and AI-related literacy) that can be learned by children?
4   How should young children learn about AI? In other words, what are the appropriate pedagogical approaches?

5 What programmes and resources can be curated for ECE educators' and parents' professional development and confidence to enable children's digital competencies?

References

Arnott, L., Kewalramani, S., Gray, C., & Dardanou, M. (2020). Role play and technologies in early childhood. In Z. Kingdon (Ed.), *A Vygotskian analysis of children's play behaviours: Beyond the home corner* (pp. 76–92). London: Routledge.

Arnott, L., Palaiologou, I., & Gray, C. (2018). Digital devices, internet-enabled toys and digital games: The changing nature of young children's learning ecologies, experiences and pedagogies. *British Journal of Educational Technology*, *49*(5), 803–806. DOI: 10.1111/bjet.12676.

Arnott, L., Palaiologou, I., & Gray, C. (2019). Internet of Toys across home and early childhood education: Understanding the ecology of the child's social world. *Technology, Pedagogy and Education*, *28*(4), 401–412. DOI: 10.1080/1475939X.2019.1656667.

Arnott, L., & Yelland, N. (2020). Multimodal lifeworlds: Pedagogies for play inquiries and explorations. *Journal of Early Childhood Education Research*, *9*(1), 124–146. https://jecer.org/wp-content/uploads/2020/02/Arnott-Yelland-issue9-1.pdf.

Australian Curriculum and Reporting Authority. (2020). *Digital Technologies F-10 curriculum*. Retrieved from https://www.australiancurriculum.edu.au/f-10-curriculum/technologies/digital-technologies/.

Australian Government Department of Education and Training. (2019). *Belonging, being and becoming – the early years learning framework for Australia*. Retrieved from https://www.dese.gov.au/child-care-package/resources/belonging-being-becoming-early-years-learning-framework-australia.

Bird, J., & Edwards, S. (2015). Children learning to use technologies through play: A digital play framework. *British Journal of Educational Technology*, *46*(6), 1149–1160.

Bølgan, N. B. (2018). *Digital praksis i barnehagen* [Digital practices in kindergarten]. Bergen: Fagbokforlaget.

Bonetti, S. (2019). *A comparative analysis using the Labour Force Survey*. A report prepared for the Education Policy institute and Nuffield Foundation.

Bowen, G. (2009). Document analysis as a qualitative research method. *Qualitative Research Journal*, *9*(2), 27–40. DOI: 10.3316/QRJ0902027.

Bradbury, A., & Roberts-Holmes, G. (2017). *The datafication of primary and early years education: Playing with numbers. Foundations and futures in education*. London: Routledge.

Bury, J., Mayer, M., Gogescu, F., Bristow, T., & Husain, F. (2020). *Understanding the early years workforce: Qualitative Research Findings*. A report prepared for the Nuffield Foundation.

Danby, S., Fleer, M., Davidson, C., & Hatzigianni, M. (2018). *Digital childhoods: Technologies and children's everyday lives (International perspectives on early childhood education and development; vol. 22)*. Singapore: Springer.

Dardanou, M., & Kofoed, T. (2019). It is not only about the tools! Professional digital competence. In C. Gray & I. Palaiologou (Eds.) *Early learning in the digital age* (pp. 61–76). Thousand Oaks and New York: SAGE.

Dardanou, M., Mossin, S. M., & Simensen, D. E. (2021). *Barnehagens digitale arenaer* [Kindergarten's digital arenas]. Oslo: Universitetsforlaget.

Dardanou, M., Unstad, T., Brito, R., Dias, P., Fotakopoulou, O., Sakata, Y., & O'Connor, J. (2020). Use of touchscreen technology by 0–3-year-old children: Parents' practices and perspectives in Norway, Portugal and Japan. *Journal of Early Childhood Literacy*, 20(3), 551–573. DOI: 10.1177/1468798420938445

Druga, S., Randi, W., Park, H. W., & Breazeal, C. (2018). How smart are the smart toys? Children and parents' agent interaction and intelligence attribution. In *Proceedings of the 17th ACM Conference on Interaction Design and Children (IDC '18)*. DOI: 10.1145/3202185.3202741.

Fjørtoft, S. O., Thun, S., & Buvik, M. P. (2019). *Datagrunnlaget til Monitorundersøkelsen 2019* [The data base for the Monitor study 2019]. Retrieved from https://www.udir.no/tall-og-forskning/finn-forskning/rapporter/datagrunnlaget-til-monitor-2019/.

Fleer, M. (2018). Digital animation: New conditions for children's development in play-based setting. *British Journal of Educational Technology*, 49(5), 943–958. DOI: 10.1111/bjet.12637.

Fleer, M. (2019). Technologies for children. Australia: Cambridge University Press.

Fotakopoulou, O., Hatzigianni, M., Dardanou, M., Unstad, T., & O'Connor, J. (2020). A cross-cultural exploration of early childhood educators' beliefs and experiences around the use of touchscreen technologies with children under 3 years of age. *European Early Childhood Education Research Journal*, 28(2), 272–285. DOI: 10.1080/1350293X.2020.1735744.

Gessiou, G., Dardanou, M., & Sakellariou, M. (2018). Comparative research on Greek and Norwegian prospective early childhood professionals' views on outdoor learning and play. In K. Tsoukala & D. Germanos (Eds.), *Children's spaces or spaces for children?* Conference proceedings (pp. 754–772). Retrieved from https://eproceedings.epublishing.ekt.gr/index.php/childspace/issue/view/82/showToc.

Hatzigianni, M., Gregoriadis, A., Karagiorgou, I., & Chatzigeorgiadou, S. (2018). Using tablets in free play: The implementation of the digital play framework in Greece. *British Journal of Educational Technology*, 49(5), 928–942.

Huber, B., Highfield, K., & Kaufman, J. (2018). Detailing the digital experience: Parent reports of children's media use in the home learning environment. *British Journal of Educational Technology*, 49(5), 821–833. DOI: 10.1111/bjet.12667.

Ilomäki, L., Paavola, S., Lakkala, M., & Kantosalo, A. (2016). Digital competence– an emergent boundary concept for policy and educational research. *Education and Information Technologies*, 21(3), 655–679. DOI: 10.1007/s10639-014-9346-4.

Inoue, M., O'Gorman, L., Davis, J., & Ji, O. (2017). An international comparison of early childhood educators' understanding and practices in education for sustainability in Japan, Australia and Korea. *International Journal of Early Childhood*, 49, 353–373. DOI: 10.1007/s13158-017-0205-5.

Kewalramani, S., Kidman, G., & Palaiologou, I. (2021). Using artificial intelligence (AI) interfaced robotic toys in early childhood settings: A pedagogy for children's inquiry literacy. *European Early Childhood Education Research Journal*, 29(5). DOI: 10.1080/1350293X.2021.1968458.

Kewalramani, S., Palaiologou, I., Arnott, L., & Dardanou, M. (2020). The integration of the Internet of Toys in early childhood education: A platform for multilayered interactions. *European Early Childhood Education Research Journal*, 28(2), 197–213. DOI: 10.1080/1350293X.2020.1735738.

Kewalramani, S., Palaiologou, I., & Dardanou, M. (2020). Children's engineering design thinking processes: The magic of the ROBOTS and the power of BLOCKS (electronics). *Eurasia Journal of Mathematics, Science and Technology Education*, *16*(3), em1830. DOI: 10.29333/ejmste/113247.

Lehesvuori, S., Ramnarain, U., & Viiri, J. (2017). In search of dialogicity: A comparison of curricular documents and classroom interactions from Finland and Hong Kong. *Education in Science*, *7*(4), 76. DOI: 10.3390/educsci7040076.

Marsh, J., Plowman, L., Yamada-Rice, D., Bishop, J., & Scott, F. (2016). Digital play: A new classification. *Early Years*, *36*(3), 242–253.

Marsh, J., Wood, E., Chesworth, L., Nisha, B., Nutbrown, B., & Olney, B. (2019). Makerspaces in early childhood education: principles of pedagogy and practice. Mind, Culture, and Activity, 26(3), 221–233.

Marty, L., Venturini, P., & Almqvist, J. (2018). Teaching traditions in science education in Switzerland, Sweden and France: A comparative analysis of three curricula. *European Educational Research Journal*, 17(1), 51–70. DOI: 10.1177/1474904117698710.

Mascheroni, G., & Holloway, D. (Eds.). (2017). *The Internet of Toys: A report on media and social discourses around young children and IoToys*. DigiLitEY. Retrieved from http://digilitey.eu/wp-content/uploads/2017/01/IoToys-June-2017-reduced.pdf.

Mascheroni, G., & Holloway, D. (Eds.). (2019). *The Internet of Toys: practices, affordances and the political economy of children's play*. Cham: Palgrave Macmillan.

Moser, T., & Martinsen, M. T. (2010). The outdoor environment in Norwegian kindergartens as a pedagogical space for toddlers' play, learning and development. *European Early Childhood Education Research Journal*, *18*(4), 457–471. DOI: 10.1080/1350293X.2010.525931.

Norwegian Directorate for Education and Training. (2017). *Framework plan for kindergartens*. Oslo: Norwegian Directorate for Education and Training. Retrieved from https://www.udir.no/contentassets/5d0f4d947b244cfe90be8e6d475ba1b4/framework-plan-for-kindergartens--rammeplan-engelsk-pdf.pdf.

Organisation for Economic and Collaboration Development. (2017). *PISA 2015 results (volume v): Collaborative problem solving*. Paris: PISA, OECD.

Organisation for Economic and Collaboration Development. (2019). *Artificial intelligence in society*. Paris: OECD.

Organisation for Economic and Collaboration Development. (2021). *OECD digital education outlook 2021: Pushing the frontiers with artificial intelligence, blockchain and robots*. Paris: OECD.

Palaiologou, I. (2019). *Child observation: A guide for students of early childhood*. London. SAGE.

Palaiologou, I., Kewalramani, S., & Dardanou, M. (2021). Make-believe play with the Internet of Toys: A case for multimodal playscapes. *British Journal of Educational Technology*, *52*(6), 2100–2117.

Palaiologou, I., and Male. T. (2019). Leadership in early childhood education: The case for pedagogical praxis. *Contemporary Issues in Early Childhood*, 20(1), 23–34. DOI: 10.1177/1463949118819100 (First published on Online First 19 December 2018).

Palaiologou, I., & Male, T. (2021). Early years foundation stage. In I. Palaiologou (Ed.), *Early years foundation stage: Theory and practice* (4th ed., pp. 19–38). London: Sage.

Pascal, C., Bertram, T., & Rouse, L. (2019). Getting it right in the Early Years Foundation Stage: A review of the evidence. Retrieved from https://earlyyears reviews.co.uk/wp-content/uploads/2020/06/EYFS-Coalition-Chris-Pascal-slides-for-sharing.pdf.

Plowman, L., & Stephen, C. (2007). Guided interaction in pre-school settings. *Journal of Computer Assisted Learning, 23*(1), 14–26.

Siraj-Blatchford, I., Kingston, D., & Melhuish, E. (2015). *Assessing quality in early childhood education and care. Sustained shared thinking and emotional wellbeing (SSTEW)s scale for 2–5 year olds provision.* London: UCL and IOE Press.

Siraj-Blatchford, I., Kingston, K., Neilsen-Hewett, C., Howard, S. J., Melhuish, E., de Rosnay, M., ... Luu, B. (2017). *A review of the current international evidence considering quality in early childhood education and care programmes – In delivery, pedagogy and child outcomes.* Sydney: NSW Department of Education.

Statistics Norway. (2021). *Kindergartens, 2021, final figures.* Retrieved from: https://www.ssb.no/en/utdanning/barnehager/statistikk/barnehager.

Stephen, C., & Edwards, S. (2018). *Young children playing and learning in a digital age: A cultural and critical perspective.* London: Routledge.

Su, J., & Yang, W. (2022). Artificial intelligence in early childhood education: A scoping review. *Computers and Education: Artificial Intelligence, 3,* 100049.

Tao, Y., Oliver, M. C., & Venville, G. J. (2012). Chinese and Australian year 3 children's conceptual understanding of science: A multiple comparative case study. *International Journal of Science Education, 34*(6), 879–901. DOI: 10.1080/09500693.2011.578679.

UNICEF Office of Research – Innocenti. (2019). *Growing up in a connected world: Global Kids online project.* Retrieved from https://www.unicef-irc.org/publications/1060-growing-up-in-a-connected-world.html.

UNICEF. (2021). *Policy guidance on AI for children.* Retrieved from https://www.unicef.org/globalinsight/stories/How-to-design-AI-for-children.

Van den Akker, J. (2003). Curriculum perspectives: An introduction. In J. van den Akker, W. Kuiper, & U. Hameyers (Eds.), *Curriculum landscapes and trends* (pp. 1–10). Dordrecht/Boston/London: Kluwer Academic Publishers.

Van den Akker, J. (2010). Building bridges: How research improve curriculum policies and classroom practices. In J. van den Akker (Ed.), *Beyond Lisbon 2010: Perspectives from research and development for education policy in Europe* (pp. 177–195). Slough, Berkshire: Consortium of Institutions for Development and Research in Education in Europe.

Voogt, J., & Roblin, N. J. (2012). A comparative analysis of international frameworks for 21st century competences: Implications for national curriculum policies. *Journal of Curriculum Studies, 44*(3), 299–321. DOI: 10.1080/00220272.2012.668938.

Williams, P., Sheridan, S., & Sandberg, A. (2014). Preschool – An arena for children's learning of social and cognitive knowledge. *Early Years: An International Research Journal, 34*(3), 226–240. DOI: 10.1080/09575146.2013.872605.

Wood, E., & Hedges, H. (2016a). Curriculum in early childhood education: Critical questions about content, coherence, and control. *The Curriculum Journal, 27*(3), 387–405.

Wood, E., & Hedges, H. (2016b). Curriculum in early childhood education: Critical Working Environment Act (2017) *Chapter 12.* Retrieved from https://lovdata.no/dokument/NLE/lov/2005-06-17-62/KAPITTEL_13#KAPITTEL_13.

Working Environment Act. (2017). *Chapter 12*. Retrieved from: https://lovdata.no/dokument/NLE/lov/2005-06-17-62.

Yang, W. (2022). Artificial intelligence education for young children: Why, what, and how in curriculum design and implementation. *Computers and Education: Artificial Intelligence*, 3, 100061. DOI: 10.1016/j.caeai.2022.100061.

3 Technological landscapes at home, but do they really play?

A case study from English homes

Introduction

There has been research in recent years which focuses on young children's interactions with technologies at home (e.g. Poveda et al., 2020; Gilen & Cameron, 2021), and although this research is valid and has given us in-depth insights into children's interactions with digital technologies at home, such research with IoToys is limited. This is especially true with children under the age of three where the research has tended to be limited to touch screen technology.

As discussed in the previous chapter, examining the research on digital technology in households and its uses by children (e.g. Chaudron et al., 2015, 2017, 2018; Rideout, 2017; Mascheroni & Holloway, 2019) has led to two key lines of discourse: whether children's interactions with technology are play or not and the "digital disconnect" between ECE and homes (e.g. Marsh et al., 2016; Edwards et al., 2017; Marsh, 2017a, 2017b). In ECE settings, dominant ideologies of play are engrossed in children's engagement with real-world objects and hands-on experience ignoring "a new generation of technologies with tangible [that is, touchable] interfaces facilitating seamless movement between digital and non-digital resources and play narratives" (Stephen & Plowman, 2014, p. 336). We have previously argued that such ideologies prevent the integration of technology in ECE (Palaiologou, 2016) despite emerging research on IoToys urging for a continuum between home and ECE (Arnott, Palaiologou, & Gray, 2019; Kewalramani, Palaiologou, Arnott, & Dardanou, 2020). Consequently, we consider it important to examine what patterns of behaviours exist when children are interacting with technology. As discussed previously in this book, IoToys have the potential to marry real and digital objects, and this conclusion makes such research important (Marsh, 2017a, 2017b). We anticipate that understanding how children are using IoToys at home will offer insights and help us to effectively integrate their use in ECE settings and create a continuum between home and ECE.

This chapter focuses on the English data and seeks to explore whether play with IoToys not only contains a physical engagement and elements of creativity and exploration but also imagination. Based on observational data, the chapter shows how children use the IoToys at home to develop play situations, either on

DOI: 10.4324/9781003185840-3

their own or with parents. We will conclude by showing that the IoToys are providing a continuum, of connectivity, bridging the digital–non-digital/physical and digital entities and spaces. Finally, it will address the implications for ECE. Currently in England (as discussed in Chapter 2), technology is not included in the statutory framework for ECE, but it will be argued that based on our findings it is even more important to integrate technology in the curriculum in playful ways. We conclude that there is a need to support parents and children to develop their learning skills not only within ECE settings but also at homes and at all times also maintaining an ethical approach to technology.

The context of the study

This chapter is based on an observational small-scale study in five English households. Findings from this project have been previously reported that it was found that children can develop make-believe play when engaging with IoToys (Palaiologou, Kewalramani, & Dardanou, 2021). It was found that children engage in imaginary situations using IoToys to facilitate their play within and beyond the functions of the IoToys. What was interesting is that, due to their transfunctional nature, children transformed the functions of the IoToys into symbolic actions and developed make-believe play to represent actions inspired by the IoToys.

So, this chapter will focus on the psychological dimensions of learning and examine what style and characteristics of play children exhibit when engaging with IoToys.

Five families participated in the project (see Table 3.1), with all households being selected as they already had IoToys at home. Data were collected from October 2018 to February 2020, but data collection was then suspended due to the COVID-19 pandemic and continuing lockdowns. As will be shown in Chapter 7, initially the parents were sending photos and videos via WhatsApp as well, but with the extension of the lockdowns these were stopped. All families were from secure socioeconomic backgrounds, and as this project was interesting to understand how children interact with IoToys, children had a degree of familiarity with them rather than being introduced to them as "new" to them, although this could also be seen as a limitation.

Data were collected with non-participant observations, with the researcher visiting each family every two weeks for about three hours and observed children during play with or without IoToys. Parents also videoed their own children if they thought a play episode was of interest and sent it to the researcher.

Because it was home-based research, the project had many ethical complexities. While it complied with the EECERA (2015) and BERA (2018) codes, ethical considerations went beyond the institutional expectations, however, and a set of reflective questions were used based on Palaiologou (2014). Actions were taken to minimise the intrusive nature of the project where the researcher was in families' private spaces by negotiating the parts of the house and the times the researcher could be present. All observational materials were shared with

Table 3.1 Overview of the participants and IoToys used in the households

England

Families	Number and age of children at the start of the study (October 2018)	Education of parents	Employment	IoToys at home
Family 1	Two boys (twins 4 years)	Both undergraduate level	Both parents	Osmo Detective, Agency Game Set, Wow Wee Mip Robot and Coji robot
Family 2	One girl (3 years and 4 months) One boy (5 years and 6 months)	Both undergraduate level	Father only, Mother not in employment by choice	Osmo Coding, Make Music and Jam Lego Boost, Creative Toolbox
Family 3	Two girls (2 years and 3 months, and 4 years and 6 months)	Mother postgraduate level Father undergraduate level	Father, Mother part time	EARSOON Intelligent & Charismatic Dancing Remote Control Robot with Music and Lights for Children, Disco & Cheering RC Robot, Wow Wee MiPosaur and Track Bell
Family 4	One boy (3 years) and one girl (4 years and 10 months)	Both parents postgraduate level	Both parents	CogniToys Dino, Wonder Workshop's Dash and Osmo Genius Kit
Family 5	Two boys (18 months, and 3 years and 8 months)	Both parents undergraduate level	Father only, Mother not in employment by choice	FUTURE ROBOT Recording Talking Robot and Fisher Price Smart Toy Bear

the families (parents and children where this was possible), and the data entered for analysis was agreed by all parties involved. Analysis of data was also shared with all participants (including children when this was possible) for approval and comments. All names in this paper are pseudonyms, and any visual data used has ensured that the families cannot be identified.

Data analysis

At an initial stage, data was analysed thematically using Braun and Clarke's (2006) approach. At a second stage, semantic analysis was employed that focused on the psychological dimensions of the characteristics of play that children exhibit (see also Palaiologou, Kewalramani, & Dardanou, 2021).

At the third stage, 46 observations were analysed. The aims were to examine play from a developmental perspective, "the state of actual" (Stephen & Edwards, 2018, p. 86), by investigating "close observation[s] of the child and emotional attunement, in other words not just listening to what the child is saying, but observing body movements and attuning to the child's emotional state" (Howes, 2010, p. 134).

Consequently, several frameworks that detail the functions of play were considered (e.g. Seagoe, 1970; Hutt, 1971; Bretherton, 1984; Rogers et al., 2002; Bornstein, 2006; Bird & Edwards, 2015). We decided to use the Children's Developmental Play Instrument (CDPI), a multidimensional psychological tool for examining children's play (Chazan, 2000, 2009; Chazan et al., 2016) as it provides a synthesis between the inner functions of play and the interactions with the environment. This tool has been developed for traditional (non-technological) play, but was chosen as it would have helped us to investigate if styles and characteristics of play are the same with playing with IoToys.

Findings

Before examining data from children's observations, it is important to report on our key findings from parents' testimonials and informal conversations when the researcher was visiting their homes for data collection.

Findings from parents

This aspect will provide a useful contextualising measure, as they represent children's social worlds and their views on the integration of IoToys in daily life.

There were varying degrees of acceptance of IoToys among parents. It was evident that IoToys were part of family life and, similar to findings on touch screen research, parents expressed concerns on how they can use them "more productively" to facilitate children's play and any potential learning, while admitting they were learning and exploring alongside their children. One mother raised the issue of educational play at home, saying that she wanted only the IoToys that her children can play as "[my children] are at school from 7:45 until 16:00 some days, when in school all they do is educational play, but when I pick them from school, I want them to play at home, so I do not want educational toys surrounding them all the time, they need a break."

Interestingly, parents mentioned that certain IoToys are suggested by the manufacturers for older children, yet younger ones enjoy them most:

> *We got [IoToy] for our older [5 years-boy], but he did not play a lot, he lost interest pretty fast, but our younger one [3 years and 4 months-girl] loved it! [...] our son has already moved to more sophisticated devices such as his games on PlayStation [...] and some of the IoToys are not attractive to him.*

(Father)

To conclude, it was evident that parents perceive children's engagement with IoToys as play "similar to his soldiers and cars." The parents especially did not see any antagonism between IoToys and non-digital toys confirming that the "distinction between digital and analogue (or non-digital) no longer has very much significance" (Buckingham, 2018, p. ix). While there were still concerns about the physical activity, social development and safety, parents appeared to want workable examples on how their children can live across a range of contexts where a "shared continuum, give rise to a new potentiality for a future, ever richer, degree of **wholeness**" (Bookchin, 1993, p. 5), "tracing the micro-temporalities of the 'craze', through the meso-temporalities of the 'experience', through to the macro -temporalities that underpin habits, routines, demeanours and collective formations such as curricula and traditions" (Thomson, Berriman, & Bragg, 2018, p. 3). Finally, it was evident that the eco-communities of children are still shaped by the binary digital–non-digital debate, instead of developing a workable continuum across children's spaces in a post-digital era where play happens.

Findings from children

Based on the CBTI instrument, the analysis of findings revealed the different styles of play when children engaged with IoToys as described in Table 3.2.

The characteristics exhibited by children when they interacted with IoToys demonstrated that they mapped to the characteristics of play with non-technological toys as shown in Table 3.3

Discussion: The case for rethinking children's play in digital landscapes

As mentioned earlier, previous discussions about the nature of digital play have focused on touchscreen technology and there is limited research about how this play is now shaped with the introduction of IoToys. Our findings showed that the binary views of digital and non-digital play are less relevant with the introduction of IoToys, as children play in the same ways across resources and

Table 3.2 Examples of play styles and descriptions

Style	Descriptions	Example
Adaptive	Anticipation	In the play, child anticipates what might happen next
	Adaptation	Child makes use of materials in the room
	Problem-solving	Child solves a problem during play
	Suppression	While playing, child intentionally avoids discomfort
	Affiliation	Child shares play activity with others
	Humour	While playing, child used humour to express himself
Inhibited	Inhibition	Activity abandoned, child moves to another one and maybe later returns to it
Conflicted	Intellectualising	While playing, child narrates an experience in matter-of-fact-tone
	Doing and undoing	While playing, child repeatedly builds and knocks down tower of blocks
	Negotiation	While at play, child begins one activity and leaves abruptly
	Reaction formation	Child enjoys activity or play object and dislikes it
	Turning aggression to the self	Child shows frustration and aggression and turns against him/her either physically or verbally (i.e. hitting his /her head)
	Avoidance	While at play, child avoids playmates or activity
Disorganised	Dedifferentiation Dispersal Dismantling (all three descriptors might be present or one of them at each time)	While playing, child throws all the pieces of a toy in the air, scattering them around the room and making no attempt to collect them
	Constriction	While playing, the child withdraws from others and engages in rigid repetitious activity
	Freezing	In the play, suddenly the child "freezes" lively characters so they cannot move or the play to progress
	Reversal of affect	In the play, a beautiful rainbow gets bigger and bigger
	Fusion	In the play, an action begins to absorb all the children, i.e. they all start screaming or running or jumping

Table 3.3 Characteristics associated with play when children engage with IoToys

Characteristics	Examples from the data
Use of objects either as they are or as replicas	Alex is playing with Wow Wee Mip Robot, then picks up the robot and says, "you are now tired" it is bed time, puts the robot on the sofa and brings a blanket and a pillow to "tuck him" in the bed to sleep. In this instance, Alex is using the robot as a doll developing symbolic play, pretending that he is putting her baby to bed.
Enthusiasm-motivation	Elliot goes to the kitchen where his father was cooking and asks him if he can play with Cosmo that was charging in the living room. His father nods positively. Elliot claps his hands and then goes and starts playing with Cosmo. He is struggling, so he goes back to the kitchen and asks his dad for help. His father says he is busy and cannot help. Elliot returns to the living room and tries to work out on his own how to code Cosmo; he manages after trying for about five minutes, and then he claps his hands showing satisfaction.
Engagement (subthemes: Experience driven by the child Concentration Absorbing activity Exploration Pursuing curiosity Pursuing their own interests)	Amy and her mother came back from the park where they had collected some leaves. Amy goes to the table where the IoToy is placed, takes out her leaves and starts observing them through the magnifier lenses of the IoToy.
	She counts the veins of the leaves through the magnifier lenses of the IoToy, and she says to herself that they are like roads; she goes and picks up a miniature toy car and brings it back and starts navigating the little car on the leaf observing it through the IoToy. Then she gets up and paraphrasing the nursery rhyme: "This little Biggy" she jumps around different areas in the house putting her leaves in different places according to the rhyme:
	This little piggy went to market
	This little piggy stayed at home
	This little piggy had roast beef
	This little piggy had none
	And this little piggy went
	Amy hides a leaf under the sofa.
	Amy hides a leaf under a pillow.
	Amy hides a leaf in the dining area.
	Amy hides a leaf under the table where the IoToy is placed.
	She stops and calls her mother to play with her; she explains to her the "new" game.
	She will chase her mother when she tries to find where she has hidden the leaves. The clues are in the nursery rhyme. She will stop chasing her once she finds the leaves.
	"Wee Wee Wee" all the way home
	She hides a leaf in her pocket, but it can be obvious, so her mother can chase her at the end.

(Continued)

Table 3.3 Characteristics associated with play when children engage with IoToys (*Continued*)

Characteristics	Examples from the data
Social and emotional growth	Andi is playing with Conji, and his sister Edith comes and asks him if she can play as well. Andi says no. Edith asks again, but Andi does not want her to play with him. Then Edith snatches Conji from the floor and starts running. Andi chases her and shouts to give Conji back to him. After about three minutes of chasing, Edith stops and returns the toy to Andi. She then asks him if she can play with him. Andi said to her that she can look at him when he is playing.
	In this instance, we can see that although Andi did not want to share with his sister, Edith does not respect this and takes the toy, but then both children found a way to negotiate and carry on with the play.
Expression of feelings (glee, delight, pleasure, surprise, anxiety, fear, frustration, disgust or boredom)	Children when playing with IoToys demonstrated a range of emotions such as happiness, frustration and fun and used their body to express these either by clapping their hands (happiness) or by stamping their feet on the floor (frustration).
Dealing with mistakes	Alex when playing with Wow Wee Mip Robot tries to balance the robot, but he is not successful. He is not giving up and tries, but after five times he shows frustration by banging his fists on the table. He stops, looks at the robot and gives it another go. At the end, he manages to balance the robot.
Risk-taking	Edith is trying to code Coji using emojis. She follows the instructions from the app; then she decided to create her own emojis on a piece of paper and tries to code Coji with her own emojis to see whether this will work.
Physicality (focusing on fine motor skills)	The manipulation of IoToys requires children to use their fingers as well as their body to follow the example of the robots.
Self-esteem and self-worth	When Edith was successfully coding Coji, she was jumping up and down and running to her mother, asking her to come and see; with a big smile, she kept saying, "Look! Look! Look! What I did." Her body language showed pride with her achievements that motivated to explore further by creating her own emojis.

(Continued)

Table 3.3 Characteristics associated with play when children engage with IoToys (*Continued*)

Characteristics	Examples from the data
Imagination and social pretend Create or change meaning, purpose, rules and actions to create a new situation	In Amy's observation above, imagination and creativity are evident as she created her chasing game. Two boys aged four (twin siblings) are using OSMO with their mother who kept instructing the boys to put pieces together according to what was on the iPad screen. Both boys were giggling most of the time, however, and were ignoring the instructions by putting things together in the way they wanted. The mother asked them to follow the instructions on the iPad screen, but the boys were a bit devious with her and carried on doing something different, creating "new" puzzles and not following the rules of OSMO. The mother gave up trying and left them on their own, and the boys carried on pretending they were creating space submarines and manipulating the pieces to pretend they were flying. (adopted from Palaiologou, Kewalramani, & Dardanou, 2021)
Fluidity	As can be seen from the above examples from the data, children during their play linked IoToys with other physical entities and used them in a fluid way to enter a play schema, then move to non-digital play continuing the theme, then back to digital play and vice versa. In all cases where children moved in and out of the digital to non-digital, they used the same theme in a fluid way.

contexts creating a play continuum. We argue that an examination of children's play in the digital world is requiring to create synergistic holistic richness in relationships between digital and non-digital that synchronise the landscapes of children's play.

The findings show that all styles and characteristics of play that have been described in non-technological play were found when children engaged with IoToys. Such findings urge us to move away from the division of children's play-scapes and try to understand children's play with IoToys and non-technological toys. From our research, we contend that arguments based on screen-based research cautioning balance in children's play between digital and non-digital activities (Nathanson, 2015; Radesky et al., 2015) should be re-evaluated in line with the context of young children's play with IoToys that has created different playscapes. The data in this project demonstrate a synchronised and synergised way between digital and non-digital, and further research is required to focus on this topic. IoToys' permanent connectivity and transfunctionality transcend from digital to non-digital and vice versa in a fluid manner.

By examining the psychological functions of play and its characteristics in relation to children's social landscapes (home and families), we can see that play with IoToys can occur in different spheres. Starting from self in relation to IoToy becomes purposeful; children attempt meaning making and move in their play as a continuum from self (playing alone) to social (playing with parents or siblings). In that sense, they use IoToys as another toy for as a "source of development" (Vygotsky, 1978, p. 138). In line with prior the analysis (Palaiologou, Kewalramani, & Dardanou, 2021), our findings show that children engage in imaginative and creative play where IoToys become objects that although they intend to initiate a playful activity due to their pre-programmed functions, the child actually can take control and move beyond the intended functions.

This movement across spheres (self-social) is context specific and is inseparable from the social world surrounding the child (the eco-community of child). Children utilise IoToys in their play by expressing themselves, making meanings, establishing rapports and reliving situations in each sphere in the same ways as with other objects and activities associated as play.

Conclusions

This study aimed to understand how children interact with IoToys in their social contexts – homes. We examined their interactions in terms of the psychological function of play and their social environment (eco-community), seeking an understanding of digital lives in the context they occur ("what-is"), rather than examining divisive discourses such as digital and non-digital play. From our findings, it became evident that IoToys (due to their multidimensionality and transfunctionality which blur physical and digital realms) can offer opportunities for children to create play situations where imaginative and creative play as a continuum can become evident. As was shown, once children engage in play with IoToys, they take control of the toy rather than the pre-programmed functions determining the play situation, as in the case of Amy using the leaves' veins as roads to create a playful situation.

Thus, it is proposed that in ECE we should consider creating multidimensional and holistic spaces which reflect the digital era and allow for potentialities to create a continuum of play when children's psychological characteristics of play (as shown in Table 3.3, e.g. motivation, self-regulation and self-worth) interact with social relationships (as shown in Table 3.2) and with the worlds they inhabit to position themselves to living in a digital eco-community.

The findings have shown that when engaging in play with IoToys, children go beyond their immediate physical surroundings as their worlds span the virtual realm. The re-conceptualisation should, therefore, revolve around an epistemological discussion on firstly, how we can achieve the creation of play spaces where there is fluidity and continuity between the digital and non-digital. Secondly, how play communities can be built and how children are attuned to play in the potentialities of the IoToys technology. We have shown in this study that IoToys allow children to transcend between physical and digital affordances in a fluid manner in their play. As IoToys develop even further and their domestication increases, ECE needs to re-imagine, reconceptualise and rebuild the spaces children inhabit and make them multidimensional multilayered inclusive spaces where physical and digital are present at two levels: ideologically in terms of teachers and children working in harmony with all playthings available (technological and non-technological) and practically in terms of the curriculum that embraces physical and digital affordances.

Research on play in digital lives in ECE can entail the use of desensitisation of the digitalisation as "new," "different" or even "external" to children's play habits and lives and focus instead on fostering the playscapes that children occupy and understanding *how children play* in the digital era.

References

Arnott, L., Palaiologou, I., & Gray, C. (2019). Internet of toys across home and early childhood education: Understanding the ecology of the child's social world, *Technology Education and Pedagogy*, *28*(4), 401–412. DOI: 10.1080/1475939X.2019.1656667.

Bird, J., & Edwards, S. (2015). Children learning to use technologies through play: A digital play framework. *British Journal of Educational Technology*, *46*(6), 1149–1160. DOI: 10.1111/bjet.12191.

Bookchin, M. (1993). What is social ecology? (essay). In M. E. Zimmerman (Ed.) *Environmental philosophy: From animal rights to radical ecology* (collection of essays with the permission of authors). Englewood Cliffs: Prentice Hall.

Bornstein, M. H. (2006). On the significance of social relationships in the development of Children's earliest symbolic play: An ecological perspective. In A. *Göncü* & S. *Gaskins* (Eds.), *Play and development: Evolutionary, sociocultural and functional perspectives* (pp. 101–129). Mahawah: Lawrence Erlbaum.

Braun, V., & Clarke, V. (2006). Using thematic analysis in psychology. *Qualitative Research in Psychology*, *3*(2), 77–101.

Bretherton, I. (1984). Representing the social world in symbolic play: Reality and fantasy. In I. Bretherton (Ed.), *Symbolic play: The development of social understanding* (pp. 1–39). Orlando: Academic Press.

British Educational Research Association (BERA). (2018). *Ethical guidelines for educational research* (4th ed.). London: BERA. Retrieved from https://www. bera.ac.uk/publication/ethical-guidelines-for-educational-research-2018.

Chaudron, S., Beutel, M. E., Černikova, M., Donoso, V., Dreier, M., Fletcher-Watson, B., … Wölfling K. (2015). *Young children (0–8) and digital technology: A qualitative exploratory study across seven countries.* Joint Research Centre, European Commission. Retrieved from http://publications.jrc.ec.europa.eu/repository/handle/JRC93239.

Chaudron, S., Di Gioia, R., & Gemo, M. (2018). *Young children (0-8) and digital technology, a qualitative study across Europe.* JRC 110359, EUR 29070 EN. Publications Office of the European Union. ISBN: 978-92-79-77767-7 (print), 978-92-79-77766-0.

Chaudron, S., Di Gioia, R., Gemo, M., Holloway, D., Marsh, J., Mascheroni, G., & Yamada Rice, D. (2017). *Kaleidoscope on the Internet of Toys—safety, security, privacy and societal insights.* Luxembourg: Publications Office of the European Union. Retrieved from http://publications.jrc.ec.europa.eu/repository/bitstream/JRC105061/jrc105061_ final_online.pdf.

Chazan, S. (2000). Using children's play therapy instrument (CPTI) to measure the development of play in simultaneous treatment: A case study. *Infant Mental Health Journal, 21*(3), 211–221.

Chazan, S. (2009). Observing play activity: The children's developmental play instrument (CDPI) with reliability studies. *Child Indicators Research, 2*, 217–436.

Chazan, S., Kuchirko, Y., Beebe, D., & Sossin, M. (2016). A longitudinal study into traumatic play activity using children's developmental play instrument (CPDI). *Journal of Infant, Child, Adolescent Psychotherapy, 15*, 1–25.

Edwards, S., Henderson, M., Gronn, D., Scott, A., & Mirkhil, M. (2017). Digital disconnect or digital difference? A socio-ecological perspective on young children's technology use in the home and the early childhood centre, *Technology, Pedagogy and Education, 26*(1), 1–17. DOI: 10.1080/1475939X.2016.1152291.

European Early Childhood Education Research Association (EECERA). (2015). *Ethical code for early childhood researchers.* Retrieved from http://www.eecera.org/about/ethical-code/.

Gilen, J., & Cameron, C. A. (2021). Importance of video-centred ethnography in a day in the life project: A case of beavers and citizenship. In *Thriving across the lifespan and around the globe.* Bentham Science. p. 19. ISBN: 9781681088815.

Howes, N. (2010). Here to listen! Communication with children and methods for communicating with children and young people as part of the assessment process. In J. Howarth (Ed.), *The child's world: The comprehensive guide to assessing children in need* (pp. 124–139). London: Jessica Kingsley.

Hutt, C. (1971). Exploration and play in children. In R. E. Herron & B. Sutton-Smith (Eds.), *Child's play* (pp. 233–251). New York: Wiley.

Kewalramani, S., Palaiologou, I., Arnott, L., & Dardanou, M. (2020). The integration of the internet of toys in early childhood education: A platform for multi-layered interactions. *European Early Childhood Research Association Journal, 28*(2), 197–213, DOI: 10.1080/1350293X.2020.1735738.

Marsh, J. (2019). The uncanny valley revisited: Play with the internet of toys. In G. Mascheroni & D. Holloway (Eds.), *The Internet of Toys: Practices, affordances and political economy of children's smart toys* (pp. 47–66). Cham: Palgrave MacMillan.

Marsh, J. A. (2017a). Russian dolls and three forms of capital: Ecological and sociological perspectives on parents' engagement with young children's tablet use. In C. Burnett, G. Merchant, A. Simpson, & M. Walsh (Eds.), *The case of the iPad: Mobile literacies in education* (pp. 31–47). Singapore: Springer.

Marsh, J. A. (2017b). The Internet of Toys and the changing nature of play. In S. Chaudron, R. Di Gioia, M. Gemo, D. Holloway, J. Marsh, G. Mascheroni, ... D. Yamanda-Rice. (Eds.), *Kaleidoscope on the Internet of Toys- safety, security, privacy and societal insights* (pp. 19–20). EUR 28397 EN. DOI: 10.2788/05383.

Marsh, J., Plowman, L., Yamada-Rice, D., Bishop, J., & Scott, F. (2016). Digital play: A new classification. *Early Years, 36*(3), 242–253.

Marsh, J., Wood, E., Chesworth, L., Nisha, B., Nutbrown, B., & Olney, B. (2019). Makerspaces in early childhood education: Principles of pedagogy and practice. *Mind, Culture, and Activity, 26*(3), 221–233. DOI: 10.1080/10749039. 2019.1655651.

Mascheroni, G., & Holloway, D. (2019). *The Internet of Toys: Practices, affordances and the political economy of children's smart play.* Cham: Palgrave Macmillan

Nathanson, A. L. (2015). Media and the family: Reflections and future directions. *Journal of Children and Media, 9*, 133–139.

Palaiologou, I. (2014). "*Do we hear what children want to say?*" Ethical praxis when choosing research tools with children under five. *Early Child Development and Care, 184*(5), 689–705. DOI: 10.1080/03004430.2013.809341.

Palaiologou, I. (2016). Teachers' dispositions towards the role of digital devices in play-based pedagogy in early childhood education. *Early Years: An International Research Journal, 36*(3), 305–321. DOI: 10.1080/09575146.2016.1174816.

Palaiologou, I., Kewalramani, S., & Dardanou, M. (2021). Make-believe play with Internet of Toys: A case for multimodal playscapes. *British Journal of Educational Research, 52*, 2100–2117. DOI: 10.1111/1467-8535.13110.

Poveda, D., Matsumoto, M., Sundin, E., Sandberg, H., Aliagas, C., & Gillen, J. (2020). Space and practices: Engagement of children under 3 with tablets and televisions in homes in Spain, Sweden and England. *Journal of Early Childhood Literacy, 20*(3), 24.

Radesky J. S., Kistin, C., Eisenberg, S., Zuckerman, B., & Silverstein, M. (2015). *Parent views about mobile device use around and by young children: Implications for anticipatory guidance.* Abstract presented at the Pediatric Academic Societies, San Diego, CA. Retrieved from http://www.abstracts2view.com/ pas/view.php?nu= PAS15L1_2195.2.

Rideout, V. (2017). *The common sense census: Media use by kids age zero to eight.* San Francisco: Common Sense Media. Retrieved from https://www. commonsensemedia.org/research/the-common-sense-census-mediause-by-kids-age-zero-to-eight-2017.

Rogers, Y., Scaife, M., Gabrielli, S., Smith, H., & Harris, E. (2002). A conceptual framework for mixed reality environments: Designing novel learning activities for young children. *Presence, 11*(6), 677–686.

Seagoe, M. V. (1970). An instrument for the analysis of children's play as an index of degree of socialisation. *Journal of School Psychology, 8*(2), 139–144.

Stephen, C., & Edwards, S. (2018). *Young children playing and learning in a digital age: A cultural and critical perspective.* London: Routledge.

Stephen, C., & Plowman, L. (2014). Digital play. In L. Brooker, M. Blaise, & S. Edwards (Eds.), *Sage handbook of play and learning in early childhood* (pp. 330–341). London: Sage.

Thomson, R., Berriman, L., & Bragg, S. (2018). *Researching everyday childhoods: Time, technology and documentation in a digital age.* London: Bloomsbury.

Vygotsky, L. (1978). *Mind in society: The development of higher process.* Cambridge: Harvard University Press.

4 Is there a space for "A" and "R" in early childhood STEM education?

Building a case for AI robotic technologies integration in Australia

Purpose of this study

The purpose of this chapter is to explore how the use of robotic technologies in ECE classrooms can support STREAM-based play experiences and STREAM literacy development. To this end, there are two questions guiding this study:

1 How do the teachers integrate robotics into ECE classrooms for STREAM-based play?
2 How do teachers integrate robotics to support children's STREAM literacy development?

What is STEM-based play?

STEM education engages learners in the exploration of real-world problems and contexts, drawing on the capabilities of science, technology, engineering and mathematics disciplines (Falloon et al., 2020) and in some cases using arts-based approaches (Liao, 2016) to bring to life what is called as STEAM education (Sullivan & Bers, 2016; Bers, 2022). As such, STEM or STEAM education is not the simple integration of these component disciplines, but an authentic and engaging approach to provoke children with the skills needed for future jobs – creativity, critical thinking, problem-solving and communication to create solutions to real-world problems (Early Childhood STEM Working Group, 2017; MacDonald, Danaia, & Murphy, 2020). This can be activated through immersing children in authentic real-world thinking scenarios through inquiry-based learning (Toh et al., 2016; Kidman & Casinader, 2017). Through STEM education, learners from the early years onwards (Fleer, 2018, 2019) can develop the knowledge and skills associated with competencies and dispositions that will enable them to become active citizens in a rapidly evolving and technology-dominated world (Zollman, 2012; MacDonald, Danaia, & Murphy, 2020).

STEM-based play can be defined as integrated STEM education (National Research Council, 2014) to expose children with tasks involving real-world phenomena and situations that require children to engage in creating solutions and draw upon their everyday experiences and existing capabilities. Children use

DOI: 10.4324/9781003185840-4

knowledge and skills from multiple disciplines – S/T/E/M. However, there are a limited number of studies that document children's abilities to make connections across concepts and practices in STEM disciplines (Fleer, 2019). Few studies have focused on capitalising on technology-constructed experiences to trigger children's interest, curiosity, imagination, creativity and problem-solving skills, and even fewer address robotics as part of STEM-based play to activate real-world thinking in the context of ECE settings.

Synergies between robotic integration and STEM-based play

In this chapter, we take the stance that STEM-based play in ECE is a human endeavour that uses the knowledge and processes of the technical disciplines (i.e. any combination of science, technology, engineering or mathematics) to help us pose, ponder and solve problems that are real and authentic to our worlds (Hunter, 2017; Murray, 2019). Taking a step further, while "T" is the "dominant player," this chapter will show that artificial intelligence (AI) and robotics can facilitate learning in ECE classrooms; thus, it is suggested to add A(=AI) and R(=robotics), and this is to be used as STREAM-based play.

The educative process of preparing young children to do so in an ever-changing technological world should consider children's existing abilities and further scaffold their engagement with real-world phenomena (Kewalramani, Palaiologou, & Dardanou, 2020; Unahalekhaka & Bers, 2022). By using technologies such as robots, creativity is boosted, unleashing playful moments and creating opportunities for productive play (Ihamäki & Heljakka, 2021; Bers, 2022). STREAM and robotic technologies are great educational tools that also harness a child's natural curiosity and sense of inquiry, especially because they offer multimodal ways of engaging and meaning making – be it through digital touch, aurally, visually, physically or digitally – that go far beyond simple screen time or printed text (Yelland, 2018; Edwards, 2021). The robots' pre-programmed storytelling functions (e.g. represent anthropomorphised characters or real/imaginary animals), together with the robots' codable features, allow the child to empathise with the problem being posed related to, for example, environmental sustainability issues (Kewalramani, Palaiologou, & Dardanou, 2020). The features are haptic (digital touch screen interface), audio-visual, tactile and movement and thus offer multimodal affordances (in contrast to monomodal play affordances or traditional toys).

When children use technologies for STREAM-based play, they make sense of their natural learning environments by blending the real world and their imagination via digital experiences (Fleer, 2018; Arnott & Yelland, 2020; Arnott et al., 2020). To date, there is limited research on how STEM and technologies, specifically robotics and AR/VR apps, can be used in age-appropriate ways with children to teach STREAM concepts and understand the emergent literacy skills. More importantly, today, young children come into the classroom already able to access information about the world around them with a swipe of a finger, further exacerbating the pedagogical problem of knowing what children need to know. More recently, studies are beginning to show, for example, how children's interactions with technologies support their learning in reading (Kucirkova & Falloon, 2016), mathematics and engineering concepts (Sullivan & Bers, 2016), and science circuitry concepts (Peppler et al., 2019). However, with technology becoming the mediator of children's everyday contexts, there have been very few studies which consider the multimodal nature of robotic technologies and how STEM-based play might enable children's STREAM literacy opportunities.

Pedagogical rationale to integrate robotics as "free-flow" STREAM-based play

Nowadays, robotic education is not only characterised as a tool for developing computational thinking skills, but also as the ability to use it wisely and in pedagogically sound ways as an instrument for children's social-emotional development (Bers, 2022). Holloway, Willson et al. (2021) affirm that children need support in pursuing the ability to use robotic toys critically and consciously, in acquiring suitable competences. In this context, STREAM education is particularly important and should be understood "as a set of activities aimed at equipping children with digital competence and multiliteracies" (Yelland, 2018). In lower primary education, robotics has been used as a comprehensive tool for creating educational space for children and performing diverse functions to aid in computational thinking skills, for example. The literature on this subject of pedagogical use of robotics provides six functions of robots by which it influences children (Ge, Ifenthaler, & Spector, 2015; Toh, Causo et al., 2016):

1　Cognitive and creative function, if a child solves difficult situations by means of critical engagement with the robot;
2　Motivating function, if using the robot enables the pursuit of one's curiosity and interests;
3　Revising function, if media allows the child to complete tasks and exercises that help the child to consolidate knowledge and abilities on their own;
4　Evaluative function, if the child's knowledge and abilities are evaluated during their work with the robot's coding programming platform;
5　Pedagogical function, if the robot creates conditions to influence the personality of the child;
6　Therapeutic function, if the media makes it possible to reduce developmental disorders.

Past educational research (Sullivan & Bers, 2016; Sullivan & Heffernan, 2016) has shown that robotics can be included for the following reasons:

- Improving a positive attitude to learning and developing curiosity in experiencing the world (Papadakis & Kalogiannakis, 2020);
- Providing friendly and safe conditions for fun and learning, for individual and group work, for developing autonomy and for promoting learning through

social interactions, negotiations, consensus building and collective decision-making "while playing to learn and learning to play" (Bers, 2008, p.4);
- Fostering the development of child's dispositional learning such as problem-solving skills necessary for active participation in future learning at school (Kewalramani, Kidman, & Palaiologou, 2021).

Even when STREAM-based play involving robotic technologies "appears" to be free-flow play, however, it is likely to be structured by adults to some degree, including permitted times for play, available resources and design of play spaces (Kewalramani, Palaiologou, & Dardanou, 2020). Some have argued that the notion of a totally "free" play environment is really a myth (Siraj-Blatchford & Brock, 2019), with adult aims shaping children's play to greater or lesser degrees, for diverse purposes and in implicit or explicit ways. Whether and how this free play can be guided or harnessed without undermining it is a point of contention in the research literature and in practice. Cowan (2020) describes free play as a "panorama" of play. That is, play should consider the unbroken viewpoint of the child who is involved as the observer as well as the partner at the heart of their play. Nevertheless, critics are concerned that play may be "instrumentalised," "pedagogised," "colonised" or "prescribed" by adults (Siraj-Blatchford & Brock, 2019). Defining free play, and play that involves robotic technologies, is therefore challenging. The United Nations (2013) defines children's free play as something that is chosen, directed and controlled by children themselves. This distinguishes it from play that is more directly led by adults and from recreation, which is understood as activities with a function, such as artistic, sporting or community engagement. In the context of STREAM-based play and robotics, free play often involves making and breaking rules, playing with possible storytelling and role-play scenarios, and acting both creatively and destructively, which Dweck (2015) calls it as experiential learning. Such qualities can mean play has an anarchic, chaotic, rebellious or purposeless appearance to adults. It may be rude, messy and noisy and may challenge expectations or conventions of teacher-directed learning environments (Siraj-Blatchford & Brock, 2019).

From this perspective, STREAM-based play as part of free play might be understood as a form of activism, where taking a "what if" or "as if" stance can help to challenge and deconstruct traditional ways of thinking (Poulsen, 2018). For instance, in the recent "makerspace" movement, playfulness is actively encouraged as a means of tinkering, experimenting, dismantling and iteratively designing (Marsh et al., 2017). This means the very "transgressive" nature of play may make it a particularly distinctive and powerful activity. These examples challenge romantic and idealised perspectives on play, showing that children may seek out experiences in free play with the robots that are taboo, risky, secretive, marginalising and disruptive, and as a result, free play may be troubling or unsettling to adults. Such play may also be unsettling to children themselves, who often appreciate fairness and a degree of safety in their play. Indeed, children can appreciate adult intervention to foster play spaces that are safe, ethical and equitable and to offer comfort and reassurance that foster safe technology-constructed play practices. Consequently, attention has focused on the role of the adults in "scaffolding" children's play so that it is aligned with intended learning objectives (Wood, 2010). Building on the idea of a "spectrum" of play, with a child's free play at one end and direct adult instruction at the other (e.g. Zosh et al., 2017), this has given rise to several concepts such as "guided play" (Zosh et al., 2017), "educational play" (Sylva, Melhuish et al., 2004), "playful learning" (Hirsh-Pasek et al., 2009) and "a pedagogy of play" (Project Zero, 2016). Although it appears that adult involvement in play can help maximise possibilities and opportunities for learning, the boundary between free STREAM-based play and adult-led play and the role of the adults in STREAM-based play involving technologies such as IoToys/robotic toys are complex and often debated (Selwyn, 2019). Drawing on these contentious issues about the role of child and the teacher in STREAM-based play involving technologies, this study in Australia endeavours to shed light on how play using robots and the interactions between the robot, children and teachers can shape the successes and challenges experienced during robotic integration. To progress our understanding of sensible use of tangible and multimodal technologies in a post-pandemic world, this study also provides insights of how teachers used robotics as a tool in the classroom to align with curriculum requirements and meet the developmental needs of children.

Links between STREAM-based play practices and children's STREAM literacy

As explained in Chapter 1, there are hierarchies of technologies (Table 1.1) available for children in the 21st century. Still, however, we do not know some of the technologies such as how robots build children's STEM literacy as part of the "panoramic suite" of STREAM-based play. Dýrfjörð and Hreiðarsdóttir's (2021) study, for example, explored how tangible robots enabled children's active participation to solve problems and engage in creative thinking, where the study's focus was on enhancing children's creative skills and actualising their collective ideas in design. Another study by Papadakis and Kalogiannakis (2020) offered real practical experiences to the students involving hands-on robotic activities and tasks, which students found fun and attractive due to their play aspect. The seminal research of Bers (2008–2022) has shown how robotics creates a creative playground for children to learn computational thinking concepts. Bers (2022) also highlights the 6Cs and 6 values learnt by children while engaging in robotics. The 6Cs include communication, collaboration, community building, content creation, creativity and conduct. The 6 values include caring, connection, contribution, competence, confidence and character.

Drawing from such studies in educational robotics, to conceptualise the positioning of STREAM-based play practices and children's STREAM literacy in ECE, a clear articulation of what enables "STREAM literacy" is required. This study's conceptualisation framework (see Figure 4.1) shows that the pedagogical considerations and aspects of STREAM-based play can act as a funnel to filter children's STEM literacy development using robotic integration. However, not all pedagogical aspects and interactions might filter to contribute to children's STREAM literacy. In the next sections of this chapter, how these characteristics

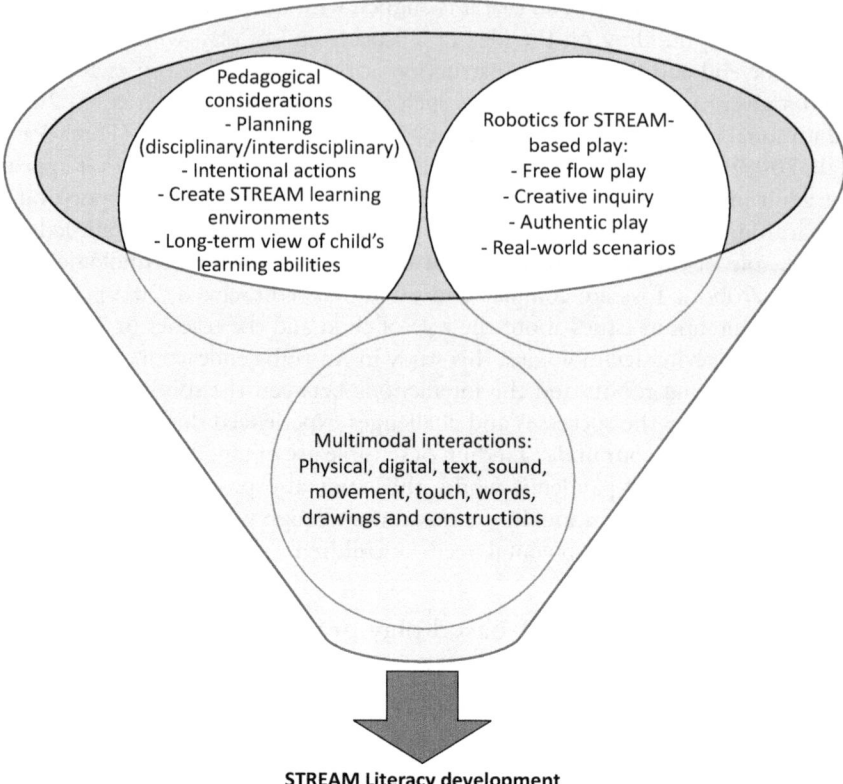

Pedagogical
considerations
- Planning
(disciplinary/interdisciplinary)
- Intentional actions
- Create STREAM learning
environments
- Long-term view of child's
learning abilities

Robotics for STREAM-
based play:
- Free flow play
- Creative inquiry
- Authentic play
- Real-world scenarios

Multimodal interactions:
Physical, digital, text, sound,
movement, touch, words,
drawings and constructions

STREAM Literacy development

Figure 4.1 Conceptual framework for children's STREAM literacy development

have been considered is explained using the Australian ECE settings as a case for children's STREAM literacy development.

Research design and context

In Australia, preschool education is provided by both private and public educational sectors, which include long day care centres, sessional and community kindergartens, family day care and Early Learning Centres (ELC) affiliated with private primary and secondary schools. The Australian EYLF (described in Chapter 2) supports all professionals who work with children aged 0–5. A design-based research (DBR) approach was employed in the current study, which is apt for small-scale educational research projects involving collaboration between educators, children and researchers (Jetnikoff, 2015). The DBR approach allows for the investigation of possibilities for educational improvement as an educational experiment by bringing about new forms of children's learning to generate, trial and refine changes to pedagogy (an integration of robotic technologies in the case of the current research) to study them.

Participants and data collection

The participants in this ongoing (2019–current) Australian study included three kindergartens, where the researcher introduced different types of robotic technologies (see Table 1.1 in Chapter 1) that can function in different styles (tangible and hybrid). A total of three teachers (females) from three different kindergartens participated. The kindergartens were a mix of private, long day care and community kindergarten services. All the teachers had a Bachelor of Early Childhood qualification and were early- to mid-career teachers. The kindergartens were situated in culturally diverse communities in the metropolitan suburbs of Victoria, Australia, and children were from English as an additional language (EAL) needs. Before the COVID-19 pandemic, the researcher together with the research assistant visited each of the kindergartens for one day a week over a fortnight to observe how the teachers used technology to engage the children in STREAM-based play. This is because it was important to understand the teachers' "naturally-inclined" intentional teaching practices and activities being planned for children's STREAM-based play. All the teaching episodes and children's experiences in each kindergarten were observed using the STREAM-based play observational protocol (Table 4.1). After reflective conversations with the participating teachers, the observational protocol was revised, which incorporated teachers' existing technology integration practices for STREAM-based play, thus accounting for teacher voice and capabilities while planning for the robotic activities.

The observation protocol comprised of the essential features for technology integration and related indicators for developing children's STREAM-based play. These pedagogical features were adapted from the Effective Early Education Experiences for Kids (E4Kids) study (Tayler, 2016) and Kewalramani and Havu-Nuutinen's (2019) study that studied teachers' technological pedagogical and content knowledge skills. E4Kids is Australia's largest four-year longitudinal study, conducted in 2010–2013, suggesting that ECE professionals use intentional teaching strategies that are always purposeful, which may be pre-planned or spontaneous, to support achievement of well-considered and identified goals. The current study extended the E4Kids study's intentional teaching strategies and identified five essential features of teachers' planning and integration of robotic technology in the context of STREAM-based play teaching practices (see Table 4.1) – teacher planning; emotional scaffolding through problem-based scenarios; building children's creative inquiry; promoting adult-child, peer-peer and child-robot interactions; and sharing of children's ideas and representations emerging from robotic free play. In addition, Table 4.1 shows how the essential features are linked to the related observed indicators for children's emergent STREAM literacy skills. This observational protocol was crucial in analysing the data together with the aspects highlighted in the study's conceptual framework.

In addition, to document the amount of children's exposure to STREAM-based play experiences along with the integration of robotic technology, the researcher collected teachers' weekly plans across the school term (10 weeks). These documents helped identify how often STREAM activities were being intentionally incorporated into teachers' planning. A total of eight weekly plans (from

Table 4.1 STREAM-based play observational protocol and pedagogical steps for robotic integration

Pedagogical step	Teacher actions	Indicators of children's STREAM literacy development
Teacher planning	• Co-design activities and provocations based on children's existing *schemes* (strengths and interests) • Curriculum goals aligned to the intentionally planned activity • Introduce the robots intentionally via play-based demonstrations • Allow children to tinker with them freely but safely.	• Children's ability to become curious about the robot • Children's ability to be emotionally aroused seeing the robot • Children express their wish to tinker with the robot • Children's ability to display range of emotions (e.g. happy, excited, not interested and move away from activity) after seeing the robot demonstrations by the teacher
Emotional scaffolding through problem-based scenarios	• Through storytelling and empathy-based situations, engage children in inquiry-based conversations • Generate a social-emotional learning environment where the robot is the central theme in the children's stories. • Encourage children to use verbal communication skills to share their ideas. For example, finding solutions to a problem centred around the robot (such as the robot might be running out of battery or a bridge might fall down on the robot) • Ask the children to initiate ideas to solve the problem encountered	• Selection of robot stimulates children's imaginative thinking • Through playful explorations such as pretend play with robots, children's ability to collaborate with their peers • Children's ability to discover new vocabulary and language while brainstorming solutions • Express emotions and behaviours in the form of words, questions, ideas and gestures • Encounter failure during beginning to code and be able to regulate emotions

(Continued)

Table 4.1 STREAM-based play observational protocol and pedagogical steps for robotic integration *(Continued)*

Pedagogical step	Teacher actions	Indicators of children's STREAM literacy development
Building children's creative inquiry	• Allow "wait, think, share" time for children to brainstorm with their peers on how to solve the posed problem • Teachers make specific links to children's everyday environment and home contexts • A variety of questions asked that promote children's inquiry skills (e.g. what do you think, I wonder what if, why did, how did, what might happen if, and how would you?) • Support the children in programming/coding the stories and tasks for the robot to perform or act out/role-play. • Ask open-ended questions to generate inquiry conversations among the children and let them think out loud while proposing solutions to the posed problem. • Key science, technology, mathematical and engineering concepts are emphasised and highlighted	• Children make links explicitly with their past experiences, the imaginary situation involving the robot and their everyday world • Children engage in asking questions and interaction with robots • Children generating hypothesis or making predictions • Children begin to visualise abstract concepts • Children begin to visualise cause-effect functions • Children provide elaborated responses about concepts being explored, and not just "Yes" or "No" responses • Children can understand their mistakes and are motivated to solve the problem • Children are motivated to code the robot • Children repeat the introduced vocabulary around science/technology/ mathematical/engineering concepts (introduced by teacher, but iteratively repeated by the children)
Promoting adult-child, peer-peer and child-robot interactions	• Note the multimodal interactions between the adult, child and the robot (the robot can also move, talk, act, smile and laugh) • Examples of interactions include children posing a question or a problem, response to a question, communicating a solution to the problem and hands-on experimentation (coding the robot) to solve a problem. • Frequent opportunities for interaction and discussion between teacher/child and among children, which encourage elaborated responses about concepts being explored	• Children understand social cues, such as turn-taking while speaking • Children can engage in coding the robot • Children regulate behaviour while communicating with their peers, teacher and/or robot • Children engage in continuous questioning, suggest ideas and pose solutions between and/or among each other (with teachers and/or peers) • Children communicate and justify explanations within the interactions and interactivity with the robots • Co-construct solutions through collaborative interactions

(Continued)

Table 4.1 STREAM-based play observational protocol and pedagogical steps for robotic integration *(Continued)*

Pedagogical step	Teacher actions	Indicators of children's STREAM literacy development
Sharing of children's ideas and representations emerging from robotic free play	• Educators should invite children to represent their thinking through drawings, storytelling through coding of the robot, and constructions using, for example, blocks and everyday materials (blending of physical and digital modalities) • Allow time for whole-group discussions • Invite children to share their emergent ideas, constructed artefacts and drawings. This enables a deeper and richer learning experience, fostered through the free-flow play and inquiry process.	• Visualising abstract concepts while building creative models (digital/physical/multimodal) • Children engage in problem-solving and come up with new imaginary ideas/innovative solutions • Children construct artefacts while drawing, reading, listening and/or speaking because of the planned activity • Children communicate and present their work to their peers/teachers/parents • Children look at their photos/artefacts and can reflect back on experiences

the three kindergarten teachers) were collected. These weekly plans incorporated sampled activities/experiences the teachers had conducted across the school term. In addition, the data collection also included photographs of children's samples of work, artefacts, children's constructed models, video observations of children's STREAM-based play and informal conversations with the teachers.

Data collection during the COVID-19 pandemic

During the COVID-19 pandemic in 2020, the data collection pivoted to remote data collection methods. In negotiation with the teachers, remotely collected observations in ECE settings were gathered, but the nature of the observations varied across the two kindergarten contexts. Further, during the pandemic, one kindergarten voluntarily dropped out of the research project. The two teachers from the remaining two kindergartens submitted self-collected video observations and photos of children's STREAM-based play with the robotic technologies. The teachers were provided with an iPad and the robots to collect the data. For the early childhood (EC) settings, the researcher provided remotely recorded stories involving empathy-based scenarios involving the robot and imaginary characters that were used as inquiry starters by the teachers in their own EC setting. The researcher had phone-based reflective conversations with the teachers to gauge how the children were reacting to the storytelling experiences as inquiry starters that involved the robot as the central character of the story. Hence, the data during the 2020 pandemic that involved a combination of reflective conversations and self-submitted videos from educators were used. In total, 20 hours of data is being analysed and reported in this chapter. As seen in the DBR approach, targeted scaffolding by the teacher as the expert adult was useful for the children to inquire, engage and interact with the robotic toys. Critical to this DBR approach was questioning and an open-ended discourse of inquiry. Throughout the play experiences, the teacher probed children's curiosities, empathy and inquiry through iterations of open-ended and reflective questions.

Ethical procedures were ensured to seek teachers' consent, being mindful that the observation sessions were not intrusive and the data collection process and methods suited the teachers' pedagogical needs, opinions and respected their professional knowledge and experiences. Parental consent was sought for their children to participate in the project. Pseudonyms have been used for the kindergarten setting and their respective teachers and children.

Data analysis

Data analysis was based on Hedegaard's (2008) wholeness approach, which involves three levels of thematic analysis. First, all video observations of the STREAM-based play with the robotic technologies and informal conversations were watched and a common sense interpretation was undertaken. The different perspectives, including the views and ideas of the children and their teachers' pedagogical actions within their natural settings and the robot's digital play environment, were considered. All the play experiences where children participate, engage, inquire and interact with the robotic toys were understood to provide valuable insights into children's inquiry thinking and the potential for shaping children's STEM literacy by making common sense interpretations (Hedegaard, 2008). These teacher-children conversations were used to track the collective emergence of children's STREAM literacy skills indicators rather than to attribute utterances to individuals. Since the children were seen to be co-constructing and contributing to classroom knowledge, we also acknowledge that such children's emergent learning does not occur in siloes. Hence teachers' actions were also considered hand in hand as part of the analytical process. Second, situated practice interpretation and sense making of the recount of the conversations that teachers have with the children and the children have among themselves and with the robots were considered. The interactions, questioning, responses and interactivity with the robotic toys were deciphered. Lastly, themes were deduced through a systematic analysis of the implementation of the play episodes that achieve the research aims, keeping in mind the theoretical understanding of how, through STREAM-based play practices, teachers can develop children's STREAM literacy development. This wholeness approach for analysis made it possible to understand deeply the emerging positive and/or conflictual play moments encountered within child–child, child–robot and teacher-child interactions that can support children's STREAM literacy development.

More specifically, the creation of themes focused on how the question-driven inquiry within the free-flow STREAM-based play interactions generated children's imaginations and on how the imaginations then stimulated children's creative inquiry, empathy, problem-solving, social interactions, communication and use of language to inquire and engage with the robots. This was in line with the theoretical understanding of interactions and the communication among the children, teachers and the robots together as a free-flow play process, and the pedagogical conditions that shape children's STREAM literacy development. The study's observational protocol was used as the analytical framework to deduce the themes. For example, indicators, such as when children made predictions, that provided explanations for why their predictions and imagined stories about their robots worked or did not work were considered under the theme of STREAM-based practices associated with creative inquiry literacy. Making connections to their own feelings and emotions while wondering about their robot's capabilities, empathising with their robots and continuing to reflect and motivate each other was classified as STREAM-based practices associated with empathy literacy. Indicators such as when children provide elaborated responses about concepts being explored, and not just "Yes" or "No" responses, children are able to understand their mistakes and are motivated to solve the problem and children are motivated to code the robot as part of the problem-solving process were classified as STREAM-based practices associated with problem-solving literacy. Collaborating to make rules and enact them as a team, use of communication and language while interacting with each other to problem-solve imagined situations, and making shared meanings together about the concept in hand were classified as STREAM-based practices associated with communication literacy. These STREAM literacies are critical to our research understandings, as illustrated in the below discussed themes.

Findings

Findings are presented mainly on video observational data and photographs of children's constructed artefacts gathered across the participating settings, on how teachers' STREAM-based play practices using real-life simulated robotic technologies prompted children to develop STREAM literacy skills – creative inquiry, empathy, problem-solving and communication. The data is presented as three themes, and within the themes are presented the STREAM-based play narratives called as learning stories. These narratives aim to unveil teachers and children's interactions and reflective inquiry-based conversations they have within the digital and physical play environments. Teachers' and children's interactions and communication of ideas and experiences are richly captured as stories because they depict lived experiences (Clandinin, 2007). The interpretation of children's learning stories is done both explicitly and implicitly, to make meaning from not only what was spoken or from the child's actions/body gestures, but also the meaning behind their words or what remained unspoken (Clandinin, 2007). This involved closely analysing children's interactions with their teacher in the environment as well as the "virtual" interactions with the robot or the digital play characters within the digital game that fostered the learning. All names have been de-identified as per the University's ethics guidelines.

Theme 1: STREAM-based play practices associated with creative inquiry literacy

The following example is from a kindergarten involving children from multicultural backgrounds that had EAL needs. The teacher adapted intentional planning and fostered children's creative inquiry as part of the pedagogical steps for robotic integration (see Table 4.1) to initiate children's STREAM-based play. In this learning story, teacher (T), Casie, a recent graduate teacher, purposefully activates children's interactions with the Sphero robot. Sphero is an AI robot that is circular in shape, has no legs or human-like features, yet has AI features and records the movements and directions of the robot. The data can then be produced as graphs or shapes and used for learning of mathematical concepts. Young children as beginning coders used block-based programming that underpins number-based concepts to be able to direct and control their Sphero robot. Children can programme the Sphero bot to roll around, jump, change colour and simulate the "driving" of the robot through environments they create. Firstly, together with the researcher, the teacher, Casie, explicitly instructs a group of eight children (four boys and four girls) about how the Sphero works and describes the functions. She also demonstrates how Sphero changes colours [cause and effect functioning]. Casie together with the researcher intentionally teaches the children how to drive the robot safely using the visual drive mode function on the Sphero Edu app. Using questioning techniques to prompt children's inquiry, Casie makes the children enquire about what sorts of things they would like Sphero to travel.

T: Where would Sphero like to go for an adventure? [Open-ended questions sparking children's imagination and creativity to think about adventurous places to visit].
CHARLIE: a palace
TOM: fire
LILLY: tower
ELLA: streets in the palace

Using Lego duplo blocks, the children begin to construct their imagined artefacts for Sphero to travel.

T: what will be inside the palace
CHARLIE: streets
T: what else will be on the streets? [activating real-world thinking]
ELLA: cars and also doors for Sphero to enter in
TOM: or a tunnel to pass through. Children continue to help each other in constructing the brainstormed ideas for their obstacle course in the palace.
T: what are you going to do so that Sphero goes inside the tunnel? Casie invited Lilly to have a go at coding Sphero and direct it to travel inside the tunnel. Lilly uses the drive mode to code.
T: how many steps do you think he [Sphero] will need? Here, Casie is probing children to think about estimating numbers and coming up with a prediction [mathematical inquiry skill].
GABY: two steps [number-based concept]

Lilly enters the code and drives Sphero into the tunnel. Although Sphero dashes the tunnel, that is because it takes a few more steps than two steps.

CHARLIE: try and make it travel straight. Lilly tries to drive Sphero again and this time Sphero makes it straight into the tunnel and into the palace garden. All children clap for Lilly.

We can see from this learning episode that Casie encourages children to manoeuvre through the obstacle course constructed by the children. In this case, the adult-directed activity becomes an introductory task, a framing activity that allows children to firstly build confidence and competence in using the robot safely and, secondly, to generate hypothesis and predictions of where Sphero would like to travel and accordingly come up with solution – constructing a palace obstacle course. Here, we notice how the interactions are transformed with children and teachers' own experience and confidence to continually scaffold the children through question-driven inquiry involving numerical thinking. Children's imaginative storytelling and mathematical inquiry become visible through the coding actions children take in a collective manner. For example, by making Sphero's journey for an adventure as the central theme of their story, children are predicting and estimating mathematical concepts such as numbers and spatial reasoning [sense of directions combined with the use of numbers]. Through the robot's coding process, children's predictions were tested visually, thus bringing mathematical inquiry into real-life action as part of the constructed palace obstacle course. During play with Sphero, children continually traverse between their own physically created space, digital space (coding app) and their real-world thinking space. The teacher joins into the play only for the purpose of triggering children's emotions by posing problem-based scenarios and questioning, thus generating creative inquiry-based solutions. Children's STREAM-based play also starts to involve spatial reasoning concepts – children taking turns to control Sphero and then subsequently using the coding functions (left, right, turn around, forward and backward) and the "imaginary" steps taken for Sphero to safely pass through the tunnel and reach the palace gardens. Here, we see the beginning of children's development of a combination of computational and numeracy skills being "carved" from children's STEM-based play opportunities by using the robot as a symbolic object into the child's multimodal play environment (see Figures 4.2, 4.3 and 4.4 for children's collaborative play with Sphero).

Figure 4.2 Teacher's explicit scaffolding and modelling how Sphero changes colours

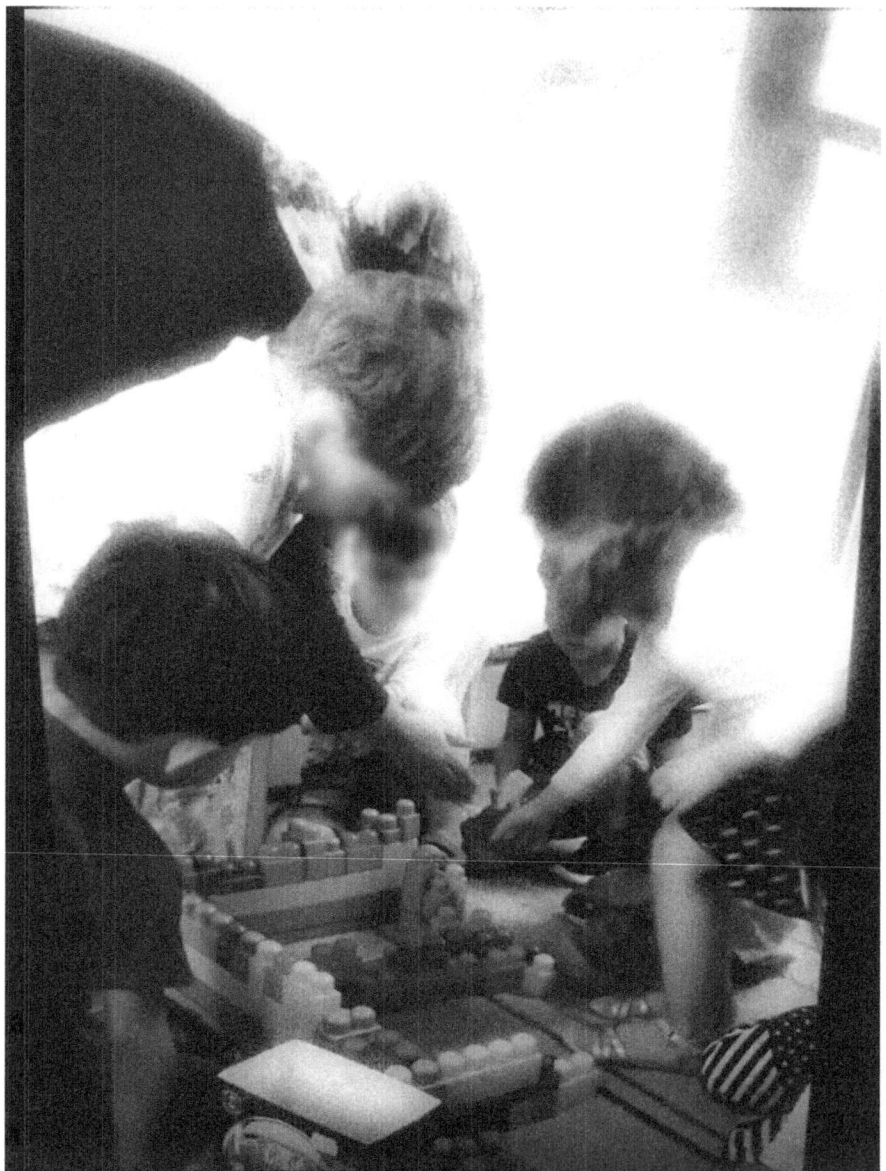

Figure 4.3 Children constructing palace obstacle course during Sphero play

Theme 2: STREAM-based play practices associated with empathy literacy

This learning story is an example of data that was collected during COVID-19 using Zoom-based instructional support provided to the teacher. The researcher provided self-recorded audio-video stories to the teacher so that she can deploy

Figure 4.4 Children taking turns to code Sphero to enter into the palace

them as per her teaching schedule and availability of children attending the kindergarten during the pandemic. Zoom-based reflective conversations between the researcher and the teacher (Lila) were also critical to the intentional planning of the robotic integration play experiences. This learning story reports data that was collected by the teacher after she introduced the remotely recorded story provocation to the 5-year-old children that was used to stimulate children's play with the robots. The social situation with the robot as the central theme was "empathised" through the telling of a story of a robot who was in danger but had characteristics to protect itself from danger. Through joint imagination and dramatisation, the children were made to get excited (empathy-based situation) with the robot. This is seen when the children show their willingness to continue interacting and coding the robot to perform actions (motivation to code). Children's expression of emotions and behaviours is seen in the form of words, questions and gestures (Figure 4.5 – child holding remote control to see how IoToys: Botley works and its characteristics, using visual cards to code). Multimodal features of the robot (tactile touch, visual code and movement of robot) enables the interactions and conversations between the teacher and the children as a group discussion with the robot as the central theme. Hands-on manipulation of the code, fail and recode afforded by the robot's multimodal characteristics fosters a feeling of emotional regulation, while also boosting empathy. The robotic story provocation culminated into children's construction

Figure 4.5 Children's numeracy skills development using visual cards during coding Botley

of a story map. The story map showed the glimpses of children's imagination being translated into representations such as which planets super bot could go with his "Robot family."

Theme 3: STREAM-based play practices associated with problem-solving and communication literacy

The following learning story is from the kindergarten that had children with EAL need. According to the teacher, the children did not speak English at home; hence, she was endeavouring to build their language (expressive and receptive), English language vocabulary, along with literacy skills in an English-speaking learning environment. The teacher (T), Anna, explicitly demonstrates how Qobo, a snail-looking robot, operates. In this play session, there were four boys and five girls. As part of an inquiry starter, Anna probes children's imagination by asking

T: tell me about Qobo
MIKSA: he was just dancing
T: oh he was just dancing

VIKTOR: he stopped when he was on the diamond.

T: repeats what Viktor said as Viktor's English language wasn't that clear for other kids to understand.

MICHAELA: Qobo goes to play in a playhouse (mutters in broken English language)

T: ahhh ... did Qobo go to the playhouse!

All the kids excitingly raising their hands up to answer.

ANOTHER GIRL DOLLY: he was going...points to the house (nonverbal language)

ANOTHER BOY, HARI: Qobo walked on the diamond and stopped (stuttering).

T added when-then sentence showing cause-effect: when Qobo walked on the diamond, it then stopped.

SID, ANOTHER BOY: stuttering – there was a police car...on the map

T: oh was there a police car on a map. [Qobo has a puzzle card with police car visual on it and when Qobo walks on that card, it makes police car siren]. That is what the child were referring to. But because the children's English language vocabulary is not fully developed, he articulates that there was police car on Qobo's map.

T: what else can anyone remember about Qobo

MICHAELA: she moves with the cards [see how another girl calls Qobo – she]

T: could she move without the cards?

ALL CHILDREN: noooo

T: could we put any cards?

MIKSA: only on the start card

ANOTHER BOY, SID: when you put all cards on the floor, she will like to dance [boys continue to attribute Qobo as 'she']

T: ok lets see how we can make it work

One child brings the cards.
    Children break into groups to see what is on the cards.

T: I wonder what will happen with these cards

ONE GIRL, TINA: Qobo wants to eat a banana (holding up the banana card)

The activity of making Qobo work becomes an inclusive activity. Where all children with varying language and speech abilities come and look at the cards (visual mode of learning).

T: come along and help us (pointing to one girl, Sheena, who had still not got into groups with other children to see the Qobo cards)

All kids look for the start card. Kids know how Qobo can start working.

T: look Sid has the start cards. Can you give Viktor another start card (sharing cards).

Anna the teacher also gets another group of two girls to go and work with the cards and Qobo (promoting collaboration).

One group of children (two boys and two girls) arrange cards and make Qobo move. When Qobo reaches at the end, they all say yay!

T: Now Viktor says he wants to make a house. Grab some wooden blocks to make Qobo house [transfer of Qobo play characteristics into the physical object space]

Two girls join into the boys play, and they also want to make a house.

Teacher looking at other group of girls: oh I can see how Michaela is working on her coding pathway for Qobo. [teacher scaffolding and generating an environment for problem-solving]

Also pointing to another girl – would you like to play with the girls on their house?

All the groups try different pathways, arrangement of cards testing different ways Qobo works, makes sounds, what makes Qobo talk, move, etc. Children help each other giving cards, sorting Qobo's QR-code operational cards and arranging pathways – demonstrating productive learning environment by sharing and social collaboration skills development (see Figure 4.6). Note the multi-interactions between the teacher, children and the robot (since Qobo, the codable snail robot can also move, talk, act, smile and laugh).

Teacher invites Miksa to show this group (a group struggling to make Qobo work/move) how to make Qobo move (Teacher modelling collaborative problem-solving behaviour and inviting children to share their discoveries, creations and generated solutions).

Another group of children had veered away making the house.

MICHAELA: hey we don't need that. We need some bricks

Teacher reminding children to be helpful to each other, giving space to make the house or spread out the card arrangements.

ANOTHER BOY, HARI: I am making a door for the Qobo house
DOLLY: see this brick – can you make a door so he [Qobo] can get in or jumps over (shows a brick that has an arch).
TINA SAYING TO THE TEACHER: after the house he can go to the playground [Here we see glimpse of Tina's imagination becoming creative activating her real-world thinking.

The entire play session results in children building a house, playground and then putting Qobo to bed. Here we see children's storytelling, frequent English language use during Qobo play, building collaborative ideas, communication and problem-solving literacy.

This learning story can be seen as building a holistic repertoire of children's STREAM literacy skills – all evoked by Qobo as the inquiry starter and multiple episodes of storytelling techniques.

The coding and manoeuvring of the robot to create actions involve children's social skills, such as social communication (the ability to socially communicate

Figure 4.6 Children play with Qobo's QR operational visual cards

and use expressive language skills such as questioning, commenting, sharing and participate in activities via a range of modalities) and social collaboration (the ability to collaborate with peers and educators on coding tasks). The children not only motivated each other to come and join the "Qobo house building project" but also put together their real-world thinking skills during problem-solving (the ability to question, pose solutions, adapt and deal with problems such as a failed code and recode). While constructing the house, the children had a road running up to it – a narrative that was associated with the children building a story about Qobo's journey. We can tell from their talk/actions the choices children made while constructing the Qobo house design – wooden blocks or bricks, thus showing how the children brainstormed all the possible designs they might have chosen to construct the house.

During STREAM-based play involving robotics, it is evident that learning occurs whenever a child spontaneously chooses to assimilate a new schema context to one or more of their established schemes (child's existing interest, emotions and ability), and this assimilation happens whenever children apply a new scheme to a familiar schema context (real-world thinking). It can be emphasised that it is every child's spontaneous and entirely natural inclination in "free-flow" play that enables the development of social communication skills (Siraj-Blatchford, 2014). Free-flow play as part of STREAM-based and robotics play provides support to pedagogues to scaffold and support these natural processes in the accommodation and development of more complex schematic operations (e.g. use of English language, numeracy skills and spatial skills). The actions and learning occurring in the above learning story may be described in the academic terms familiar to constructivist psychology, or alternatively in the terms of cultural historical activity theory. Nevertheless, there is a very strong academic empirical evidence base that includes a much wider range of perspectives including the most recent advances in neuroscience (Siraj-Blatchford & Brock, 2016).

Conclusions: A framework for deploying robotic technologies for STREAM-based play

This Australian study provides rich empirical evidence of how through free-flow play, children explore the "educational content" of the robotic technology and, while doing so, enact their real-world thinking into practice. Such playful explorations do not happen in siloes, however, and the teacher plays a critical part in intentionally planning and introducing children to such robotic technology-constructed experiences. The children actively engage with the coding app to explore educational patterns (coding exercises, number-based concepts and spatial reasoning) and thus also employ a flipped classroom approach by teaching other children what they had previously learned (social communication and collaboration literacy development). By predicting and evaluating their coding choices made, children learn new ways to be able to regulate emotions while encountering failure when beginning to code and recode (empathy literacy). Problem-solving through collaboration with teachers and their peers also becomes visible. Children engage in continuous questioning, suggest ideas and pose solutions between and/or among each other (with teachers and/or peers), thus demonstrating development of problem-solving literacy. Children link their own constructions to facilitate collaborative knowledge building and translate imaginative thinking to real-world thinking (creative inquiry literacy development).

Through this study, we have highlighted that all new literacy and numeracy activities offered to children must be meaningful. This requires activities to be based on what children can already do (their schemes – interests and abilities) and/or know (their schemas). It is crucial to support children's emergent learning in free play, even if they are playing and tinkering with advanced technologies such as robots. When educators build upon what a child "can do," they provide emotional scaffolding to the child's emergent learning. For example, we saw in the case of the kindergartens where children with diverse language needs demonstrated the ability to connect to everyday world and be able to socially communicate using English language that needs explicit scaffolding – facilitated most naturally through the robotic technologies free play and dramatised storytelling. Robotic play gives children agency, develops their self-esteem and helps them see themselves as active learners and problem-solvers in their own enacted stories. It gives them multimodal opportunities to learn numeracy skills through observing, modelling and imitating of behaviours, when appropriately scaffolded by educators. The robot, when placed within children's learning environment, provides a "schema" – a context to generate empathy-based situations and problems – keeping the robot as the central character at the heart of children's self-generated inquiry (Siraj-Blatchford & Brock, 2016).

This study provides examples to educators in ECE settings of how to effectively integrate robots as "toys and/or tools" that do have educational value and can support children's STREAM-based play – which is the most effective context for learning. Through this study, we build a case for further understanding children's STREAM literacy development by deploying robotic technologies safely and ethically into ECE settings. By using the robotic toys, teachers have an exceptional capacity for developing children's STREAM literacy in sophisticated ways. The five pedagogical steps (Table 4.1) can be integrated while activating children's STREAM-based play using robotics. Further studies are recommended to investigate pre- and in-service teachers' beliefs and attitudes towards robotic technologies and what training they might require, as past research has observed diminished use in specific interventions when negative attitudes or a lack of training exists (MacDonald, Danaia, & Murphy, 2020). Research on building ECE teachers' and leaders' capacities should also include those who are also responsible for the organisation of their teaching staff's professional learning to embrace nuanced ways for teachers to integrate technologies. There is a need to build assessment tools that can measure, both quantitatively and qualitatively, children's developing STREAM literacy. Policymakers and curricula stakeholders need to reimagine ways while adapting the STREAM-based play, robotic integration teaching and learning framework when considering cultivating high possibility classrooms in ECE (Hunter, 2017). As both peak international bodies OECD and UNICEF (2021) recommend, in seeking to meet quality education and social growth of young children with diverse needs, policymakers and education providers can no longer afford to ignore the untapped potential that the latest tangible technologies, such as robotics, have to offer. Robotic technologies offer one solution to the lack of technology-constructed tools and resources in ECE settings, particularly serving those children with diverse needs such as EAL, or being neurodiverse. While robot technologies cannot replace caregivers and educators, integration of technologies should be combined with non-technological interventions to assist in the child's interests and imagination.

We propose that STREAM-based play with tangible technologies such as robot and coding toys should be (re)conceptualised as multimodal playscapes (places and spaces for children's STREAM-based play). As these toys have pre-programmed functions, sensors and codable instructions, they generate a cyclic loop of various modes of acting, expressing, communicating (mathematical/scientific ideas), collaborating, creating, empathising through which they spark children's creative inquiry. Although this study has limitations in terms of its size and sample selection, our findings indicate that such an approach has implications at policy and practice level. At policy level, there is scope for extending this research to a wider sample of disadvantaged socioeconomic and cultural backgrounds. Future research also needs to focus on examining how children engaging in robotic play can impact on how developmentally vulnerable children might be seeking their own agency and/or develop their academic skills (e.g. school-based literacy and numeracy skills). Further implications lie in understanding and analysing robots as objects of study, which open the doors to pragmatics of children's cognitive learning such as mathematical and scientific inquiry, real-world problem-solving, decision-making, and spatial reasoning and computation thinking skills.

References

Arnott, L., Kewalramani, S., Gray, C., & Dardanou, M. (2020). Role play and technologies in early childhood. In Z. Kingdon (Ed.), *A Vygotskian analysis of children's play behaviours: Beyond the home corner* (pp. 76–92). London: Routledge.

Arnott, L., & Yelland, N. (2020). Multimodal lifeworlds: Pedagogies for play inquiries and explorations. *Journal of Early Childhood Education Research*, *9*(1), 124–146. https://jecer.org/wp-content/uploads/2020/02/Arnott-Yelland-issue9-1.Pdf.

Bers, M. U. (2008). Blocks to robots: Learning with technology in the early childhood classroom. New York: Teachers College Press.

Bers, M. U. (2022). *Beyond coding: How children learn human values through programming*. Cambridge, MA: MIT Press.

Clandinin, D. J. (Ed.). (2007). *Handbook of narrative inquiry: Mapping a methodology*. Thousand Oaks: Sage.

Cowan, K. (2020). *A panorama of play – A literature review. Digital futures commission*. London: 5Rights Foundation.

Dweck, C. (2015). Carol Dweck revisits the "growth mindset". *Education Week*, *35*(5), 20–24.

Dýrfjörð, K., & Hreiðarsdóttir, A. E. (2021). Digital play objects as part of preschool children's imaginative play. In D. Holloway, M. Willson, K. Murcia, C. Archer, & F. Stocco (Eds.), *Young children's rights in a digital world* (pp. 205–219). Cham: Springer.

Early Childhood STEM Working Group. (2017). *Early STEM matters: Providing high-quality STEM experiences for all young learners.* A Policy Report by the Early Childhood STEM Working Group. Retrieved from http://d3lwefg3pyezlb. cloudfront.net/docs/Early_STEM_Matters_FINAL.pdf.

Edwards, S. (2021). Digital play and technical code: What new knowledge formations are possible? *Learning, Media and Technology.* DOI: 10.1080/17439884. 2021.1890612.

Falloon, G., Hatzigianni, M., Bower, M., Forbes, A., & Stevenson, M. (2020). Understanding K-12 STEM education: A framework for developing STEM literacy. *Journal of Science Education and Technology, 29*(3), 369–385. DOI: 10.1007/ s10956-020-09823-x.

Fleer, M. (2018). Digital animation: New conditions for children's development in play-based setting. *British Journal of Educational Technology, 49*(5), 943–958. DOI: 10.1111/bjet.12637.

Fleer, M. (2019). Scientific playworlds: A model of teaching science in play-based settings. *Research in Science Education, 49*(5), 1257–1278.

Ge, X., Ifenthaler, D., & Spector, J. M. (Eds.). (2015). *Emerging technologies for STEAM education.* Springer. DOI: 10.1007/978-3-319-02573-5.

Hedegaard, M. (2008). Principles for interpreting research protocols. In M. Hedegaard, M. Fleer, J. Bang, & P. Hviid (Eds.), *Studying children: A cultural-historical approach* (pp. 46–64). Maidenhead: Open University Press.

Hirsh-Pasek, K., Golinkoff, R. M., Berk, l., & Singer, D. (2009). *A mandate for playful learning in preschool: Presenting the evidence.* New York: Oxford AcademicUniversity Press. DOI: 10.1093/acprof:oso/9780195382716.001.0001.

Holloway, D., Willson, M., Murcia, K., Archer, C., & Stocco, F. (Eds.). (2021). *Young children's rights in a digital world, children's well-being: Indicators and research.* DOI: 10.1007/978-3-030-65916-5_15.

Hunter, J. (2017). High possibility classrooms as a pedagogical framework for technology integration in classrooms: An inquiry in two Australian secondary schools. *Technology, Pedagogy and Education, 26*(5), 559–571. DOI: 10.1080/1475939X.2017.1359663.

Ihamäki, P., & Heljakka, K. (2021). Internet of Toys and forms of play in early education: A longitudinal study of preschoolers' toy-based learning experiences. In D. Holloway, M. Willson, K. Murcia, C. Archer, & F. Stocco (Eds.), *Young children's rights in a digital world* (pp. 193–204). Cham: Springer.

Jetnikoff, A. (2015). Design based research methodology for teaching with technology in English. *English in Australia, 50*(3), 56–60.

Kewalramani, S., & Havu-Nuutinen, S. (2019). Preschool teachers' beliefs and pedagogical practices in the integration of technology: A case for engaging young children in scientific inquiry. *Eurasia Journal of Mathematics, Science and Technology Education, 15*(12). DOI: 10.29333/ejmste/109949.

Kewalramani, S., Kidman, G., & Palaiologou, I. (2021). Using artificial intelligence (AI) interfaced robotic toys in early childhood settings: A pedagogy for children's inquiry literacy. *European Early Childhood Education Research Journal, 29*(5). DOI: 10.1080/1350293X.2021.1968458.

Kewalramani, S., Palaiologou, I., & Dardanou, M. (2020). Children's engineering design thinking processes: The magic of the ROBOTS and the power of BLOCKS (electronics). *Eurasia Journal of Mathematics, Science and Technology Education.* DOI: 10.29333/ejmste/113247.

Kidman, G., & Casinader, N. (2017). *Inquiry-based teaching and learning across disciplines: Comparative theory and practice in schools.* London: Palgrave Macmillan.

Kucirkova, N., & Falloon, G. (Eds.). (2016). *Apps, technology and younger learners: International evidence for teaching.* London: Routledge.

Liao, C. (2016). From interdisciplinary to transdisciplinary: An arts-integrated approach to STEAM education. *Art Education, 69*(6), 44–49. DOI: 10.1080/00043125.2016.1224873.

MacDonald, A., Danaia, L., & Murphy, S. (2020). *STEM education across the learning continuum.* Springer Singapore Pvt. Limited. DOI: 10.1007/978-981-15-2821-7.

Marsh, J., Kumpulainen, K., Nisha, B., Velicu, A., Blum-Ross, A., Hyatt, D.... Thorsteinsson, G. (2017). *Makerspaces in the early years: A literature review.* University of Sheffield: MakEY Project. Retrieved from http://makeyproject.eu/wp-content/uploads/2017/02/Makey_Literature_Review.pdf.

Murray, J. (2019). Routes to STEM: Nurturing science, technology, engineering and mathematics in early years education. *International Journal of Early Years Education, 27,* 219–221.

National Research Council. (2014). *STEM integration in K-12 education: Status, prospects, and an agenda for research.* Washington, DC: National Academies Press.

Organisation for Economic and Collaboration Development. (2021). *OECD digital education outlook 2021: Pushing the frontiers with artificial intelligence, blockchain and robots.* Paris: OECD.

Papadakis, S., & Kalogiannakis, M. (Eds.). (2020). *Handbook of research on using educational robotics to facilitate student learning.* Hershey, PA: IGI Global.

Peppler, K., Wohlwend, K., Thompson, N., Tan, V., & Thomas, A. (2019). Squishing circuits: Circuitry learning with electronics and playdough in early childhood. *Journal of Science Education and Technology, 28*(2), 118–132. DOI: 10.1007/s10956-018-9752-2

Poulsen, M. (2018). *CounterPlay Manifesto.* CounterPlay. Retrieved from http://www.counterplay.org/counterplay-manifesto/.

Project Zero. (2016). *Towards a pedagogy of play* [Project Zero Working Paper]. Retrieved from http://www.pz.harvard.edu/sites/default/files/Towards%20a%20Pedagogy%20of%20Play.pdf.

Selwyn, N. (2019). *Should robots replace teachers? AI and the future of education.* Cambridge, UK: John Wiley & Sons.

Siraj-Blatchford, I. (2014). Early childhood education (ECE). In T. Maynard & N. Thomas (Eds.), *an introduction to early childhood studies* (pp. 172–184). Thousand Oaks, CA: Sage.

Siraj-Blatchford, J., & Brock, L. (2016). *Early childhood digital play and the Zone of Proximal Developmental Flow (ZPDF).* In *Proceedings I Congreso Internacional de Innovacion Y Tecnologia Educativa en Educacion Infantil, Seville, April.*

Siraj-Blatchford, J., & Brock, L. (2019). How to scaffold learning through free-flow play. *Early Years Educator, 21*(3), 31–33.

Sullivan, A., & Bers, M. U. (2016). Robotics in the early childhood classroom: Learning outcomes from an 8-week robotics curriculum in pre-kindergarten through second grade. *International Journal of Technology and Design Education, 26*(3), 3–20. DOI: 10.1007/s10798-015-9304-5.

Sullivan, F., & Heffernan, J. (2016). Robotic construction kits as computational manipulatives for learning in the STEM disciplines. *Journal of Research on Technology in Education, 48*(2), 105–128. DOI: 10.1080/15391523.2016.1146563.

Sylva, K., Melhuish, E. C., Sammons, P., Siraj-Blatchford, I., & Taggart, B. (2004). *The effective provision of pre-school education (EPPE) project: Technical paper 12—The final report: effective pre-school education*. London: DfES/Institute of Education, University of London.

Tayler, C. (2016). E4Kids. Retrieved March 4, 2019, from https://www.vic.gov.au/effective-early-education-experiences-e4kids-study.

Toh, L. P. E., Causo, A., Tzuo, P.-W., Chen, I.-M., & Yeo, S. H. (2016). A review on the use of robots in education and young children. *Educational Technology & Society, 19*(2), 148–163.

Unahalekhaka, A., & Bers, M. U. (2022). Evaluating young children's creative coding: Rubric development and testing for ScratchJr projects. *Education and Information Technologies*. DOI: 10.1007/s10639-021-10873-w.

UNICEF. (2021). *Policy guidance on AI for children*. Retrieved from https://www.unicef.org/globalinsight/stories/How-to-design-AI-for-children.

United Nations. (2013). *General comment no. 17 on the right of the child to rest, leisure, play, recreational activities, cultural life and the arts (art. 31)*. Committee on the Rights of the Child. Retrieved from https://www.refworld.org/docid/51ef9bcc4.html.

Wood, E. (2010). Reconceptualizing the play–pedagogy relationship. In L. Brooker & S. Edwards (Eds.), *Engaging play* (pp. 11–24). Maidenhead: Open University Press.

Yelland, N. J. (2018). A pedagogy of multiliteracies: Young children and multimodal learning with tablets. *British Journal of Educational Technology, 49*(5), 847–858. DOI: 10.1111/bjet. 12635.

Zollman, A. (2012). Learning for STEM literacy: STEM literacy for learning. *School Science and Mathematics, 112*(1), 12–19.

Zosh, J. M., Hirsh-Pasek, K., Hopkins, E. J., Jensen, H., Liu, C., Neale, D., … Whitebread, D. (2017). *Learning through play: A review of the evidence*. LEGO Foundation. Retrieved from https://www.researchgate.net/publication/325171106_Learning_through_play_a_review_of_the_evidence.

5 The technological landscapes with IoToys in early childhood education in Norway

Introduction

As demonstrated elsewhere in this book, children live in a digital society and interact with technology from birth. Children's play has evolved in various ways that include technology. Norway is one of the countries that has come the furthest when it comes to digitalisation. Families in general are continuously connected and available via mobile technology, and information is available online whenever it is needed (Dardanou, Mossin, & Simensen, 2021). Children observe uses of technology in their everyday lives and social relationships (Stephen & Edwards, 2018). Studies on children's use of internet have showed that Norwegian children have access from early age (Staksrud, 2011; Staksrud & Olafsson, 2018; Fjørtoft, Thun, & Buvik, 2019).

Studies have showed that personal data can be exchanged by Internet of Toys (IoToys) to related or third-party services (Geneiatakis et al., 2017; Chaudron, Di Gioia, & Gemo, 2018). EUKids Online report (Smahel et al., 2020) showed that in Norway, children spend more time on the internet than other European children (3.6 hours compared with 2.8 hours on average). At the same time, Norwegians feel safer on the internet than other European children. 42 per cent of Norwegian children aged 9–16 state that they always feel safe online (compared with the European average of 29%), and most Norwegian children think that other people are kind and helpful on the internet. The Norwegian research results reveal that more Norwegian children state that they feel safe online, than at home and at school. In addition, recommendations for screen time, for example, "can take into account some other risks associated with technology use such as phishing, cyber-bullying, accessing unsafe material or pornography, and communication with unknown persons that can open the door for grooming or radicalization" (WHO, 2015; OECD, 2019).

Children's interaction with IoToys and with other children around IoToys is related to digital and non-digital spaces (Arnott, Palaiologou, & Gray, 2019, p. 153). Play with IoToys as a social practice should be contextualised in the context and relation to children's everyday lives. Framing and mentoring to support children as part of their digital lives are crucial factors in looking at how IoToys can be integrated into children's social world. The principles of children's

DOI: 10.4324/9781003185840-5

privacy when using IoToys should be considered so that personal information about children is considered (Bergsjø et al., 2020). At the same time, there are good opportunities to reflect on privacy that contributes to the development of children's critical thinking and digital judgement (Dardanou & Kofoed, 2019).

Theoretical underpinnings

Children's play in the Norwegian context

There is an ongoing debate about the form, meaning and role digital play can have in children's lives. Some researchers claim that children need free play that is separate from interaction with screens or digital tools. On the other hand, digital play has positive effects, such as relaxation, entertainment, learning and the development of many skills (Marsh et al., 2015). Digital play is a new concept in the kindergarten context that is related to the emergence of the digital age. Today, young children are growing up in a context where the development of technology has created new opportunities for play. Research is currently aimed at theorising digital play and understanding the convergence of traditional play, where technological activity is a form of digital play. This new understanding of play is required as parents, actors and communities increasingly engage with young children growing up with technology as a dominant aspect of their lives. Touch technology (tablets, etc.) allows young children to use games, apps and websites in a relatively simple way, yet not all children find touch screens easy to use and some apps are not intuitive (Merchant, 2014; Dardanou, Mossin, & Simensen, 2021).

Resnick (2017) argues that people of all ages must learn to think and act creatively and believed that the creative process used by children in kindergarten can be illustrated with a creative learning spiral (see Figure 5.1). Resnick (2017) then discusses new technology and new strategies to motivate children and adolescents to creative learning experiences. By giving children opportunities to collaborate with peers on exciting projects, we can prepare them for a world where creative thinking is more important than ever. Children learn to develop their own ideas, try them out, experiment with alternatives, get input from others and create new ideas based on their own experiences. As children move through the spiral, they gain new ideas and move on to the next interaction of the spiral, with another cycle in which they imagine, create, play, share and reflect. With each interaction of the spiral, the ECE teachers or parents get new opportunities to support the children in their creative learning (Dardanou, Mossin, & Simensen, 2021).

According to Resnick (2017), children engage in all aspects of the creative process around play. Children's social experiences during digital play presuppose different degrees of social participation and occupy children's different technological positions and social roles. Together with the children, the ECE teacher must construct play in a way that facilitates the use of technology to improve play, instead of seeing digital play as a central activity. By critically reflecting

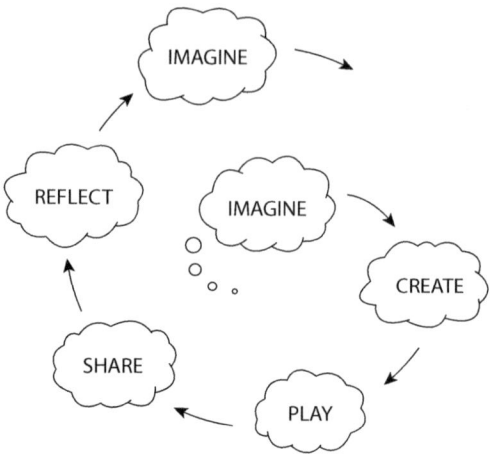

Figure 5.1 The creative learning spiral

Source: Resnick (2017, p. 12).

on their own practice, the ECE teacher can plan and engage in the theoretical foundations and frameworks for decoding how children's play develops in the face of digital technology.

Forms of play

Play primarily has a social form. Children are interested in playing with others and sharing experiences. Social interaction and learning through exploration and play are valuable for quality in children's learning (Dardanou, Mossin, & Simensen, 2021). We make assessments when we interact with, play with and create things in interaction with other people. We share ideas, get reactions from other people and build on each other's ideas (Resnick, 2017). Children's playful exploration proves children's multimodal learning and encourages the use of a variety of media and resources that are part of this learning and are at the same time artefacts and objects for the learning process (Yelland & Gilbert, 2017, p. 33). Kucirkova (2020, p. 73) emphasises that considered the use of digital technology only based on children's motivation and engagement, it could be underestimating the technology's contribution to learning opportunities.

Children's play is just for them (Kleeman, 2020; Sakr, 2020). Children develop their play culture in relation to the time and space they live in. In the same way as culture, play changes over time and new economic and technological conditions are adapted (Johansen, 2015). Shapiro (2018, pp. 37–40) gives an example of how sandboxes as a playground were met by society at the end of the 20th century. Play in the sandbox was as digital play is in our time. Like screen time, playing in a sandbox was new and controversial and represented radical economic, social and cultural changes. Over the years, the sandbox became just a normal part of young children's lives. Both kindergarten (as an ECE setting) and sandbox play were at that time radically new for children and education Therefore, it is often accepted as the type of play that is remembered from one's childhood and is accepted as good for children, but this has not always been the case (Shapiro, 2018).

Children's participation in kindergarten's everyday activities

The UN Convention on the Rights of the Child (United Nations, 2003) obliges national states to acknowledge children's rights, respecting the view and voices of children. The Norwegian Framework for Kindergartens has the UN Convention as its founding starting point. ECE shall and must recognise children's right to participation in all the activities and everyday life in the kindergartens. An essential part of the framework plan dictates and highlights the importance of children's active involvement explicitly "in planning and assessing the kindergarten's activities regularly" (Norwegian Directorate for Education and Training, 2017, p. 27).

The Norwegian Framework Plan for Kindergartens underlines that the importance of children's participation must be in accordance with their age and their premises (Norwegian Directorate for Education and Training, 2017). The concepts of involvement and active participation are complex. Nevertheless, the framework plan considers the encouragement of children to self-play an active role in self-determination and co-determination, as well as the involvement in everyday situations and experiences as a democratic right (Dardanou & Gamst-Nergård, 2020). As the framework plan states, the ECE educators must focus on children's interests and give the children varied experiences (Norwegian Directorate for Education and Training, 2017). The basis for children's learning is mainly based on the totality of the experiences that the children make (Bøe et al., 2018). The ECE teacher can facilitate and contribute so that the children can make new experiences. In this context, it is necessary for the children to have access to various materials, tools and equipment that they can explore, play and experiment with.

Holistic development and learning

The concept of holistic development and learning has a strong tradition in the Nordic ECE pedagogy (Karila, 2012), as the concept has been "classified as belonging to the social pedagogical tradition which encourages play, relationship, curiosity, and the desire for meaning making based on activities that value both children and educators in a co-constructing environment" (p. 588). The Article 1 of the Kindergarten Act underlines that kindergarten shall "in cooperation and understanding with the home, take care of the children's needs for care and play, and promote learning and formation as a basis for a holistic development" (Ministry of Education and Research, 2005). The framework states that ECE teachers are the professionals and are responsible for "facilitating holistic learning processes such as promotes children's well-being and holistic development" (Norwegian Directorate for Education and Training, 2017, p. 22). Holistic development includes social, linguistic, cognitive, ethical, emotional and physical development.

A study report by Bøe et al. (2018) investigated the characterises of ECE teachers' professional practices in relation to a holistic approach to learning and how these practices are integrated in children's play, learning, care and formation. Formation is a normative concept that expresses something about what values, actions, knowledge and skills a society should strive for when it comes to forming (*Bildung*) of citizens. Formation (*danning in Norwegian*) is a process that occurs in dialogical, reflective situations that contribute to the development of critical thinking and self-decision-making. Therefore, it is important to provide children with opportunities to think independently, to seek knowledge, reflect upon and assess adopted ideas or principles, ask questions and give opposition for themselves and on behalf of others. Hence, children's formation (*danning*) is about developing knowledge, values and attitudes *together*, through dialogue, to be recognised as an independent person with feelings and thoughts in common process with others (Straume, 2013). More importantly, formation is comprehended as a person's self-determination, co-determination and skills for solidarity and countercultural thinking. This understanding is linked to cultural and societal norms and values. When it comes to formation processes, one usually means individual and social preconditions and conditions for achieving formation (Løvlie, 2011). There, formation is discussed closely related to the law's concepts of care and play in contrast to the more aim-oriented learning concept. Formation of oneself (self-formation) is an aspect that can be related to participation aspects, through experiences. Ødegaard and Krüger (2012) provide a description on how ECE settings, through a variety of activities, create conditions for children's formation. Through different forms of conversation and dialogue, everyday activities and routines, children participate and experience elements of formation. However, the implementation and realization of the concept in ECE practices created mix reactions from the field because it was provided more explanations related to how the ECE settings could or should work with practices of formation.

Children learn in a social interaction with others and their environment (Wittek, 2014; Gray & MacBlain, 2015). Vygotsky (1978) emphasizes on the contribution of a competent person's knowledge, skills and competence in children's learning processes. A holistic approach to learning is understood as an integrative concept that binds the key concepts together in a way that is particularly relevant to the ECE teachers' professional practice. ECE teachers should balance here and now practices with future requirements and expectations and built their professional practices on both care and professionalism and orient themselves towards the ideals of formation. This must be realised with the help of pedagogical values and guidelines that are not based on prescribed dividend formulations (Bøe et al., 2018).

What is digital judgement?

Judgement refers to the ability to understand how knowledge and skills can be used in new situations that come up to practise a new action. When judgement takes place in a digital context, it is referred as digital judgement (Bergsjø et al., 2020, p. 24).

According to the framework plan (Norwegian Directorate for Education and Training, 2017, p. 44), digital judgement is underlined as one of the perspectives inside digital praxis that children shall be introduced during their ECE activities. The aim of these activities for children shall be to develop an incipient ethical understanding connected to digital media. Furthermore, the focus is to "exercise digital judgement regarding searching for information, be conscious of copyright issues, critically analyse sources and safeguard the children's privacy" (Norwegian Directorate for Education and Training, 2017, p. 45).

ECE teachers often search the internet for pictures, films, text and music. It is wise to be aware that anyone can publish almost anything on the internet. The supply of data/information today is much greater than it has ever been, and this can create challenges. It also means that it is even more important to be critical of what we encounter on the internet. For ECE teachers, this means that they must be able to assess and understand the information they collect and use (Dardanou, Mossin, & Simensen, 2021).

Ethical reflections and critical thinking

One of the interdisciplinary learning areas of the framework plan (Norwegian Directorate for Education and Training, 2017) is *Ethics, religion and philosophy*. In the learning area, it is highlighted a connection between judgement and reflection.

> By talking about and wondering at existential, ethical and philosophical questions, the children shall be enabled to formulate questions, listen to others, reflect and find answers. This way, kindergartens shall help steer the children towards critical thinking and sound judgement.
>
> (Norwegian Directorate for Education and Training, 2017, p. 54)

Judgement refers to the use of common sense, as well as how to practise common civility, regardless of whether one meets face to face or uses for example digital media (Dardanou & Kofoed, 2019). Children's reflections about ethical issues such as privacy or safeguarding personal information are about what is ethically right and good. Reflection is related to how to think critically, listen, discuss, recognise, wonder and formulate questions and to being able to participate in conversations under dialogic and democratic conditions. According to Arendt (Mahrd, 2004), the woven of interpersonal relationships precedes individuals' actions; at the same time, Arendt (1954) clarifies that judgement is needed for these actions. It is through own judgement that one orients in the world. Arendt (1954) connects judgement to common sense and imagination. Being able to imagine something, visiting own thoughts and imagining something is a prerequisite for orientation in the world (Mahrd, 2004). Hence, imagination contributes to the creation of identity as well as the ability to think independently.

In consequence, critical thinking refers to judgement and classification of reasons in one's actions, seeking for arguments and grounds. Critical thinking as an aspect of formation includes a process where the individual thinks together, thinks about and thinks alone, a process that circulates in order to become a critical thinker. Aristotle argued that *fronesis* is important in order that a person will act wisely in a society and is connected to a reflective judgement over own decisions and practices and is also connected to knowledge about life (Aristotle, Bartlett & Collins, 2011). Moreover, Arendt (1954) discussed that the formation of meaning, dialogue, disagreement and plurality is essential for individual's political development. Arendt (1954) argued that individuals need skills to think reflectively in their interaction with others. Self-reflexivity occurs both on an individual and collective level. Kindergarten teachers must help and strengthen the child's understanding of what rights and duties they have, and the staff must be able to practise safeguarding in relation to children's right to privacy and be able to process the children's personal data in accordance with the legislation. All children have the right to have their say and to be heard (United Nations, 2003, Article 12). Activities and practices that highlight children's point of view will be a good starting point for further conversation and reflections with the children. Children must be able to gain an understanding of their own duties and rights.

Furthermore, ECE teachers have the responsibility to comply with the laws and rules that apply to the processing of personal data (Dardanou, Mossin, & Simensen, 2021). The children's personal data must be processed in a secure manner. This means that the kindergarten staff must have knowledge of how the children's personal data is protected. ECE settings should have a system for the systematic obtaining of consent from parents and ECE teachers to use personal information in the pedagogical work (Bølgan, 2018). In addition, it is also necessary for ECE teachers to have common ethical guidelines that apply when it comes to the use of digital technology. Information security is often mentioned in connection with privacy. Information security is about information being secured regarding confidentiality, integrity and accessibility (Hardersen, 2016). It is mainly a matter of taking care of information that you have access to and making sure that it does not go astray.

The late years after the Norwegian Framework Plan for Kindergartens' context and task came in force in 2017 (Norwegian Directorate for Education and Training, 2017), a developmental work in ECE in Norway has focused especially on the concept of digital judgement. The Norwegian Directorate for Education and Training (n.d.) has published online training packages for ECE teachers to reflect and train on implementing this concept in the daily practices and activities.

Children's meaning making

By participating in activities that make meaning, children are supported to their own identity development and positive self-understanding. Children have different needs, different experiences, different meanings and perspectives, and all of those will be visible in kindergarten activities and everyday practices. When children are invited in a variety of conversations, they have opportunities to exchange experiences, meanings and perspectives. Children practise ways of thinking and reflections about what is true and not true, about similarities and differences or about what is ethically right or not. Reflection about actions and their consequences contributes to an understanding of others' perspectives and standpoints (Dardanou, Mossin, & Simensen, 2021, p. 45).

Studies have illustrated that in a technology-mediated, creative and play-centred activity and process, meaning making occurs as an entwined activity between non-digital and digital activities and is often based on children's previous experience with technology (Burnett & Daniels, 2016; Undheim, 2020). These technologies – and in this case IoToys – can play an important role in introducing children in complex concepts like internet, digital safety or information technology.

Purpose of this study

The purpose of this study is to explore how the use of IoToys in ECE settings supports children's play and meaning making that emerge children's reflections on ethical perspectives of the use of digital technology. To examine this objective, two guiding questions were addressed:

1 *In what ways do IoToys support children's digital judgement in the form of ethical reflection and critical thinking?*
2 *How can play activities with IoToys support children's participation and holistic development?*

Method and ethics

The study builds upon and extends the findings and the qualitative methodology of previous research on IoToys (see Arnott, Palaiologou, & Gray, 2019; Kewalramani et al., 2020). The data collection reported here spans from January 2019 to March 2020 with data having been collected with a naturalistic multimethod approach: semi-structured interviews or focus groups lasting up to 30 minutes with the educators, observations of interactions with IoToys (narrative and video), multimedia messages (digital images, videos and short written reflections submitted by educators to the researchers) and informal discussions (consultations) with the children (Table 5.1). Field notes were used to document the context, routines and procedures, alongside of the rapport building with the children.

Children's participation was voluntary, and parents were advised that children's lack of engagement was a reasonable finding and not to force participation.

Table 5.1 Overview of periods, participants, IoToys integrated and data

Period	Children's age group	EC setting	Educators (term is used collectively to describe all qualifications in each country)	IoToys used	Data
January 2019 To June 2019	Six children, five years old	One ECE setting	One Bachelor of Education EC degree-trained teacher; three EC assistants with a one-year pedagogical training	Osmo: Coding Jam, Awbie and Monster Robotic toys: Dash (xylophone) Dot	Interviews = 1.5 hours Observations = 7 hours Photographs = 263 Voice recordings = 203 minutes with children and educators
August 2019 to March 2020	Eight children, three to five years old	One ECE setting	One Bachelor of Education EC degree-trained teacher; two EC assistants with a one-year pedagogical training	Osmo: Coding Jam, Awbie and Monster Robotic toys: Dash (xylophone) Dot Blue-bot Botley	Observations = 8.5 hours Photographs = 217 Voice recordings = 184 minutes with children and educators

The EECERA Ethical Code of Practice (2015) was followed, and the project was approved by the Norwegian Centre for Research Data (NSD). Additionally, all the protocols were inherent to the conduct of research in an ethical manner. Ethical procedures were considered and followed during the entire research process so that educators', parents' and children's consent was ensured (NESH, 2016). Pseudonyms have been used for the respective educators and children.

Findings and analysis

A deductive thematic analysis based on Braun and Clarke's (2021) approach was employed to explicitly analyse the key themes underpinned by the theoretical underpinnings of the study. More specifically, the generation of codes was focused on whether and how IoToys as a motivational pivot can activate conversations between children and teachers and/or among children and to what extent children develop an early ethical understanding of digital media such as safety and the internet through situations that led to IoToys play-type situations.

Theme 1: Defining the internet

This story is an example on how the IoToys provide opportunities for children to reflect on the concept of the internet and its functions related to play. The teacher, Solveig, is participating in the activity.

Marisa (4 years and 8 months), Andrew (4 years and 11 months) and Solveig (kindergarten teacher).

MARISA: I can click on Blue-bot.

ANDREW (*holds the iPad*): I can see Blue-bot in the iPad.

SOLVEIG: You can move Blue-bot with the iPad. You can press on the arrows and the button in the middle and Blue-bot will move.

ANDREW: Can I do it? Can I choose where will go? Can he go to the other room where Thea and Christin play (*Figure 5.2: Andrew programming Blue-bot*)?

SOLVEIG: Yes, you can, but you have to calculate how many times you will press on the buttons, so Blue-bot actually makes it to the other room.

MARISA: I can count to 30, does it take more than that?

SOLVEIG: We can try to test first inside the room here, and then you can try to calculate how much it is needed to make it to the other room.

ANDREW: Solveig, how does blue bot know where to go? Why when I press on the iPad the buttons Blue-bot moves?

SOLVEIG: Well, it is because they synchronise. When you press the arrows on the iPad, through something we call Bluetooth and internet that comes to Blue-bot.

MARISA: My mother says that we must be careful on internet. Children should not be on internet without someone older together.

SOLVEIG: Yes, that is right Marisa. Internet can be both for children and gown-ups.

ANDREW: My father says that YouTube is not for children, he has fixed that I can watch what I want.

SOLVEIG: The same have we done here in the kindergarten with the iPads. One should be careful with what can come when you search to watch a video on YouTube.

ANDREW: It can come a scary monster!

MARISA: Or blood?

SOLVEIG: It can be. One should be careful and search exactly one wants to watch. Especially children. Why do you think? Do we know who is putting up the videos?

MARISA: I don't know

ANDREW: Me either. Do you Solveig?

SOLVEIG: Difficult often to know. Normally there is a name, but not always. That's why it is good to ask an adult to help you if you are unsure.

MARISA: I will ask always my mother and father.

ANDREW: Me too.

SOLVEIG: And us here in the kindergarten.

MARISA: Ok, now Blue-bot is going in the next room! (Andrew and Marisa left the room).

In this example, we see that children wonder about how Blue-bot connects with the iPad. The teacher is using concepts like "Bluetooth" to explain to children

Figure 5.2 Andrew programming Blue-bot

the way the iPad and Blue-bot connect (Figure 5.3: Testing the Bluetooth, and Figure 5.4: Blue-bot on iPad). The use of the concepts "Bluetooth" and "Internet," which are concepts children have heard before in their everyday lives at home, provides associations with earlier experiences (Dardanou, Mossin, & Simensen, 2021). Meaning making of the concept of "Internet" expands through children's previous experiences with the use of YouTube at home. The dialogue between children and the teacher develops an opportunity for the teacher to provide children information about internet search. Based on that, children reflect that on internet (YouTube) one can be exposed to things that can be scary and unsure of who is behind it. Critical thinking when one is on internet or YouTube is essential as the presence of an adult (Bergsjø et al., 2020). The children in ECE settings must be included in reflections related to the use of digital tools and technology. According to the Norwegian Framework Plan (Norwegian Directorate for Education and Training, 2017), ECE teachers should invite children to different types of conversations where the children can wonder, reflect and ask questions.

Figure 5.3 Testing the Bluetooth

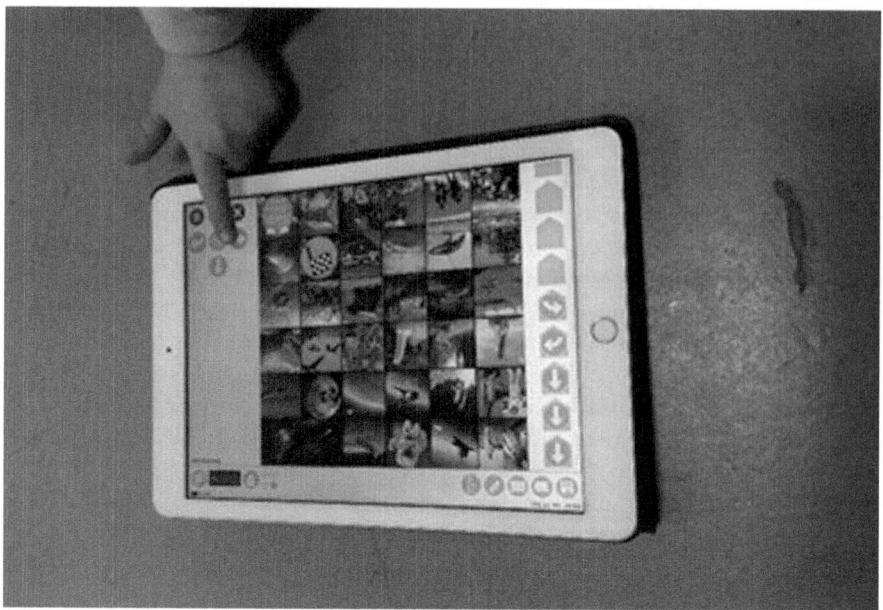

Figure 5.4 Blue-bot on iPad

Theme 2: "Can I take a picture of you? Yes, you can ... today"

Sivert (5 years and 3 months), Markus (4 years and 11 months) and Kathrine (kindergarten teacher) are having an activity with Osmo Monster Mo (Figure 5.5). The app requires the Osmo base and a whiteboard. The app features Mo, a furry orange monster, who asks you to draw various things, which are then brought onto the screen and become part of Mo's world.

KATHRINE: Do you remember last time you played with Monster Mo?
SIVERT: Yes, I remember I drew a bathtub and Monster took it up inside!
MARKUS: I was not here last time.
KATHRINE: Yes, Markus. That's right. You were home that day. Sivert, do you
    want to explain Markus how that works?
SIVERT: Sivert, it is easy. Monster is asking us to draw something here in this
    board with the marker and then Monster drags it inside the iPad.
MARKUS: Wow! How can Monster do that?
KATHRINE: It is because there is a mirror, a reflector (shows on the red clip on
    the iPad) that connects the board with the iPad. It reflects on the screen.
SIVERT: Yes, mirror, like when you see yourself in the mirror.
KATHRINE: Exactly.
MARKUS: I want to try it.

Figure 5.5 Monster Mo

(*Kathrine starts a new session of Monster Mo, and Markus is following the instructions of Mo with the help of Kathrine and Sivert*).

SIVERT: Now Mo wants you to draw a table for the kitchen.

MARKUS: I can do that. Can I put many different colours, Kathrine?

KATHRINE: Yes, you can do that.

MARKUS: Right, ok, I think I will use red and blue (*Markus is drawing the table*, Figure 5.5).

KATHRINE: Sivert, do you want to take a picture of Markus drawing?

SIVERT: Yes! (*takes the digital camera from Kathrine*).

KATHRINE: Remember what we have said about taking picture of others.

SIVERT: I remember! Markus, can I take a picture of you?

MARKUS: Picture of me? Ok, you can take a picture of me … today.

SIVERT: Ok.

KATHRINE: What do you mean Markus? Why only today?

MARKUS: I mean it is ok today.

SIVERT: Maybe he means that I have to ask again another time? Like you and Solveig do?

KATHRINE: Yes, I think that is what Markus means Sivert. That we must ask. Like me and Solveig do when you played yesterday on the trip to the forest, and we had the cameras with us.

MARKUS: I think it is done. Take a picture of my drawing Sivert, want to show to my mother. Can you send it Kathrine?

(*Sivert takes picture of Markus and his drawing*, Figure 5.6 and Figure 5.7)

KATHRINE: Yes, of course.

(*The activity continues*).

Figure 5.6 Sivert takes photo of Markus

The teacher in this example refers to the other teachers in the same ECE setting who have been developing a praxis to ask the children if it is all right to take photos of them during various activities. Through interaction, dialogue, play and exploration, the ECE contributes to the children developing critical thinking, ethical judgement, ability to provide resistance and action competence, so that they can contribute to change. Because the children must practise good attitudes and contribute to change, this is also an important aspect for the ECE teachers. Understanding that digital tools and technology can be used for so

Figure 5.7 Photo of Markus' drawing of the table during Monster Mo play

much more than just getting to know the tool – in this case Osmo – itself is about attitudes, interest and not least experience. By introducing earlier practices, like asking each other if it is all right to take a photo, it provides children with experiences that they can build on (Dardanou, Mossin, & Simensen, 2021).

Conclusions: Towards a holistic approach on digital

The Norwegian study provides evidence about the development of the aspect of digital judgement in children's play and exploration with IoToys. Digital judgement refers to the use of digital tools, media and resources in a responsible manner, as well as having a conscious relationship with privacy and ethical use of the internet. Children's experiences with IoToys in the learning examples from the Norwegian study are related to the concept of digital judgement in both attitudes and actions based on knowledge and information. These experiences are connected to legal, technological and social aspects for safeguarding intellectual property, privacy and interpersonal relationships in digital media (Kelentrić, Helland, & Arstorp, 2017, p. 14). An ethical understanding has not often to do with what man *can do* and what man *should do* (Staksrud, 2019, p. 228). Children's participation in discussions during play situations provided opportunities for reflections on safety issues and approaches to understand abstract concepts like the internet.

Through this study, children's formed processes through opportunity to participate in activities that are perceived as meaningful and can support their own identity development and positive self-understanding (Bøe et al., 2018). Different needs, opinions and perspectives must be both made visible and valued in ECE practices. The blended digital experiences that included elements from children's previous experiences at home settings, or their ECE setting, launch conversations that develop these experiences and expand their meaning making on other levels (Arnott et al., 2020). Relations are important in children's participation in dialogue. Therefore, as ECE settings are a place where those close relations occur (relationships between teachers and children as well as among children), teachers' presence in the development of those relationships is fundamental. Through this relational network and through actions and values, all participants influence each other. Children's participation in this community of relationships is developing their rationality and self-identity through being and acting as a part of a group in a community of practices, actions, values and relations.

Implications for ECE practices are related to the use of IoToys in children's free play activities and exploration, and/or in planned activities by ECE educators (Johansen, 2015). As these toys are often connected with internet and Bluetooth, they can generate exploratory conversations that challenge children's ideas, experiences and reflections and invite for further understanding of complex concepts by children, like the internet. When participating in play activities with IoToys, children are given opportunities to express their meanings and ideas about matters that are important to them (Norwegian Directorate for Education and Training, 2017).

Moreover, the integration of IoToys in kindergarten activities and pedagogical practices is related to the educators' knowledge and ability to reflect and make critical choices about if, when and how these toys could or should be included to support children's play and exploration and/or the frameworks' aims and purposes.

References

Arendt, H. (1954). *The Crisis in Education*, Retrieved from http://learningspaces.org/files/ArendtCrisisInEdTable.pdf.

Aristotle, Bartlett, R. C., & Collins, S. D. (2011). *Aristotle's Nicomachean ethics.* Chicago: University of Chicago Press.

Arnott, L., Kewalramani, S., Gray, C., & Dardanou, M. (2020). Role play and technologies in early childhood. In Z. Kingdon (Ed.), *A Vygotskian analysis of children's play behaviours: Beyond the home corner* (pp. 76–92). London and New York: Routledge.

Arnott, L., Palaiologou, I., & Gray, C. (2019). An ecological exploration of the Internet of Toys in early childhood everyday life. In G. Mascheroni & D. Holloway (Eds.), *The Internet of Toys. Practices, affordances and political economy of children's smart play* (pp. 135–157). Cham: Palgrave McMillan.

Bergsjø, L. O., Eilifsen, M., Tønnesen, K. T., & Vik, L. G. V. (2020). *Barn og unges digitale dømmekraft. Verdiløft i barnehage og skole.* [Children and young people's digital judgment. Value increase in kindergarten and school]. Oslo: Universitetsforlaget.

Bøe, M., Steinnes, G. S., Hognestad, K., Fimreite, H., & Moser, T. (2018). *Barnehagelæreres praktisering av en helhetlig tilnærming til læring* [Kindergarten teachers' practice of a holistic approach to learning]. Universitetet i Sørøst-Norge, Retrieved from https://nettsteder.regjeringen.no/barnehagelarerrollen/files/2018/12/Barnehagel%C3%A6reres-praktisering-av-en-helhetlig-tiln%C3%A6rming-til-l%C3%A6ring.pdf.

Bølgan, N. (2018). *Digital praksis i barnehagen. Nysgjerrig, eksperimentell og skapende* [Digital practice in kindergarten. Curious, experimental, and creative]. Bergen: Fagbokforlaget.

Braun, V., & Clarke, V. (2021). *Thematic analysis: A practical guide.* Los Angeles, London, New Delhi, Singapore, Washington DC: Sage.

Burnett, C., & Daniels, K. (2016). Technology and literacy in the early years: Framing young children's meaning-making with new technologies. In S. Garvis & N. Lemon (Eds.), *Understanding digital technologies and young children* (pp. 18–27). London and New York: Routledge.

Chaudron, S., Di Gioia, R., & Gemo, M. (2018). *Young children (0–8) and digital technology: A qualitative study across Europe.* [EUR 29070]. European Union. DOI: 10.2760/294383.

Dardanou, M., & Gamst-Nergård, E. (2020). The role of the kindergarten in children's well-being and resilience: The case of Norway. In Z. Williams-Brown & S. Mander (Eds.), *Childhood well-being and resilience: Influences on educational outcomes* (pp. 190–203). London and New York: Routledge.

Dardanou, M., & Kofoed, T. (2019). It is not only about the tools! Professional digital competence. In C. Gray & I. Palaiologou (Eds.), *Early learning in the digital age* (pp. 61–76). Los Angeles, London, New Delhi, Singapore, and Washington DC: Sage.

Dardanou, M., Mossin, S. M., & Simensen, D. E. (2021). *Barnehagens digitale are-naer.* [Kindergarten's digital arenas]. Oslo: Universitetsforlaget.

European Early Childhood Education Research Association (EECERA). (2015). *Ethical code for early childhood researchers.* Retrieved from http://www.eecera.org/about/ethical-code/.

Fjørtoft, S. O., Thun, S., & Buvik, M. P. (2019). *Datagrunnlaget til Monitorundersøkelsen 2019* [The data base for the Monitor study 2019]. Retrieved from https://www.udir.no/tall-og-forskning/finn-forskning/rapporter/datagrunnlaget-til-monitor-2019/.

Geneiatakis, D., Kounelis, I., Nai-Fovino, I., Steri, G., & Baldini, G. (2017). Security and privacy issues for an IoT based smart home. In *2017 40th International Convention of Information and Communication Technology, Electronics and Microelectronics (MIPRO)* (pp. 1292–1297). Retrieved from https://ieeexplore.ieee.org/stamp/stamp.jsp?tp=&arnumber=7973622.

Gray, G., & MacBlain, S. (2015). *Learning theories in childhood.* Los Angeles, London, New Delhi, Singapore, Washington DC: SAGE.

Hardersen, B. (2016). *App' legøyer og app' estreker? Profesjonsfaglig digital kompetanse i barnehagen* [App fun and app strokes? Professional digital competence in kindergarten]. Oslo: Cappelen Damm Akademisk.

Johansen, S. L. (2015). *Barns liv og lek med medier* [Children's lives and play with media]. Oslo: Cappelen Damm Akademisk.

Karila, K. (2012). A nordic perspective on early childhood education and care policy. *European Journal of Education, 47*(4), 584–595.

Kelentrić, M., Helland, K., & Arstorp, A.-T. (2017). *Rammeverk for lærerens profesjonsfaglig digitale kompetanse.* [Framework for the teacher's professional digital competence] Oslo: Senter for IKT i utdanningen.. Retrieved from https://www.udir.no/contentassets/081d3aef2e4747b096387aba163691e4/pfdk-rammeverk-2018.pdf.

Kewalramani, S., Palaiologou, I., Arnott, L., & Dardanou, M. (2020). The integration of the internet of toys in early childhood education: A platform for multi-layered interactions. *European Early Childhood Education Research Journal, 28*(2). DOI: 10.1080/1350293X.2020.1735738.

Kleeman, D. (2020). Five things that haven't changed (much). In C. Donohue (Ed.), *Exploring key issues in early childhood and technology. Evolving perspectives and innovative approaches* (pp. 16–19). London and New York: Routledge.

Kucirkova, N. (2020). Personalized education and technology. How can we find an optimal balance? In C. Donahue (Ed.), *Exploring key issues in early childhood and technology. Evolving perspectives and innovative approaches* (pp. 71–78). London and New York: Routledge.

Løvlie, L. (2011). Dannelse og profesjonell tenkning. Utfordringen i lærerutdanningen de neste tiårene education and professional thinking [The challenge in teacher education in the coming decades]. In B. Hagtvet & G. Ognjenovic (Eds.), *Dannelse: Tenkning, modning, refleksjon. Nordiske perspektiver på allmenndannelsens nødvendighet i høyere utdanning og forskning* [Formation: Thinking, maturation, reflection. Nordic perspectives on the necessity of general education in higher education and research] (pp. 735–753). Oslo: Dreyers Forlag.

Mahrd, H. (2004). Hannah Arendt: Dannelse til humanitet [Formation to humanity]. In K. Steinsholt & L. Løvlie (Eds.), *Pedagogikkens mange ansikter. Pedagogisk idehistorie fra antikken til det postmoderne* [Pedagogy's many faces. Pedagogical history of ideas from antiquity to the postmodern] (pp. 541–554). Oslo: Universitetsforlaget.

Marsh, J., Plowman, L, D., Yamada-Rice, J.C., Bishop, J., Lahmar, F., Scott, ... Winter, P. (2015). *Exploring play and creativity in pre-schoolers' use of apps*. Final Project Report. Retrieved from www.techandplay.org/reports/TAP_Final_ Report.pdf.

Merchant, G. (2014). Apps, adults and young children: Researching digital literacy practices in context. In R. H. Jones, A. Chik, & C. Hafner (Eds.), *discourse and digital practices: Doing discourse analysis in the digital age* (pp. 144–157). London and New York: Routledge

Ministry of Education and Research. (2005). *Kindergarten act*. Oslo: Norwegian Ministry of Education. Retrieved from http://www.lovdata.no/all/nl-20050617-064.html.

NESH. (2016). *Guidelines for research ethics in the social sciences, humanities, law and theology* (4th ed.). Oslo: The Norwegian National Research Ethics Committees.

Norwegian Directorate for Education and Training. (n.d.). *Støttemateriell til rammeplan for barnehage* [Support material for the framework plan for kindergarten]. Retrieved from https://www.udir.no/laring-og-trivsel/stottemateriell-til-rammeplanen/.

Norwegian Directorate for Education and Training (2017). *Framework plan for kindergartens*. Oslo: Norwegian Directorate for Education and Training. Retrieved from https://www.udir.no/contentassets/5d0f4d947b244cfe90be8e6d475ba1b4/framework-plan-for-kindergartens--rammeplan-engelsk-pdf.pdf.

Ødegaard, E. E., & Krüger, T. (2012). Studier av barnehagen som danningsarena – sosialepistemologiske perspektiver [Studies of kindergarten as a formation arena-social-epistemological perspectives]. In E. E. Ødegaard. (Ed.). *Barnehagen som danningsarena*. [The kindergarten as a formation arena] (pp. 19–47) Bergen: Fagbokforlaget.

Organisation for Economic and Collaboration Development. (2019). *Impacts of technology use on children: Exploring literature on the brain, cognition and well-being*. OECD Education Working Paper No. 195. Retrieved from http://www.oecd.org/officialdocuments/publicdisplaydocumentpdf/?cote=EDU/WKP%282019%293&docLanguage=En.

Resnick, M. (2017). *Lifelong kindergarten. Cultivating creativity through projects, passion, peers, and play*. Cambridge, MA, and London: The MIT Press.

Sakr, M. (2020). *Digital play in early childhood. What's the problem?* Los Angeles, London, New Delhi, Washington, DC, and Melbourne: Sage.

Shapiro, J. (2018). *The new childhood. Raising kids to thrive in a connected world*. New York, Boston, MA, and London: Little, Brown Spark.

Smahel, D., Machackova, H., Mascheroni, G., Dedkova, L., Staksrud, E., Ólafsson, K., ... & Hasebrink, U. (2020). *EU kids online 2020: Survey results from 19 countries*. EU Kids Online. DOI: 10.21953/lse.47fdeqj01ofo.

Staksrud, E. (2011). Norske barn på Internett: Høy risiko – liten skade? [Norwegian children on the Internet: High risk - little harm]. *Nordicom Information*, 33(4), 59–70. Retrieved from https://www.nordicom.gu.se/sites/default/files/kapitel-pdf/344_staksrud.pdf.

Staksrud, E. (2019). Digital dømmekraft og etiske refleksjoner i barnehagen [Digital judgment and ethical reflections in kindergarten]. In H. Jæger, M. Sandvik, & A.-H. L. Waterhouse (Eds.), *Digitale barnehagepraksiser. Teknologier, medier og muligheter* [Digital kindergarten practices. Technologies, media and opportunities]. (pp. 213–231). Oslo: Cappelen Damn Akademisk.

Staksrud, E., & Olafsson, K. (2018). *Tilgang, bruk, risiko og muligheter. Norske barn på Internett. Resultater 2fra EU Kids Online- Undersøkelsen i Norge 2018* [Access, use, risk and opportunities. Norwegian children on the Internet. Results 2 from the EU Kids Online Survey in Norway 2018]. Institutt for medier og kommunikasjon. Retrieved from https://www.uio.no/english/research/strategic-research-areas/nordic/research/research-groups/living-the-nordic-model/news/eu-kids-online-hovedrapport-for-norge-2019.pdf.

Stephen, C., & Edwards, S. (2018). *Young children playing and learning in a digital age. A cultural and critical perspective.* London and New York: Routledge.

Straume, I. S. (2013). Cornelius Castoriadis. Danning som ansvar [Cornelius Castoriadis. Formation as responsibility]. In I. S. Straume (Red.), *Danningens filosofi-historie* [History of the philosophy of formation]. Oslo: Gyldendal Akademisk.

Undheim, M. (2020). "We need sound too!" Children and teachers creating multimodal digital stories together. *Nordic Journal of Digital Literacy, 15*(3), 165–177.

United Nations. Committee on the Rights of the Child (CRC). (2003). *General measures of implementation of the convention on the rights of the child.* General comment no. 5 (2003). CRC/GC/2003/5. Retrieved from https://www.refworld.org/docid/4538834f11.html.

Vygotsky, L. S. (1978). *Mind in society. The development of higher psychological processes.* Cambridge, MA: Harvard University Press.

Wittek, L. (2014). Arven fra Vygotsky [The inheritance from Vygotsky]. In J. H. Stray & L. Wittek (Eds.), *Pedagogikk. En grunnbok* [Pedagogy: A primer book]. (pp. 286–300) Oslo: Cappelen Damm Akademisk.

World Health Organization. (2015). Public health implications of excessive use of the internet, computers, smartphones and similar electronic devices: Meeting report, Main Meeting Hall, Foundation for Promotion of Cancer Research, National Cancer Research Centre, Tokyo, Japan, 27–29 August 2014. World Health Organization. Retrieved from https://apps.who.int/iris/handle/10665/184264.

Yelland, N., & Gilbert, C. (2017). Re-imagining play with new technologies. In L. Arnott (Ed.), *Digital technologies and learning in the early years* (pp. 32–43). Los Angeles, London, New Delhi, Singapore, Washington DC, and Melbourne: Sage.

6 IoToys and social-emotional literacies

Introduction

As domains of everyday functioning, such as academic achievement and social skills, rely heavily on children's ability to socially communicate, interact with their peers and emotionally regulate, lack of social and emotional skills can have significant consequences for children with diverse needs (Sukkar, Dunst, & Kirkby, 2017). Children that learn and think differently (neurodiverse children) may not be able to express their emotions or are unable to make social connections with peers at an early age.

For example, for children from culturally and linguistically diverse (CALD) and English as an additional language (EAL) backgrounds, English can be a barrier to children's smooth social assimilation into their natural learning environments (Phillipson, Phillipson, & Kewalramani, 2018; Kewalramani, Phillipson, S. & Belford, 2020). For children with EAL needs, the "foreign" learning environment may present challenges, which may not be experienced by non-CALD families. These challenges might be in relation to children's friendship building and socially communicating with their peers, educators and/or community-based environments (Sukkar, Dunst, & Kirkby, 2017).

Additionally, there are many children with chronic illnesses who are hospitalised either for long periods of time or spend substantial time in hospitals. Advancement of medical treatments for chronic illnesses means that more and more children are spending time in hospitals, unable to attend mainstream education and thus in need of education at either hospital or home. An earlier study by Bsiri-Moghaddam et al. (2011), on the effects of hospitalisation of children, found that hospitalisation brings some degree of emotional disturbance to them. Especially, prolonged and repeated hospitalisation increases the chance of later problems in life, especially mental health-related issues. Research has shown strong evidence that supporting children to stay connected with education and social activities during hospitalisation reduces difficulties during school re-entry, helps children to cope with their medical illness and manage it in better ways, provides children with a sense of normalcy and helps them to avoid maybe later potential mental health issues due to their absence from "normal" life, especially for children that have spent long periods

DOI: 10.4324/9781003185840-6

of time in hospital (Cane, 2016; Kendall & Taylor, 2016;; Wade, 2016; Boles et al., 2017).

These children are likely to be at risk of growing up of having some difficulty in understanding a sense of coping and resiliency in adulthood (Allen, 2003; Garvis et al., 2016). Cultivating social-emotional health and well-being should not only be part of education agendas but also part of citizenship so that every single child has the right to embrace and be encouraged to advocate their views and understandings of belonging, being and becoming in their world (Australian Government Department of Education and Training, 2019). Hence, we underpin our study through decades of research in positive psychology that social and emotional competencies are significant indicators for successful learning (Seligman, 2011), with the premise that "All" children including those with diverse needs (e.g. neurodiverse, EAL and chronic illnesses) have the right and opportunity to learn to socially communicate, collaborate and interact with their peers and adults, express emotions and be able to participate in their everyday learning environments that include digital technology-based interactions (UNICEF Office of Research – Innocenti, 2019)).

Thus, in this chapter, based on research findings from Australia and England, we explore how IoToys and robotic technologies might enable children's social and emotional competency development.

Children with diverse needs

Research has shown growing attention to the use of technologies as an affordance to build young children's social-emotional well-being – one of the significant indicators for successful learning (Grynszpan et al., 2014; Sandbank et al., 2020). But for neurodiverse children (with diverse learning needs) such as attention deficit hyperactivity disorder (ADHD) or those from EAL backgrounds or those who hospitalised for very long time, having the capacity to make social connections as they transition into formal schooling contexts is fundamental for positive social-emotional well-being (Goff & McLoughlin, 2017; Australian Institute of Health and Welfare, 2018; Atkinson et al., 2020). A 2015 survey of the mental health of Australian children and adolescents, Young Minds Matter, identified that 40.5% of children and young people aged 4–17 were identified as having emotional or behaviour problems (Department of Health, 2015). Research by OECD Health has also shown that effective approaches to promote social and emotional competencies and prevent mental health problems should be prioritised, given the scale of human suffering such as physical and psychological health (McDaid, Hewlett, & Park, 2017). In addition, the Australian early childhood (EC) sector including the early childhood early intervention (ECEI) community service providers has been identified as having depleted resources for catering for the social and emotional competencies of young children with a disability/developmental delay (Be You, 2019). Recent research has shown that insufficient resources and tools are available for EC professionals as well as parents to support social and emotional competencies in young children

(Sukkar, Dunst, & Kirkby, 2017; Phillips, Phillipson, & Tyler-Merrick, 2021). A large proportion of families feel inadequate or unqualified to support social and emotional learning opportunities for young children (Hancock et al., 2012).

A foundational gap addressed by this study is the need to equip families to be able to feel apt in building children's social and emotional competencies as a lifelong learning skill. By tapping on the unmet potential of IoToys and robotic technologies, this study explores the use of technologies such as interactive AI robotic toys and how these robotic technologies might shape children's (age 4–8 years) social-emotional competencies. Studies in the UK and the USA have found that children can develop social and emotional skills through interactions with robots. For example, Huijnen et al.'s (2016) study showed how for a typical autism spectrum disorder (ASD) child, preschool skills such as collaborative play and joint attention, as well as turn-taking behaviour, were often improved by robotic intervention.

The *robot therapy* acts as a platform focusing on robot-child interactions (operated by the caregiver/EC professional) rather than a fully robot-assisted intervention. The robot's prompting (e.g. talking, smiling, laughing and expressing emotions) provides an interesting stimulant for children who have difficulties engaging socially. While the presence of a robot in a learning environment offers a 3D embodiment, recently Lahiri (2020) also found that children with autism interact with robots, express concern for them and focus on them in ways that are often similar to their typically developing peers. The children are more likely to easily learn to code the robot to perform a set of social-emotional actions, which can then be transferable when they are engaged in playing with their peers, siblings and/or other key persons including role-playing in imitating the robot actions and utterance (McReynolds et al., 2017; Luckin & Cukurova, 2019). Such robot-child interactions are novel and stimulating and have been found to be motivating for the child engaging in playful social and emotional learning. Another study conducted by Hjorth et al. (2020) found that technology-based gaming platforms such as Minecraft "seriously" situate children's digital play as a creative and cultural practice. Addressing the issues of how to manage and augment children's media and digital literacy skills, Hjorth et al. (2020) suggest researchers should not ignore considering complex ways in which Minecraft occupies the daily lives of children as players engaging in cultural and generational contexts, fostering a "spectrum of multimodal, sociomaterial and sensory literacies" (p. 5). As such, this international study also considered Minecraft as a multimodal digital tool to understand how children with neurodiverse needs play in virtual 3D world gaming platforms that can also be seen as a suite of IoToys play. Engineering and technology industry experts have also researched how Minecraft can bridge the gap as being a multimodal and assistive technology-based resource that uses computer-aided design (CAD) building blocks to provide children with tangible ways to create, communicate and problem-solve in virtual world-based scenarios and construct solutions (Schaul, 2013).

In Johnson et al.'s (2016) study, Minecraft players construct elaborate virtual structures that allow users to bring these into the real world using 3D printers.

Players build their digital monuments – whether they're the Taj Mahal – in the game itself. Then, they place obsidian, diamond, gold and iron blocks at set points to define the 3D area to be printed.

Minecraft, a popular multiplayer online game in which players use blocks to design structures, is of academic interest as a natural experiment in collaborative 3D design of very complex structures. Virtual teams of up to 40 simultaneous designers have created city-scale models with total design times in the thousands of hours.

The role of technologies in home and hospital education (HHE) and especially the use of robotic technology or AI robotics is emerging (Soares, Kay, & Craven, 2017). Three major research studies – Keeping Connected in Australia, the Bednet project in Belgium and the Learning at Home and in the Hospital (LeHo) project – have emphasised the beneficial role that digital technologies can play in HHE.

As part of a more effective approach to the provision of education support for children with chronic health conditions, the potential to use technologies to connect children with their schools and their peers and contribute to a learning culture within a hospital setting is increasingly being realised. For example, in England, the Oxfordshire Hospital School is using telepresence robots to help children with medical needs to stay connected with their home schools (Robots in School Project – Oxfordshire Hospital School (ohs.oxon.sch.uk)). Such technology allows children to join their class from the hospital bed so they do not miss out on their education, but at the same time it offers a sense of socialisation which is of great importance for children with chronic medical conditions. In Australia, the Missing School project is also using telepresence technology to support either hospitalised children or homebound children due to medical conditions (MissingSchool – Robots). Findings from both projects have shown the value of such technology not only in the continuation of children's education and their academic outcomes but also in their socioemotional developmental outcomes. However, such potential gains have not yet been fully explored by research in early childhood education (ECE), and there still appears to be some scepticism around the use of technologies in HHE.

Similar to these projects, The Bednet project in Belgium, based on the principles of individualised learning in HHE, is using synchronous internet education (SIE). SIE makes use of the internet to connect children who are hospitalised with their home schools. It is available for preschool children from the age of five and all pupils in primary and secondary education. HHE, families and the home schools are equipped and supported with free adequate devices for the period that the children are hospitalised. The Bednet programme supports children to "attend" lessons from the hospital bed to their home school class. The aim of the programme, supported by the legislation across Belgium, is to prevent children missing lessons and learning when unable to attend home school. It creates a live connection between hospitalised children and the home schools' classroom teacher and classmates. Children can see their classmates and the teacher during the lesson through an audio-video link with the help of the internet. The children can direct the camera in any direction they wish enabling them to "attend" the lesson in their hope schools and at the same time to participate in any activities that take place in the classrooms. This way children feel connected with their home school and its social life of the school (https://bednet.be/bednet-english).

An earlier project, the LeHo, examined the role of information communication technology (ICT) and how it can be embedded in the curriculum for HHE. The project team, based on their analysis of studies such as Lombaert et al. (2006) and Tielen (2003), proposed that ICT can become a valuable tool in assuring continuity in education. Children with medical conditions who are unable to attend school and are either hospitalised or homebound might not want to continue attending mainstream school due to lack of social contact with peers (Fels & Weiss, 2001; Searle, Askins, & Bleyer, 2003). They also proposed that children with medical conditions can follow classes live from home by using educational software and interactive learning (Capurso & Dennis, 2015a, 2015b).

Such innovative projects and emerging research have shown that the anthropomorphised nature of robotic technology helps children to establish a sense of normalcy (e.g. Newhart, Warschause, & Sender, 2016) to overcome isolation and meet socioemotional needs of these children. However, there is limited research examining the use of robotics on the benefits using such technology with young children in their social and emotional development.

Thus, in this chapter, we focus on Australia and English studies to examine the role of robotic technology in relation to neurodiverse children's social and emotional development.

Theoretical underpinnings

Understanding children's social-emotional development is a complex phenomenon which begins with considering child's emotional state as a repertoire of highly effective actions and feelings (Ziegler & Baker, 2013). For example, for a child, expressing emotions as facial gestures is a cognitive domain-specific adaptation to their environmental conditions, which needs to be modelled and increasingly developed by the adult in the child's learning environment (Ziegler & Baker, 2013). Findings emerging from the field of neuropsychology show strong links between brain development and expression of emotions. Brown et al. (2019) argue that emotions are energy in action (=e-motions) and explains that we use embodied language to express emotions, for example, when a child feels fear their bodies might freeze, when they are angry they might engage in a fight, or when they are feeling excitement they start clapping their hands. The limbic mammalian system of the brain which is responsible for emotions and memory impacts on the neocortex cognitive brain. Although here we examine social-emotional development, it is important to stress that we cannot separate them from other aspects of development such as physical and cognitive development. Moreover, social-emotional development in education cannot be neglected. Social-emotional development is particularly important in adult-child and child-child interactions. As has been mentioned elsewhere in this book, the anthropomorphised nature of the robotic technology makes them attractive to young children.

In the past, studies supported the idea that human interaction with computers is fundamentally social in nature (Nass, Steuer, & Tauber, 1994; Takeuchi & Katagiri, 1999). Research has shown that users tend to treat computers and robots as if they were humans without even being conscious of it (Luczak, Roetting, & Schmidt, 2003). In a previous study with very young children (under the age of five), Palaiologou (2016) found that children using touch screen technology apply human emotions and social behaviours to the characters of the application they were playing with. In our previous work about examining robotic toys and as indicated in Figure 6.1, we found that the playful interactions with the robotic toys were social and emotional in nature and can form the means by which children practise and engage in collaborative activities with their peers, the focus being to support children's self-efficacy in forming social relationships and boost their confidence to participate in future learning opportunities as children transition from preschool environments to formal schooling adapted from the (Arnott et al., 2020; Kewalramani, Kidman, & Palaiologou, 2021, Palaiologou, Kewalramani, & Dardanou 2021). In this chapter and in line with our theoretical conceptualisation that was discussed in Chapter 1, extending previous work, we argue that the "intelligent" robot can act as a therapeutic tool when placed within the child's natural learning environment to foster multimodal interactions and subsequently facilitate social-emotional behavioural characteristics (Kewalramani, Kidman, & Palaiologou, 2021). For example, the interactions and the communication between the child and the robot and the manipulation of the robot to perform certain tasks act as a "natural" stimulus to provide the child with motivational pleasure and psychologically triggered actions to continually interact with the robot, thus shaping skills such as social communication, social collaboration, emotional inquiry and self-regulation, problem-solving and resiliency. The anthropomorphic nature of the robot works as a "real-life model" to stimulate the child's emotional skills and behaviours, leading to their socioemotional competency development.

The research from Australia

We employ a participatory Arts-Based Educational Research (ABER) approach. The ABER approach allows for the investigation of possibilities for educational improvement as an educational intervention by bringing about new forms of learning to generate, trial and refine changes to learning and news forms of children's play and multimodal interaction (integration of technologies such as IoToys in our case) in order to generate new knowledge and practices. ABER is a child-centred methodology which includes artistic representations and aligns with the play-based approach in ECE (Australian Government Department of Education and Training, 2019; Arnott et al., 2020). Employing the ABER approach in this research, well-grounded in our conceptual framework, will enable us to understand the neurodiverse child's ways of knowing and preferred

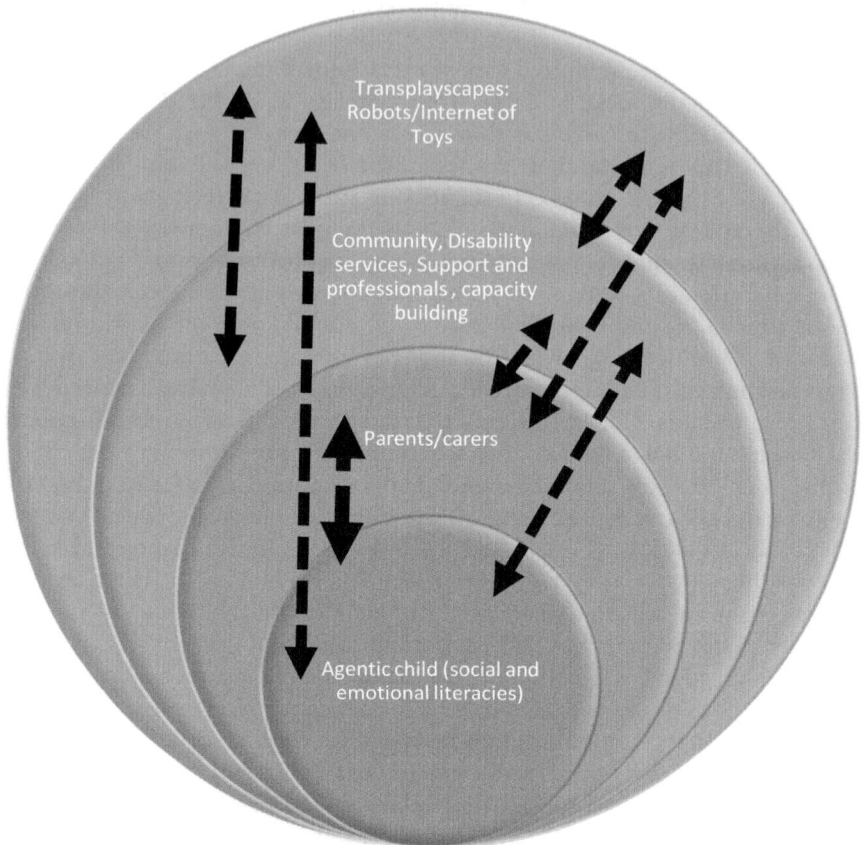

Figure 6.1 The interplay of social-emotional development and robotic technology

ways of communicating, through a range of techniques – such as storytelling, storyboarding, drawings, painting, sculptures, photovoice, photo stories, dance and drama, thus catering to a broad range of child abilities (Arnott et al., 2020; Blaisdell et al., 2019). Furthermore, our previous research in international EC settings has shown that ABER diminishes the power relationships that may exist when researching with families of children of diverse abilities and considers children as capable research participants and in some cases, such as this study, children as co-researchers (Arnott et al., 2020; Blaisdell et al., 2019).

In order to co-design activities with children and parents that will allow the researchers to study children's interactions and behaviours in line with the study's conceptual framework, we adapted the evidence-based framework (Kewalramani & Havu-Nuutinen, 2019; Kewalramani et al., 2020; Kewalramani, Palaiologou, & Dardanou, 2020), encompassing the five steps to the essential features for the integration of technologies in an inclusive manner that fosters children's social-emotional learning (Table 6.1).

Table 6.1 All-inclusive teaching and learning framework to integrate IoToys/robots in children's play

Step	Activity/actions
Planning	Co-design activities and provocations based on reflective conversations with children's existing schemes (strengths and interests), thus employing a child-centred approach. Introduce the robots intentionally via play-based demonstrations and allow children to tinker with them freely, but safely.
Emotional scaffolding through posing problem-based scenarios	Through storytelling and empathy-based situations, scaffold children and engage in inquiry-based conversations. Encourage children to use verbal communication skills to share their ideas. Example of inquiry starters can be about picking up a problem-based situation using the robot as the central character (such as the robot might be in danger of the battery dying – How can we save the robot from dying?)
Building children's inquiry skills	Allow "wait-think-share" time for children to brainstorm with their peers on how to solve the posed problem. Generate a social-emotional learning environment where the robot is the central theme in the children's stories. The teachers then support the children to program/code the stories and tasks for the robot to perform or act out/role-play. Enable time for children's understanding of social cues such as turn-taking while speaking, and regulating behaviour while communicating with their peers. Continue the free flow of children's inquiry using open-ended questioning techniques to generate inquiry conversations among the children and let the children think out loud while proposing solutions to save the robot.
Adult-child, peer-peer and child-robot interactions	Within the reciprocal and multi-interactions between the adult, children and the robot (remember the robot can also talk, move, act, smile, laugh, etc.). Consider children's construction of artefacts and drawings as a qualitative measure for children's symbolic representation of their developing social emotional skills.
Culminating with a performance by the robot and children	Allow time for whole-group discussions and children's presentations of their constructed artefacts and drawings. This enables a deeper and richer learning experience translating to making real-world connections and physical modalities, fostered through a social and emotional inquiry process.

These five steps as part of the ABER approach guided the researchers to understand children's social-emotional competencies that are formed from the interactivity and relations, as well as the social, emotional and collaborative actions children participate in while playing with the IoToys and robots, thus offering a nuanced and an ideal methodology to understand the development of children's social-emotional skills by using an all-inclusive teaching and learning framework that integrates IoToys.

Participants and methods

Five neurodiverse children (age 4 to 7 years) participated in the study: two diagnosed with autism, one with intellectual disability, one gifted learner and one with language developmental needs. Two parents shared the detailed reports of their children's assessments of learning and developmental needs, and three confirmed verbally about the neurodiverse needs of their children. The detailed assessment reports of the children are not considered as part of the data for the purpose of this chapter. We are rather reporting on children's play with the IoToys (the variety of family of IoToys children engaged with). Families were a mix from immigrant and non-immigrant backgrounds and from low to mid socioeconomic backgrounds within the Australian context. Through purposeful sampling and after discussions with EC educators that the research team has previously worked with, only families those who identified their child needing additional and/or enrichment learning support activities were contacted to participate in this study. The project was also promoted by a not-for-profit (NFP) organisation who promotes STEM and technology education opportunities for those communities and children from diverse needs and backgrounds.

The initial research plan in conjunction with the NFP organisation was to run workshops for parents and children to ascertain the impact of the AI robotic toys on children's social-emotional development. However, due to COVID-19 lockdown periods (June 2020–Nov 2021), the project reverted to an online workshop delivery mode. Five parents agreed to attend the workshop with their children via Zoom. The remaining two families chose to use the toys and engage the child at home as per their convenience. Hence, the data analysed and reported here is a combination of both Zoom video workshops and children's play that was guided by their parents in home settings. The robots and IoToys were sent home to each family. Using COVID-19 sanitation and quarantining procedures, the toys were rotated and used by the children at least once during the lockdown period of six months. Data were generated through Zoom video observations of the workshops (50 hours), self-generated video observations of children's and parents' play experiences (10 hours), reflective and informal conversations with the children during the Zoom workshops and children's constructed artefacts and drawings. We were interested in how the children engaged and interacted with the robotic toys and how this shapes their social-emotional competencies. WhatsApp conversations with parents (which were treated as field notes in an online format of the research project) were used to document the context, routines and procedures, alongside the rapport building and supporting the parents. The data reported and analysed in this paper are the self-generated video observations of parent-child play at home.

Ethics

This project conformed to University Human Ethics Committee guidelines and relevant local authorities including the de-identification of participants' data. In accordance to our previous research with robotic technologies and IoToys, the research team considered ethical procedures, including

1   The children's own perceptions of the uses of data from this project, the permanency of data collected and their associated consent;
2   The role of internet safety in children's play.

Our previous participatory research with young children has shown that children are reliable and voluntary participants in research (Groundwater-Smith, Dockett, & Bottrell, 2014), providing grounds for negotiating consent directly with children. Furthermore, the researchers worked in partnership with parents to encourage discussion and learning experiences designed around safe internet use (while playing with the robots that run using apps for coding) in order to raise awareness. The safe internet use policy was employed at all times while playing with the robots both at home and community-based settings.

In relation to the moral panic around using technologies such as robots with young children, research has acknowledged that technologies are useful in helping to identify the main influences driving children's play and development in the era of IoToys (Arnott, 2016; Edwards et al., 2017). But we suggest that the child's digital life is not so neatly confined, and so evidence of childhood needs to document its messiness (Arnott et al., 2020). When technologies connect children to multiple realms and contexts, children's digital lives cannot be compartmentalised or separated into various systems. Instead, children's digital worlds need to be viewed more holistically, in an interconnected albeit ethical manner, wherein the robot is a tool/facilitator only and not designed to replace social and emotional relationships (I'Anson, 2013).

Data analysis and findings from Australia

One of the strengths of the participatory ABER approach is in meaning making of the robot-child interactions and the role of parents and other significant persons such as siblings that may be present in the child's learning environment. Hence, we analyse these interactions within the "parent–child" dyad or "child–sibling" dyad taken together, rather than interpreting them separately. This combination of information in parent-child dyad has a higher communicative power to unfold how the interactions with the AI robots and related experiences could be internalised by the children and shape children's social-emotional competencies. This data analysis strategy placed an importance on the experiences of the parent-child dyad as signified by the repetition of words, body gestures, facial expressions and/or themes within and between the data, which was the real focus of the study (Bryman, 2012). Further, the study's theoretical ideas of socioecological lens do include a view of the child having agency in expressing their emotions, tone of voice, ways of communication and the modalities involved (e.g. haptic, visual, text based and digital) and the dialogues they may have with the AI robots that may affect their social-emotional state, thinking and actions. However, because of the nature of the study being a qualitative one, we cannot determine a plausible cause and effect and confirm predictions or directional relations using a qualitative approach (Bryman, 2012). Nonetheless, the core of this research lies in revealing the interactions a child may have with the AI robots in conjunction with parents and other significant persons in the neurodiverse child's home environment.

Considering the full richness of the interpretation of the data and those in position of influence (parents and siblings), the data is presented in the form of narrative passages. The narrative passages aim to unveil children's thoughts, feelings, expressions, interactions and experiences as stories. The interpretation of their stories is done both explicitly and implicitly to make meaning not only of what was spoken or children's drawings, but also of the meaning behind their words, constructed artefacts or what remained unspoken (Clandinin, 2007). This involved closely analysing the parents' self-generated data of their child playing with the robot. The below narratives presented as dyads highlight the social-emotional perspectives of the child together with those who were immediately involved in the play experiences and might have an impact on children's social-emotional development.

Parent-child dyad 1: Children's emotional inquiry and problem-solving skills

Learning story – Feeding my cat while he listens and make me happy

The below vignette introduces a scenario of how through Minecraft play Milan, a six-year-old child with autism, engages in social interactions that enable Milan to potentially acquire skills for social and emotional adjustments and practise embodying of emotions and feelings.

Milan co-creates a scenario in the Minecraft (a virtual 3D world application and AI-interfaced coding platform that uses codable building blocks). Together with the parent (Milan's mother), Milan imagines to build a house and a yard for his cat, Sam. Sam becomes the central imagined character and a virtual pet that Sam can play with in his house and the yard.

MOTHER – What are you building?
MILAN – I am trying to build a house, there is normally like a regular house and
    I trying to see where my Cat Sam to live
MOTHER – Did you build a space for Sam
MILAN – Sam is going to live in the yard, in the Cat house

MOTHER – what will Sam have in his cat house?

MILAN – Let me go to settings, and look for items for his yard [i.e. in the Minecraft Inventory].

MOTHER – Oh are there are other animals in the yard? Is Sam lonely in the yard?

MILAN – No, I am his friend.

MOTHER – That is very nice of you to be Sam's friend.

MILAN – Yes, he is my Cat, Sammm come sit there [Milan tried to make Sam in the yard using the Minecraft game controls].

MOTHER – Is Sam listening to you?

MILAN – Sammy, listen to me [Milan pats Sam]. Come, on Sammy we got some work to do!

MOTHER – What else do you have in your yard?

MILAN – It has a swimming pool.

MOTHER – Does Sam make you feel happy when he listens to you?

MILAN – I am taking care of Sam and that makes me feel happy. I am giving him whatever he wants. That makes him feel happy too

MOTHER – That is so nice of you making Sam have happy feelings too!

MILAN – I will now build my pool. Minecraft is all about blocks. Nothing is circle in Minecraft.

And Milan continues his house and yard building using the different shapes – squares and rectangles. Milan is aware of the shapes and spatial awareness of how the blocks connect to each other, which is in essence block play and construction play in a physical environment. However, Minecraft allows children to visualise the shapes in a virtual playspace environment. In the above learning story, it is evident that Milan notices his pet's actions as modelling feelings of showing red love

Figure 6.2 Milan feeding Sam, the cat with some fish to make the cat feel happy

Figure 6.3 Milan's inventory with shapes and real-world objects as visuals

hearts when being fed fish – Sam's favourite food (see Figure 6.2). These feelings demonstrated by the cat then allow the child to verbalise their own feelings and communicate those feelings during play (let's feed the hungry cat some more fish such as raw cod). The pet cat acts as a potential partner to drive the child's emotional thought process, triggering empathy as seen in the playful dialogues. The child co-creates a "self-generated" empathetic situation where Milan wants to continue feeding the Cat Bot new items and continue building a safe place for both of them to play such as the yard and also be cautious not to play outside when it rains (empathy-based feeling being realised and communicated in a social virtual environment). During the house construction process, through parent-child inquiry-based interactions (parent scaffolding and asking open-ended questions such as why, how and where together with child commenting), Milan begins to realise the importance of listening as an important skill and attribute to make someone (his virtual pet cat) feel happy. Milan also begins to connect real-world objects and shapes such as squares and rectangular shapes into his imaginative house and yard construction, thus prompting his problem-solving skills of making right choices of shapes from the Minecraft inventory tools – see Figure 6.3.

Parent-child dyad 2: Children's social communication and social collaboration

Learning story – My robot buddy crashing play

ARGUS – Mummy, can you hold my robot [Iron Man – physical Toy] near Coji [App-operated robot that shows emojis through coding]

MOTHER – okay, what do you want to do next

ARGUS – While you hold my robot, I will use ipad for Coji. But I am scared of those [pointing to the emojis panel of the Coji app that has an angry face].

MOTHER – Its okay, try and see what happens

[Argus imagines that Coji is angry and codes it to display angry face and crash into the Iron Man toy robot].

ARGUS – And now mummy, you hold the Iron Man back up and shoot the gun at Coji. [Argus imagines that Iron man is upset and holding a toy gun].

MOTHER – You know I don't like holding guns!

ARGUS – Just do it and you will see COJI's face

MOTHER – Pichhu....Pichhu....[the mother pretends to join into the 'destruction play' and shoots at Coji].

Argus codes Coji to display a surprised face [see Figure 6.4].

MOTHER – why does Coji have that face?

ARGUS – Because you killed him!

Mother and Argus have a laugh about their robot buddy crashing play.

ARGUS – Now I make Coji feel a cheeky face and then happy face. And he can have a shield to face the gun. Can you hold the shield please?

And the play continues where Argus codes Coji to crash into Iron Man physical toy where Coji is wearing the "imaginative" shield. Subsequently, Coji is displaying a variety of emojis (as seen in Figure 6.5).

Figure 6.4 Argus codes Coji to display a surprised face

Figure 6.5 Argus codes Coji to have an angry face during imaginative destruction play with Iron Man toy

Research from England

In England, school age children (starting age 4 years) who are hospitalised for long periods of time have the right to education within the premises of the hospital. Hospital education

> *means education provided at a community special school or a foundation special school established in a hospital, or education provider under any arrangements made by the local authority under section 19 of the Education Act 1996 (exceptional provision of education), where the child is being provided with such education by reason of a decision made by a medical practitioner*

(Department for Health and Social Care, 2015)

There are several hospital schools located in hospitals that have paediatric wards where the teachers either go to the children's beds to carry out lessons or, if the children can move from their bed, they go to the school which normally is located in a close proximity to the paediatric ward.

The current small case project aimed to investigate what technology was being used in these schools and for what purposes. The project employed qualitative methodology to collect data. Interviews were undertaken at eight hospital school sites in England. Face-to-face interviews were held with a range of hospital school service staff, parents and children: ten heads and deputy heads, 41 teachers, ten parents and 13 children (3 to 8 years old).

Data collection started in October 2019, however, although the aim was to undertake observations to see how technology especially robotic one was used; the project had to stop due to the COVID-19 pandemic in March 2020 as visits were not allowed anymore in hospitals. It is aimed to "re-start" the project once researchers are allowed in hospitals as there is limited research on how it can be used effectively. As it will be shown in the findings, the use of robotics has a lot of potentialities.

Data analysis and findings from England

From the eight hospital schools, only two had started using robotic technology. The rest were using technology mainly tablets for academic subjects, and on some occasions when the medical condition was allowing them to connect online with their home school's classes, so the children feel that they are part of the class, but these attempts were very limited and sporadic. There were concerns raised about the potential interference of mobile technology with the idea that students were now in a time or space focused on school work and that for some children with mental health problems digital technology can be a way of avoiding interpersonal contact. A teacher at one service noted that

> *A lot of the young people we get through the mental health services are already behind their bedroom door, they are already on far too many screens. They are disengaging from many things, including human beings. And I feel very strongly that trust has to be built up, relationships have to be built up.*

Two services had started embracing robotic technology and augmentative communication technology with those pupils who would benefit from using communication aids. Both schools found that the use of such technology allowed remotely linking isolated children on wards with lessons such as phonics and also facilitated linking the children with their home school classes.

> *the children being on a bed all day isolated from their friends and peers thought the robot can now 'go' to their classes, see their friends and even 'go' to the school playground and play with them*, it is a great way to maintain contact and make them feel some form of normality
>
> (Teacher)

> *the use of such technology allows children helps them with their academic basic skills such as phonics and maths but also help them to learn to code and programme, they can make and record music, produce their own videos, they learn editing, all these activities are essential for these children and takes away their mind from their physical illness*
>
> (Teacher)

This school has purchased an internet-connected robot in an attempt to keep children connected with the home schools of children:

> *It's early stages for us as we still learning how to use the robot, but what, well I don't know how tall it is, a metre, a metre and a half, I don't know. It's*

not huge. So, it's free standing and it can move around the school room, it can walk, it can be part of a session. We noticed that using something like a robot or even a dog, a real dog, the children really relaxed. They could see almost the humour in it, but the fact that they're relaxed means that their interaction between the teacher and the other students is more relaxed. Or they might interact with the robot as opposed to another child or a teacher but at least they're interacting. So, it was that engagement factor that we think will work. I think the robot will be used, they'll be able to programme the robot to do certain things.

So there'll be a computing element to the curriculum. You'll be able to use it for all sorts of subjects because it might be about interviewing, the robot talks, so it might be about a child with early language communicating with the robot. Very early stages, you'll have to come back and see. I'm not sure how it will develop

(Headteacher)

The two head teachers of the schools that had started using robotic technology found that it helps children as one of them commented that

Within the functions of the robot a child can be present in the class or a class trip without the child being seen or his or her voice can be altered if they do not feel confident to speak directly in the class.

The second hospital school had purchased an AV1 internet-connected robot produced by a Norwegian company. The robot aims to help children to stay connected with their home schools and end loneliness when children are hospitalised or stay home unable to attend school. It does not aim to replace human contact. It is an avatar device designed to sit on a desk with its head down until a remote user signs on at home through their tablet or phone. Then, the head comes up and lights go on behind the eyes, where there is also a camera, speaker and microphone. Unlike a phone, however, AV1 has no screen. The user can choose from pre-programmed selection of expressions to convey their emotions.

This school was in contact with the company, and they are willing to try alternative technologies, compared to the traditional use of tablets.

Parents were also positive with the use of the robotic technologies. One mother that has a lot of experience in hospital schools with both her children with medical conditions mentioned that for their children "was cool as they could 'come' [with the use of robot] to the school with their pyjamas and this made them 'cool' when they were back in school." Data from the parents showed that the use of robotics provided their children support not to discontinue engagement with their schools and not lose out on their education. But what they valued most was that it was helping children with their well-being, emotional and social development as "despite being in tubes, my son can still play with his friends."

In conclusion, the parents at both schools showed high levels of satisfaction and they were appreciative of the benefits that the use of robotic technology has in their children's education and well-being.

Data from the children revealed that using the robots helps them to create normalcy around their lives when they are hospitalised as they offer "exciting" learning activities and they can stay "in touch" with their friends, and it also offers opportunity to follow classes live from home, to stay in touch with the real world. In the testimonials below, we can see how the robot helped to offer them some form of normality and also takes their minds away from their mental needs:

> *missed my friends at school and it was nice to see them and be able to play with them*
>
> (5 year old)

> *the robot makes my life fun, he brings me my medication*
>
> (6 year old)

> *I do not have hair anymore and I was afraid that my friends will tease me but when they showed me they asked me why and the next day all the boys had saved their heads*
>
> (7 year old)

> *it is lonely here and cannot event go to the class* [meaning the hospital school class] *to play so the robot keeps me company*
>
> (7 year old)

> *the robot made me get up from bed, forgot my pain and enjoyed chasing him*
>
> (5 year old)

As it can be seen the robot became a therapeutic aid, their medical needs were met in the hospital, but the existence of the robot helped them with their emotional and social skills. We do not make the case here that robots can replace human contact; however, under adverse circumstances, they support the children to get a sense of normalcy.

Children also shared how they felt when interacting with the robot and described it as "fun," "laughed when it was falling down," "loved we could sing together," and "loved being able to attend school with them." The top response in all children was that they enjoyed being able to see their friends and be able to play with them despite the fact that they were in hospital.

To conclude, all participants in these two schools valued the use of robotic technology not only for the academic activities but as it allowed opportunities apart from the core subjects such as phonics and maths to offer children a richer curriculum including arts and music. But what they valued most was that it was helping children to stay connected with the outside world, and this had a therapeutic element for their well-being and their social and emotional development.

Discussion

Both studies' findings show how through playful explorations with robots, children are provided with opportunities to collaborate with their peers (e.g. via role-play or by exercising choice and control when coding the robot to perform tasks), and this was mostly evident with the English data, communicated feelings and emotions, and regulated behaviour – important for social-emotional learning and communication skills development. Just like physical toys and play-based resources act as mediational signs and cultural tools, a robotic toy, when placed meaningfully in a child's environment, becomes a manipulative artefact and aids the child's process of communication and social-emotional functioning. It as shown in the English study holds a therapeutic role as it helped children to stay connected with the "real" world.

The playful interactions that a child has with IoToys, including virtual multi-modal environments, depend upon their emotions and imagination, which then mediates the child's cognitive thinking process as they encounter the physical and digital (through robotics and coding) worlds. Children participate in social and emotional imaginative situations, role-play scenarios, storytelling opportunities and collaborative actions while playing with the robots.

The findings show that within the adult-child-robot, robot-child and child-sibling interactions, a new multimodal environment is created for the child to learn social and emotional skills such as communication, gestures and expressing feelings of empathy. The AI robot's coding features, digital touch interface and audio-visual movement features (Milan's learning story play in Minecraft virtual world) allow for a seamless approach to facilitate social-emotional actions, joint attention (looking at the codable building blocks and observing how the enacted code produces an action) and social collaboration with parent and virtual imaginative pets as "real" characters. The robot (as seen in learning story dyad 1) exhibits a "resilience-building event," when Argus tries to code and imagines for Coji to follow the code and demonstrate the variety of feelings while either being hurt and come back with positive feelings during the robot buddy play, thus consequently communicating their emotions. At the same time, the child manifests an "agentic behaviour" to continually be motivated to interact with the robot, thus fostering child's emotional capital (Ziegler & Baker, 2013). This study builds a case for exploring the pedagogical *know-hows* to foster a pedagogy that safely and ethically integrates robotic technologies that have the potential to enhance children's social and emotional development. Implications lie in understanding how can AI robotic toys and AI-interfaced virtual worlds such as Minecraft be effectively integrated as "transfunctional play approach" in ECE. Further studies are recommended in investigating what kinds of training, professional learning opportunities and resources are needed for pre-/in-service ECE teachers' IoToys integration competency development. Building parental capacities (as one of the significant adult) also needs research attention as parents are also responsible for the organisation of child's learning environments and related learning experiences that might be rooted in IoToys play. Additionally, there is an urgent need to build forms of assessment tools that can be used to further understand the strengths, needs and barriers for developing neurodiverse children's social-emotional capital as a core success and pathway for future academic learning. This study has shown how by using AI robotic toys children have an exceptional capacity for developing and using sophisticated social and emotional communication skills which can be harnessed by adults, siblings and peers (including virtual peers) in their lives (Salamon, 2017, p. 2015). Thus, it is possible to consider degrees of participation of children with diverse needs, and a first step to supporting a more holistic view of understanding the ways children can become socially-emotionally literate. Understanding children's development of social-emotional capital will help frame adults (EC professionals and parents) co-develop ways that can better facilitate and reconcile concepts of social communication, emotional inquiry, children's self-efficacy and agency within the platform of robot-child interactions that children engage in. Policymakers and curricula stakeholders need to reimagine ways to create an inclusive play-based teaching and learning framework and related transfunctional play resources for integrating AI robotics and IoToys in the light of cultivating children's social and emotional competencies. An inclusive teaching approach that encompasses the five steps for IoToys integration also needs to be widely researched to test the applicability and feasibility in diverse community, ECEI services and health contexts. We need professional development programmes for EC professionals that specifically targets their understandings and practices to support culturally appropriate IoToys technology experiences for parents/carers and to consistently support their children's social and emotional competencies.

As the OECD Health (2017) recommends, in seeking to meet the mental health and social growth of young children with diverse needs, policymakers and health and education providers can no longer afford to ignore the untapped potential that latest technologies have to offer to solve health problems early on. Robotic toys and IoToys technologies offer one solution that the current international study has piloted to cater to the lack of social and emotional tools and resources in EC settings, particularly serving those children with neurodiverse needs. However, this is not to undermine the role of parents as primary caregivers in child's home environment, and EC educators in child's formal learning environment can be replaced by robots and IoToys technologies. Integration of technologies should be that parents and educators combine elements of child's social-emotional interests and imagination and blend in the codable virtual play characteristics of the robots to intentionally devise the robot-child play, as well as considering children's perspectives (Hakkarainen et al., 2013). It will also be interesting to follow these neurodiverse children to see their actions and reactions in the absence of a robot and how far do these interactions translate into real-world learning environments. Additionally, understanding children's cognitive behaviour and intentions when they react to the action performed by the AI robots and characters that children interact with remains an area of further research in ECE.

Conclusions and further research

In line with our theoretical conceptualisation that play and learning are transformed with the robotic technology and based on the findings of the two studies discusses here, we propose that we need to rethink the use of such technology and examine ways of how we can explore this technology to meet the needs of the neurodiverse children. We suggest that we should value an approach based on the neurodiverse child's interests to promote the agentic nature of children who are able to partake and have a voice in all facets of their learning and development during playful interactions with the therapy robots. As shown elsewhere in this book, our transnational research considers the child's natural learning and socioecological environment to be comprised of key persons such as the parents (child's first educator) and siblings/peers with whom the child interacts, inquires and co-constructs their learning together during play. We also place an emphasis to reveal how the IoToy/robot acts as a manipulative artefact to "jump-start" children's social-emotional competency development. We conceptualise that, like mediational signs and cultural tools, an IoToy such as a robot and/or virtual multimodal learning environments, when introduced meaningfully and with a specific learning intention in a child's environment, become a transfunctional resource and model the child's process of socioemotional development. The transfunctional (visual, digital, tactile and haptic) interactions that a child has with the robot depend upon their imagination and support in shaping social communication, social collaboration, emotional inquiry and self-regulation, and problem- solving and resiliency, which then mediates the child's socioemotional development process as they encounter the physical and virtual worlds (Kewalramani et al., 2020; Kewalramani, Palaiologou, & Dardanou, 2020). These skills and characteristics are learned from the interactivity and relations, as well as the social, emotional and collaborative actions and communications children participate in while playing with the therapy robot. A direct stimulus-response interaction framed by the robot, when encoded and embodied by the child, can influence children's socioemotional competency development. For example, social communication (ability to socially communicate, such as questioning, commenting and sharing, and participate in activities via a range of modalities), social collaboration (ability to collaborate with peers [including virtual peers and imaginative characters in virtual learning environments], siblings, parents and educators on certain tasks), emotional inquiry and self-regulation (ability to express emotions, empathy and persistence on tasks) and problem-solving and resiliency (ability to question, pose solutions, adapt and deal with problems, making connections with real-world learning environments and physical modalities) – all of which when sparked by the therapeutic nature of robots' interactions provide the basis for children's positive social-emotional competencies to participate in their natural learning environments (home and preschool or other learning environments such as hospital school) and communities.

The key benefits of such technology (IoToys and AI) play for social and emotional learning are summarised:

- Imaginative play with the robot enables children to experiment with social and emotional skills such as empathy and demonstrate expressive language and communication skills for social interaction and engagement with peers and imagined characters.
- Purposeful, child-led imaginative play supports resilience.
- IoToys play has been found to facilitate collaboration and shared goal setting.
- IoToys play allows for children to test problem-solving skills and pose solutions.

Key outcomes for children

Our study is conceptualised on the premise that children's learning skills of building respectful social-emotional relationships are deeply connected to the quality support system available in their natural learning environments. The study demonstrated a glimpse of evidence-based strategies to achieving children's development of the following:

- Express emotions and behaviours in the form of words and questions;
- Embody resilience during manipulative play with the toys and collaborating with peers to achieve a shared goal;
- Evaluate encountered problems and pose solutions;
- Engage in continuous questioning, suggest ideas and pose solutions between and/or among each other (with adults and virtual imagined peers);
- Learn about negotiation, conflict resolution, understanding social cues and listening to each other's (adults' and peers') perspectives.

As discussed in Chapter 2, our study findings also support the Australian EYLF, Norwegian DigiCompEdu framework and EYFS in England curricula's implementation of harnessing the potential of using digital technologies and multimedia resources to plan for children's play-based experiences; particularly, for skills such that children can communicate their emotions and create and display their understandings and expressions of their everyday world. As children's social-emotional development advances, they become increasingly able to form and sustain positive relationships, experience, manage and express emotions, and explore and engage with their environment.

Educators can scaffold the unique attributes of each child, be they cultural, behavioural, intellectual or social-emotional (Australian Government Department of Education and Training, 2019, 2019, p. 6). Educators can use their digital judgement in adapting the evidence-based learning stories and the 5-step all-inclusive teaching and learning framework in their intentional planning and delivery of quality learning experiences to support multimodal interactions with neurodiverse children. For example, through multimodal play affordances (digital, dance, movement, drawings, text and sound), educators can teach children to make sense of, become aware of, and construct creative ideas about the social and natural worlds.

We recommend next steps of research in the field of IoToys use in which ECE should also consider supporting EC professionals, intervention community service providers and allied health professionals to

1   Gain confidence in deploying robotic resources and IoToys-based learning interventions and inclusive strategies to engage children in social-emotional learning;
2   Improve their confidence in deploying multimodal teaching and learning opportunities for children and build their capacities in supporting children to use oral language to communicate and express themselves socially and emotionally;
3   Gain confidence in employing a child-led and strength-based approach that is concerned with the educators'/parents' co-investigation with children as agentic learners and reflecting on the improvement of new forms of children's social-emotional learning growth;
4   Enable EC professionals' technological and pedagogical knowledge development for IoToys and robotic technology integration by providing support for the challenges and difficulties faced by the educators, children and families through continuous reflection and collaboration with colleagues and families.

References

Allen, C. (2003). Desperately seeking fusion: On "joined up thinking", "holistic practice" and the new economy of welfare professional power. *British Journal of Sociology, 54*, 287–306.

Arnott, L. (2016). An ecological exploration of young children's digital play: Framing children's social experiences with technologies in early childhood. *Early Years: An International Journal, 36*(3), 271–287.

Arnott, L., Kewalramani, S., Gray, C., & Dardanou, M. (2020). Role play and technologies in early childhood. In Z. Kingdon (Ed). *A Vygotskian analysis of children's play behaviours: Beyond the home corner* (pp. 76–92). London. Routledge.

Australian Government Department of Education and Training. (2019). *Belonging, being and becoming – The early years learning framework for Australia*. Retrieved from https://www.dese.gov.au/child-care-package/resources/belonging-being-becoming-early-years-learning-framework-australia.

Australian Institute of Health and Welfare. (2018). *Mental health services: In brief 2018*. Retrieved from https://www.aihw.gov.au/getmedia/0e102c2f-694b-4949-84fb-e5db1c941a58/aihw-hse-211.pdf.aspx.

Be You. (2019). Evaluation and research. Retrieved from https://beyou.edu.au/about-be-you/evaluation-and-research.

Blaisdell, C., Arnott, L., Wall, K., & Robinson, C. (2019). Look who's talking: Using creative, playful arts-based methods in research with young children. *Journal of Early Childhood Research, 17*(1). doi: 10.1177/1476718X18808816.

Boles, J. C., Winsor, D. L., Mandrell, B., Gattuso, J., West, L. L., & Grissom, S. M. (2017). Student/patient: School perceptions of children with cancer. *Educational Studies*. DOI: 10.1080/03055698.2017.1312288.

Brown, J., Blackshaw, E., Stahl, D., Fennelly, L., McKeague, L., Sclare, I., & Michelson, D. (2019). School-based early intervention for anxiety and depression in older adolescents: A feasibility randomised controlled trial of a self-referral stress management workshop programme. *Journal of Adolescence*, 71(1), 150–161. DOI: 10.1016/j.adolescence.2018.11.009.

Bryman, A. (2012). *Social research methods* (4th ed.). New York: Oxford University Press.

Bsiri-Moghaddam, K., Basiri-Moghaddam, M., Sadeghmoghaddam, L., & Fazlollah Ahmadi, F. (2011). The concept of hospitalisation of children from the view point of parents and children. *Iranian Journal of Pediatrics*, 21(2), 201–208.

Cane, F. (2016). Whose problem? Everyone's solution: A case study of a systemic and solution-focused approach to therapeutic intervention in a secondary school. *Educational and Child Psychology*, 33(4), 66–79.

Capurso, M., & Dennis, J. (2015a). *Focus groups. ICTs and education of children with medical needs*. Final public report. LeHoproject. Retrieved from http://www. lehoproject.eu/jdownloads/Public/International%20community/LeHo_-_Focus_Groups_Final_Public_Report_June_2015.pdf.

Capurso, M., & Dennis, J. (2015b). *The Key Educational Factors for the education of children with medical needs*. LeHoproject. Retrieved from http://www. lehoproject.eu/jdownloads/Public/International%20community/LeHo_-_Key_educational_factors_for_the_education_of_children_with_medical_needs.pdf.

Clandinin, D. J. (Ed.). (2007). Handbook of narrative inquiry: Mapping a methodology. Thousand Oaks, CA: Sage.

Department of Health. (2015). *The mental health of children and adolescents*. Retrieved from https://www.health.gov.au/resources/publications/the-mental-health-of-children-and-adolescents.

Department for Health and Social Care. (2015). *Children with special educational needs and disabilities*. Retrieved from https://www.gov.uk/children-with-special-educational-needs.

Edwards, S., Henderson, M., Gronn, D., Scott, A., & Mirkhil, M. (2017). Digital disconnect or digital difference? A socio-ecological perspective on young children's technology use in the home and the early childhood centre. *Technology Pedagogy and Education*, 26(1), 1–17. Doi: 10.1080/1475939X.2016.1152291.

Fels, D., & Weiss, P. L. (2001). Video-mediated communication in the classroom to support sick children: A case study. *International Journal of Industrial Ergonomics*, 28, 251–263.

Garvis, S., Phillipson, S., Belford, N., Kewalramani, S. C., McMahon, K., & Meyer, C. (2016). Time for reflection on maternal child health assessments in Australia: Making a case for a three-way partnership. *Journal of Nursing & Patient Care*, 1(1), 1–4. Retrieved from https://research.monash.edu/en/publications/time-for-reflection-on-maternal-child-health-assessments-in-austr.

Goff, W., & McLoughlin, J. (2017). Working with families in schools. In H. Sukkar, C. Dunst, & J. Kirkby (Eds.), Early childhood intervention: Working with families of young children with special needs (pp. 164–174). London: Routledge.

Groundwater-Smith, S., Dockett, S., & Bottrell, D. (2014). Participatory research with children and young people. London: Sage. DOI: 10.4135/9781473910751.

Grynszpan, O., Weiss, P. L., Perez-Diaz, F., & Gal, E. (2014). Innovative technology-based interventions for autism spectrum disorders: A meta-analysis. *Autism: The International Journal of Research and Practice*, 18(4), 346–361. DOI: 10.1177/1362361313476767.

Hakkarainen, P., Brėdikytė, M., Jakkula, K., & Munter, H. (2013). Adult play guidance and children's play development in a narrative play-world. *European Early Childhood Education Research Journal*, 21(2), 213–225.

Hancock, K., Lawrence, D., Mitrou, F., Zarb, D., Berthelsen, D., Nicholson, J., & Zubrick, S. (2012). The association between playgroup participation, learning competence and social-emotional wellbeing for children aged four-five years in Australia. *Australasian Journal of Early Childhood*, 37(2), 72–81.

Hjorth, L., Richardson I., Davies, H., & Balmford, W. (2020). Exploring minecraft: Ethnographies of play and creativity. London: Palgrave Macmillan.

Huijnen, C. A. G. J., Lexis, M. A. S., Jansens, R., & de Witte, L. P. (2016). Mapping robots to therapy and educational objectives for children with autism spectrum disorder. *Journal of Autism and Developmental Disorders*, 46(6), 2100–2114. DOI: 10.1007/s10803-016-2740-6.

I'Anson, J. (2013). Beyond the child's voice: Towards an ethics for children's participation rights. *Global Issues of Childhood*, 3(2), 104–114.

Johnson, M., Hofmann, K., Hutton, T., & Bignell, D. (2016). *The Malmo platform for artificial intelligence experimentation*. DOI: 10.5555/3061053.3061259.

Kendall, K., & Taylor, E. (2016). "We can't make fit into system": Parental reflections on the reasons why home education is the only option for their child who has special educational needs. *Education 3-13*, 44(3), 297–310.

Kewalramani, S., & Havu-nuutinen, S. (2019). Preschool teachers' beliefs and pedagogical practices in the integration of technology: A case for engaging young children in scientific inquiry. *Eurasia Journal of Mathematics, Science and Technology Education*, 15(12). DOI: 10.29333/ejmste/109949.

Kewalramani, S., Kidman, G., & Palaiologou, I. (2021). Using artificial intelligence (AI) interfaced robotic toys in early childhood settings: A pedagogy for children's inquiry literacy. *European Early Childhood Education Research Journal*, 29(5). DOI: 10.1080/1350293X.2021.1968458.

Kewalramani, S., Palaiologou, I., Arnott, L., & Dardanou, M. (2020). The integration of the Internet of Toys in early childhood education: A platform for multilayered interactions. *European Early Childhood Education Research Journal*. DOI: 10.1080/1350293X.2020.1735738.

Kewalramani, S., Palaiologou, I., & Dardanou, M. (2020). Children's engineering design thinking processes: The magic of the ROBOTS and the power of BLOCKS (electronics). *Eurasia Journal of Mathematics, Science and Technology Education*. DOI: 10.29333/ejmste/113247.

Kewalramani, S., Phillipson, S. & Belford, N. (2020). How parents engaged and inspired their young children to learn science in the later years: A story of 11 immigrant parents in Australia. *Research in Science Education*. DOI: 10.1007/s11165-020-09919-9.

Lahiri, U. (2020). Scope of virtual reality to autism intervention. In U. Lahiri, A computational view of autism: Using Virtual Reality Technologies in Autism Intervention (pp. 83–130). Cham: Springer.

Lombaert, E., Veevaete, P., Schuurman, D., Hauttekeete, L., & Valcke, M. (2006). A special tool for special children: Creating an ICT tool to fulfil the educational and social needs of long-term or chronic sick children. In A. Méndez-Vilas, A. Solano Martín, J. A. Mesa González, & J. Mesa González (Eds.), Current developments in technology-assisted education (pp. 1075–1080). Badajoz: Formatex.

Luckin, R., & Cukurova, M. (2019). Designing educational technologies in the age of AI: A learning sciences-driven approach. *British Journal of Educational Technologies*, 50, 2824–2838. DOI: 10.1111/bjet.12861.

Luczak, H., Roetting, M., & Schmidt, L. (2003). Let's talk: Anthropomorphization as means to cope with stress of interacting with technical devices. *Ergonomics*, 2003 Oct 20-Nov 15; 46(13-14), 1361–74. DOI: 10.1080/00140130310001610883. PMID: 14612325.

McDaid D., Hewlett E., & Park A.-L. (2017). Understanding effective approaches to promoting mental health and preventing mental illness. OECD Health. https://doi.org/10.1787/bc364fb2-en.

McReynolds, E., Hubbard, S., Lau, T., Saraf, A., Cakmak, M., & Roesner, F. (2017). Toys that listen: A study of parents, children, and Internet-Cconnected Toys. DOI: 10.1145/3025453.3025735.

Nass, C., Steuer, J., & Tauber, E. (1994). Computers are social actors. *Proceedings of the SIGCHI Conference on human factors in computing systems*, pp. 72–78. https://doi.org/10.1145/191666.191703.

Newhart, V., Warschause, M., & Sender, L. (2016). Virtual inclusion via telepresence robots in the classroom: An exploratory case study. *The International Journal of Technologies in Learning*, 23(4), 9–25.

Palaiologou, I. (2016). Children under five and digital technologies: Implications for early years pedagogy. *European Early Childhood Education Research Journal*, 24(1). DOI: 10.1080/1350293X.2014.929876.

Palaiologou, I., Kewalramani, S., & Dardanou, M. (2021). Make-believe play with the Internet of Toys: A case for multimodal playscapes. *British Journal of Educational Technology*, 1–18. DOI: 10.1111/bjet.13110.

Phillips, J., Phillipson, S., & Tyler-Merrick, G. (2021). Growing children's social and emotional skills: Using the TOGETHER programme (1st ed.). London: Routledge.

Phillipson, S., Phillipson, S. N., & Kewalramani, S. (2018). Cultural variability in the educational and learning capitals of Australian families and its relationship with children's numeracy outcomes. *Journal for the Education of the Gifted*. DOI: 10.1177/0162353218799484.

Sandbank, M., Bottema-Beutel, K., Crowley, S., Cassidy, M., Dunham, K., Feldman, J. I., … Woynaroski, T. G. (2020). Project AIM: Autism intervention meta-analysis for studies of young children. *Psychological bulletin*, 146(1), 1–29. DOI: 10.1037/bul0000215.

Salamon, A. (2017). Infants' practices: Shaping (and shaped by) the arrangements of early childhood education. In S. Kemmis, K. Mahon, & S. Francisco (Eds.), Exploring educational and professional practice: Through the lens of practice architectures. Dordrecht: Springer.

Schaul, T. (2013). A video game description language for model-based or interactive learning. *2013 IEEE Conference on Computational Intelligence in Games* (pp. 1–8). DOI: 10.1109/CIG.2013.6633610.

Searle, N. S., Askins, M., & Bleyer, W. A. (2003). Homebound schooling is the least favorable option for continued education of adolescent cancer patients: A preliminary report. *Medical and Paediatric Oncology*, 40, 380–384.

Seligman, M. (2011). Flourish: A visionary new understanding of happiness and well-being. New York: Free Press.

Soares, N., Kay, J. C., & Craven, G. (2017). Mobile robotic telepresence solutions for the education of hospitalized children. *Perspectives in Health Information Management, 14*(Fall), 1. Retrieved from https://sap.mit.edu/press-clip/want-learn-computer-aided-design-cad-play-minecraft.

Sukkar, H., Dunst, C. J., & Kirkby, J. (2017). Early childhood intervention working with families of young children with special needs. Routledge. DOI: 10.4324/9781315688442.

Takeuchi, Y., & Katagiri, Y. (1999). Social character design for animated agents. *8th IEEE International Workshop on Robot and Human Interaction* (pp. 53–58). DOI: 10.1109/ROMAN.1999.900313.

Tielen, L. (2003). ICT en kinderen met chronische ziekten. Een studie naar de bijdrage van ICT-voorzieningen aan de kwaliteit van leven van kinderen en jongeren met chronische ziekten. Utrecht: VSB Fonds, stichting Nederland Kennisland.

UNICEF Office of Research – Innocenti. (2019). *Growing up in a connected world: Global Kids online project.* Retrieved from https://www.unicef-irc.org/publications/1060-growing-up-in-a-connected-world.html.

Wade, C. (2016). Therapeutic practice within educational psychology: The discursive construction of therapeutic practice from the perspective of educational psychologists new to the profession. *Educational and Child Psychology, 33*(4), 8–27.

Ziegler, A. & Baker, J. (2013). Talent development as adaption: The role of educational and learning capital. In S. Phillipson, H. Stoeger, & A. Ziegler (Eds.), Exceptionality in East-Asia: Explorations in the Actiotope model of giftedness (pp. 18–39). London: Routledge.

7 Children's agency

Mentally linked and digitally connected, but are they heard?

Introduction

In the current age, technologies such as the Internet of Toys (IoToys) and artificial intelligence (AI) are being developed by commercial developers and companies. In essence, the adults are the ones who build such technologies; thus, there is a need to ensure that these adults consider children's needs and their agency. UNICEF stated that

> The Convention on the Rights of the Child applies to the digital world, therefore, when AI interacts with children and young people. AI systems, must now and in anticipation of the future, be researched, designed, developed, implemented and used to respect, promote and fulfill child's rights as a part of child-centred design.
>
> (Baroness Beeban Kidron, 5Rights Foundation, as cited in UNICEF, 2019)

A review of government policies (UNICEF, 2019) examined 17 ethical frameworks that have been produced by intergovernmental and non-profit organisations, as well as technology companies. It was not surprising that this review again revealed that little is said about children and what they hope to do and learn while engaging with these modern IoToys/AI technologies. OECD (2021) also indicates that more needs to be done to unpack what ethics mean for child rights and specifically for technology-constructed play. Ethics within a broader human rights framework encourage and provide a foundation to build on understanding children's voices and what types of learning or "fun" children encounter during IoToys/AI technologies, such as robotic toys play.

Consequently, this chapter aims to report on children's voices and perceptions of what they think and do with IoToys during play. By reporting on children in this way, this chapter addresses both the gaps and opportunities to put child rights at the heart of AI policies and systems development in relation to children's holistic learning and development in ethical and safe ways. Given the rapid pace of technological change, this window of opportunity will be short.

DOI: 10.4324/9781003185840-7

When it comes to ensuring AI works for children, time is of the essence. Hence, the data reported in this chapter from our research conducted in ECE international settings about children's agency, perceptions and voices during playful encounters with the IoToys is critical and timely.

State of the art about AI technologies/ IoToys and children's voices

According to Wohlwend (2016), when young children gain exposure to technology and its methods of interaction over time, they do so by observing others (e.g. adults and peers) engaged in conventional touchscreen navigational practices and get motivated to participate themselves. As mentioned in Chapter 1 of this book, the multimodal (visual, haptic, aural and movement) characteristics of smart technologies (IoToys and robots) and immersive digital games design also facilitate self-taught learning opportunities for children as they test their imagined hypothesis and problem-solving through actions like tapping and swiping (Bailey, 2016). Studies have explored how young children perceive their use of IoToys as toys that talk and listen (e.g. McReynolds et al., 2017), involving children in content control (Ihamäki & Heljakka, 2021). While children typically do not have a role in the design of new technologies such as apps, robots or immersive games, their position as a growing consumer group makes their input increasingly important to the development of technologies they find useful and meaningful. We argue that children can be a part of the design process at each stage of development. Roles such as the user, the tester, the informant and the design partner offer different ways to engage children and iterate based on their feedback (D'Mello, 2021). Research has also been done to understand how parent-child relationships in families shape co-design processes such that sociocultural familial values are also considered by technology creators and industry stakeholders to reshape technologies through co-design (Holloway, Green, & Livingstone, 2013). For example, studies have explored such sociocultural perspectives of parent and teen perspectives on technologies that allow parents to monitor their children (Czeskis et al., 2010).

Reflecting on our research, our goal in this chapter is to investigate the child's agency, voice/s and perceptions of IoToys, the choices children make and the roles they adopt while playing with them. This chapter builds a conversation around empirical investigation of children's interactions with IoToys at homes to a degree where we provide a continuum of research debates in an under-researched area of AI technologies. To that end, we examined the following research questions:

1 How do children interact with IoToys?
2 What are the roles children perceive to adopt during interactions with IoToys?
3 What are children's perceptions of robotic toys they play and interact with?

The international research context and participants of this study

As mentioned in Chapter 2, the three countries in this study have many cultural differences and values that underpin the pedagogy of the education system, their curriculum, policies and the sociocultural perspectives that impact the choices children might make during IoToys play. It is not our intention to present a comparative study, but to investigate the roles children perceive to adopt during interactions with IoToys. This international study reports on children who played with IoToys both at home and at formal ECE settings. Across the three countries, the IoToys used were integrated to varying degrees (see Table 1.1 in Chapter 1). Although there was some degree of familiarity of children with IoToys in the home, no ECE settings owned any prior to the start of this study. IoToys across countries varied depending upon available resources and funding, and the toys used were specifically bought for the study based on negotiations with the educators and parents of each setting and the potential educational benefits they might have for children. These benefits described by Mascheroni and Holloway (2017) are as being engaging, encouraging playful learning (i.e. coding, language and mathematical skills) and promoting collaboration, physicality and imagination, with their pre-programmed functions allowed a blending between the physical and online environments and context in which the children lived.

Ethics

Although the ethics of the project have been discussed in the introductory chapter, it is important here to explain that the project was guided by principles of participatory research. Children's participation was voluntary, with parents and staff being advised that children's lack of engagement was a reasonable finding and not to force participation. Ethical procedures were ensured to seek educators', parents' and children's consent and assent, being mindful that the observation sessions were not intrusive and the consultation questions suited the child's opinions, while respecting the types of interactions they might have had with the IoToys. Pseudonyms have been used for the children, the EC settings and their respective educators and parents. Guided by the work of Chaudron et al. (2017) attention was given to the safety, security and privacy of children's data, and no personal information of children was used. The "Settings Safe Internet Use Policy" was always followed.

Children's voices of play with robotic toys in home settings: Australian study

Three children (aged 4–7 years old) participated in the Australian study. During the 2020–2021 COVID-19 pandemic lockdowns, the Australian study reverted to remote data collection. The robotic toys/IoToys/apps (see Table 7.1) were sent to the children's homes. The children were invited to take part in Zoom-based

Table 7.1 Overview of children's data reported in this chapter from Australia, Norway and England

Country/child's name	Age (years)	IoToys children played with	Data collection
Australia/Myra	5	Osmo, COJI and Lego We do 2.0	Video observations and consultation questions
Australia/Riya	6.5	Alpha Mini, Lego We do 2.0 and Scratch Jr	Video observations and consultation questions
Australia/Niya	6.5	Alpha Mini and Lego We do 2.0	Video observations and consultation questions
Norway/Kristofer, Eirin and Johan	5.5, 4.10 and 5.3	Osmo Monster	Participatory video observations and pictures
Norway/Thea and Johan	5.8 and 5.3	Osmo Monster, Osmo Coding Jam and Osmo Coding Awbie	Participatory video observations, field notes and photos
England/ Neave, Elliot, Harry and Albus	4.3, 4.5 5 and 5.3	Osmo Newton Osmo Words Osmo Monster Cosmo	Observations, videos, photos and field notes

storytelling and story-making sessions every Friday evening for about eight weeks. Parental consent was sought for the children to take part in the study. Not all children came to all weekly live sessions because it was made clear that taking part in the sessions was completely voluntary and based on child's readiness and interest to come, thus adhering to a child-centred learning approach. A private WhatsApp group was also set up for parents to communicate with each other and reflect upon their children's play and interactions with the robotic toys. Parents were also invited to share the audio-video recordings of their play interactions with the IoToys, if it was feasible for them. The researchers ensured that the child's voices, wonderings and thoughts would drive the agenda for the following week's live play session. At the end of the eight weeks, the children were consulted for about 10 minutes to reflect upon their play experiences, their perceptions of robotic toys and the expectations they had if they were to play with the robots in the future in their own preschool/school setting. The consultation questions were as follows:

1   How did the robots work? Did you ask them questions? Did you ask them to play with you?
2   What did you like about the robots?
3   What would you talk about with the robot?
4   What would you build for the robot?
5   Do you think the robot can remember what you say to it?
6   Is there anything else you would like to share about your play with the robots and the other apps you have been playing with?

Children's voices in ECE settings: Norwegian study

Eight children (aged 4–5 years old) and two pedagogical assistants and one kindergarten teacher participated in activities that included *Osmo Monster, Osmo Coding Awbie* and *Osmo Coding Jam* during the period spring 2019 to autumn 2020. The activities were planned once a week by the educators and included both free play and exploration by the educators and planned activities. Parental consent was sought, but children's participation was voluntary and the children were free to pull out from the activities at any time. The researcher was participating often actively in the activities, especially after the first time as the children were used to her presence. Consequently, the researcher was often asked by the children for assistance in the planned activities or in the exploration of the Osmo. That provided the opportunity for unplanned discussions between the researcher and the children which were covered by ethical approval as it was clearly stated that it was in our intention to ask some questions that they will emerge when we are in the field. These "unofficial" conversations gave the researcher an insight on children's views about Osmo and what they think about using it in play (see example in Theme 4 story).

The key questions emerged during these conversations between the researcher and the children are as follows:

1   Do you like to play with Osmo?
2   What do you like about Osmo most?
3   Do you think you like to play with Osmo more often?

Children's voices of play with IoToys in home settings: English study

The data reported in this chapter were collected in four households. All the households were having IoToys and thus were selected. The researcher was visiting each household for two to three hours a day per week for a period of a year (February 2019–March 2020). During these visits, observations, videos, photos and field notes constituted the key methods for collecting data. Unfortunately, the data collection was stopped during the lockdown period caused by the Covid pandemic, but the parents of the children kept sending the researcher messages via WhatsApp with short videos on how children were playing with the IoToys. However, after a while and as the lockdowns became longer, the parents eventually stopped sending these videos.

There were four children ranging from the ages of 4.4 to 5.3 at the start of the project. The observations took place during children's play times within the home environment. As part of the ethical approach, it was important that the researcher showed sensitivity in children's spaces and private places, so the researcher always asked whether the children wanted to be observed. All observations were shown to the children afterwards, and all pseudonyms were agreed with the children.

After every observation, the children were asked about their play when engaging with IoToys. The questions that emerged were as follows:

1 Did you enjoy playing with Cosmo/Osmo?/What did you not like playing with Cosmo/Osmo?
2 What were your favourite parts?
3 What have you created with Cosmo/Osmo?
4 What other toys are your favourite ones?

Data analysis

To analyse the multimodal data, we used an approach associated with grounded theory (Glaser & Strauss, 1967) in which we developed a set of themes, via an iterative process. We first transcribed the audio-video observations and children's voices and analysed the children's answers to our structured questions. Each researcher then independently coded each of the set of interviews in their respective country, while iteratively developing a codebook through discussions with the rest of the research team. We conducted member checking of each other's transcripts, codebook and iterating until we began to see broader themes in children's responses. Conflicts between coders were resolved through discussion to arrive at full consensus of the emerging themes.

Findings

We present our findings in the form of narratives as stories within the themes, which aim to reveal children's voices inclusive of their emotions, wonderings, interests, imagination and creativity while engaging with the IoToys. Children's interactions and communication of ideas and experiences during play and in response to the interview questions are captured as stories because they depict lived experiences (Clandinin, 2007). The interpretation of children's stories is done both explicitly and implicitly, to make meaning from not only what was spoken or from the child's actions/body gestures, but also the meaning behind their words or what remained unspoken (Clandinin, 2007). This involved closely analysing children's interactions with their adult in the environment as well as the "virtual" interactions with the robot or the digital play characters within the digital game/app that fostered the learning. Although we present the themes separately, as will be shown, the themes are intermingled as during children's play episodes children moved to all these different roles.

We found the following themes:

- Child as digital observer and digital motivator;
- Child as tactician;
- Child as explorer;
- Child as designer.

Theme 1: Child as digital observer and digital motivator

From digital observer to digitality motivated to digital tactician

Analysis of the data showed that children spent time observing their siblings or adults when they were playing not only with IoToys but also with other digital devices and asking questions about their uses as shown in the observation below from the English data.

> Harry is observing his older brother when he plays Butterfield 1 in the PlayStation. The game is about a battle and Harry's brother plays with his friends online. Harry asks questions about the game and his brother willingly answers him, but not at all times, ignoring him when the "moment" of the game becomes "heated".
>
> Harry then picks up OSMO and chooses the creative kit. He is designing a battlefield and is lying on the floor on his belly. He pauses the digital drawing and starts looking at the drawing. He raises up his half leg in the area moving it in cycles. He inhibits his play on OSMO and asks his mother for a cereal box. His mother asks why he wants it and said that he wants to make an armour. He uses scissors to cut two sides as semi-circles, then asks his mother to tie it around his chest. He finds a sword and wears a knight's helmet and starts a battle on his own, pretending he is a soldier (Figure 7.1), going up and down the stairs, then ends up in his bedroom where the IoToy was and falls pretending he is "dead" [sic] (Figure 7.2). He gets up and says: "Haha! I have another life"

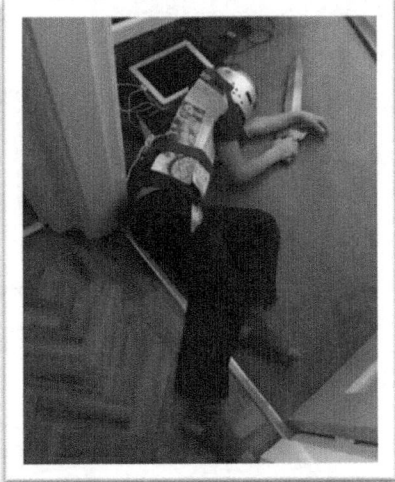

Figure 7.1 Harry pretends he is a soldier   *Figure 7.2* Harry pretends he has died

Then he picks up Cosmo and the cubes and creates a "battlefield", using his drawing where he starts his own battle either chasing Cosmo or being chased by Cosmo. The staircase of the house became a mountain and once on the top of the stairs he pretends he is falling (as one of the soldiers who fall from a mountain on his brother game). He starts shouting "Cosmooooo help, help".

In this instance, we can see that Harry started as an observer and was then motivated to use IoToys to create his own play (tactician). The start of his play and elements of his play were based on what he has observed when his brother was playing with the PlayStation.

Digital motivator

In the case of the Norwegian observations (adopted from Kewalramani et al., 2020), three children are using Osmo Monster with the presence of two pedagogical assistants (Figure 7.3). That was the first time the group of children were introduced to Monster, for which all instructions were provided in the English language. Two of the participant children (Kristofer and Eirin) in this observation are monolingual Norwegians, and the third child, Johan, is bilingual with English as one of his mother languages and Norwegian as his second language. When the participant pedagogical assistants Marianne and Christina are introducing Osmo Monster to the children, the following dialogue occurs:

Figure 7.3 Children collaborating in Osmo Monster play

MARIANNE: [addressing to the children] Wait, wait, you must listen what Monster says

CHRISTINA: What language is he talking?

JOHAN: I understand, I understand, he speaks English! He says that we will have an adventure

MARIANNE: What is an adventure? [Adventure pronounced in English]

JOHAN: We will go on a trip.

KRISTOFER: You must help us understand what he says.

JOHAN: We will go in a door [door pronounced in English].

MARIANNE: Does anyone want to draw a door? [door pronounced in English]

The children continued to work together to draw, and the multilingual child had the opportunity to translate and interpret the language to English. Initially, only two of the children were actively involved (Johan and Eirin); the third child Kristofer was observing the other two and seemed uncertain as he claimed that he could not draw anything other than a potato. After a few minutes, Kristofer found motivation to play with the others. The play Osmo Monster is the digital motivator for playing. During the Monster activity, the multilingual child, Johan, was given the opportunity to demonstrate his competence as an interpreter for the other children. Johan was leading the activity by using his knowledge in English and became the mediator for the play. This experience was positive for Johan as he provided a motivation factor for him. On the other hand, Kristofer had the opportunity to follow Johan's instructions, to observe Eirin and Johan interact with the IoToy, before he decided to participate actively. When he felt more confident about the activity, he was motivated to participate. Time was important for Kristofer, and it was an aspect for his participation. These child-child interactions made play with Osmo Monster in a way possible for the three children. The role of the Osmo Monster as drawing back from a leadership role gave the opportunity for motivation to be developed.

In the above examples, we can see that when children are in the sphere of a digital play landscape, they hold several roles where the entanglement of digital and non-digital is evident.

Once the children were interested in tasks with IoToys, they appeared to be in control, choosing with which task they would engage. The self was in motion in terms of their cognitive, physical and affective aspects, bridging "the gap between real events in the changing world and the imagination within one's head" (Preissler, 2006, p. 233) as in the examples above. This epitomised to us the agency and voice/s in children's play with IoToys. Despite research cautioning that technologies physically constrain children (Miller et al., 2017), the analysis of the play episodes of children revealed that physical movement was present and children's bodies were in motion in relation to the IoToys; for example, moving their legs according to the music of the robot, intentionally moving their body according to the movements of the character in the activity and running after the robot or using fine motor cross movements to build blocks.

Depending either on the elements of the task of the IoToy (such as the colours, images, speech, speed of internet connection or the difficulty of the task), children used their body to

- Express emotions (happiness by raising their hands up or frustration by hitting their head);
- Solve a problem by moving pieces of the IoToys to resolve a task;
- Walk and balance their body to facilitate their play with IoToys.

Children, based on the observation of others' use of technology, facilitated progression to be motivated where children engage with them. For example, in the case of Harry, his observations from his brother's play came into action to use the IoToy as an object beyond its intended functions within the child's own structure, as Nikolopoulou (1993) described.

Just as we were interested to investigate children's agency when playing with IoToys, equally we were interested in researching how children engage with IoToys within their surroundings (spaces, places and cultures) as it was considered fundamental to understanding their agency during play. Examining children's play with IoToy indicates how they take the device beyond the initial confined space in which it started and engage with the space around them.

Although critiques of children's use of technology claim that children become passive and limit their agency (e.g. Palmér, 2015; Radesky et al., 2015), we found that play with IoToys was social, reciprocal and cooperative and does not limit their agency. From our research, we contend that arguments based on screen-based research cautioning that is limiting children's agency (Nathanson, 2015; Radesky et al., 2015) should be re-evaluated in line with the context of young children's play with IoToys. Children utilise IoToys in their play by expressing themselves, making meanings, establishing rapports and reliving situations showing their agency.

Theme 2: Child as digital tactician

The story of Myra, girl aged 5 years old

Before Myra started to interact with the IoToys, the Australian researcher had a 10-minute informal discussion with her parents, both mother and father, to understand Myra's prior engagement with technologies. The parents believed that Myra was "tech-savvy," curious to touch buttons and explore the apps (such as Reading Eggs) and familiar with IoToys and games such as Osmo. Myra knew where the home button was and how Osmo, the coding game, worked. Myra's parents encouraged her to interact with the logical thinking techniques while using Osmo in the coding mode. They hoped by using games such as Osmo, Myra would learn how to put things together (in essence basic coding), build resilience and advance Myra's computational thinking skills (e.g. get the carrot or the strawberry to the obstacle course). The parents also encouraged Myra to play with Lego WeDo 2.0 robotic kits, with the hope that she could use such technologies in her preschool class for teamwork and interact with her peers during the building and coding process work. Below is a conversation between the researcher (R) and Myra at the end of the 8-week period of her interactions with the IoToys.

MYRA: Look what I made, a spy bot – press the button sensor that shines light.
R: How did you build it?
MYRA: I built it with mumma. Well we first made the body, then we made the head and then we plugged it in, it's a spy bot, it can spy on people. He says hellooo
R: Wow does it speak as well
MYRA: Not exactly speaks because it's a robot [here we can see that Myra understands the difference between human speaks and robots don't). But it shines light
R: How did you make it work Myra?
MYRA: Well mum connected it to her computer, then we put the blocks and told it what to do, and then pressed go and that is what we needed it to do. But it doesn't work on carpet, only works on floorboards.
R: Which other robot have you played with?
MYRA: Lots of robots
R: Which is your fav?
MYRA: Coji
R: What did you play with it
MYRA: It made different faces and stuff and we emailed Coji to become a spy bot. [the email button is actually the go button to enact the code command given by the child.
R: What about Osmo? Do you like that one better or the robot?
MYRA: Robot
R: Remember the snail robot. How was that one?
MYRA: You just have to build it and it works same as the spy bot [here we see Myra enjoyed building and constructing artefacts more than the coding game Osmo]
R: Which other robots would you like to build?
MYRA: Mia and Max. I would like to help them build robots. [Mia and Max are the characters in the Lego We Do App]
R: Tell me why your bot shines light? What is inside it?
MYRA: You press the button that has a battery. And these two help it to shine light. Mummy and I put the blocks together and when it sees some pass by it sings happy birthday in Chinese [Myra demonstrates her voice singing Happy Birthday song in Chinese].
R: Would you like to play with spy bot at school with your friends
MYRA: Yes, we can have a spy bot race [Myra makes actions of bot actions as if racing]

In this story and consultation sessions with Myra, it is evident that robotic toys and tangible coding games such as Osmo that operate via apps encourage Myra to tactfully play with the IoToys and developed an interest to construct and design robots (such as spy bot) rather than giving Myra a "sugar rush" during IoToys tactful play. Myra tended not to give up, persist and ask her mother for help to bring her imagined spy bot to fruitful creation. Myra indeed was a tactician, partly because she was exposed to technology play since the age of two. In fact, her interests in becoming a digital tactician because of building robots only grew as she realised through the multimodal interactions how robots can perform the actions (speak, move and sing) and can be controlled through coding and its processes. With a few robotic creations (see Figure 7.4 for spy bot creation) under her belt, Myra explored on her own terms and the individual space that was afforded by the Lego pieces and computer use became a safe space for her to tactfully discover the features of the robot. Based on the previous coding strategies that worked, this allowed Myra to construct her own meaning and perceptions of how robots work, thus bringing real-world concepts of how robots work into real-life action.

Theme 3: Child as digital designer

Story of Riya and Niya, girls aged 6.5 years old

Before the COVID-19 pandemic began, this play episode was captured among three girls playing with the robot Alpha Mini. However, the consultation sessions with the children occurred via Zoom-based conversations. The Australian researcher had provided the children with a demonstration of how Alpha Mini works, and then the girls explored through free flow play interactions, taking turns to code the robot. One child Riya gave the command for Mini (the robot) to sing and dance the "Twinkle Twinkle Little Star" song. Mini's voice singing the song got the girls excited, and they started dancing and mimicking Mini's steps. Another girl, Niya, made Mini burp and "fart" [sic] because the storyline the girls had co-created was that Mini had too many cupcakes, too much food at the party. Children saw and understood how robots work through a series of block commands put together. Researchers encouraged them to see the different types of commands – for example, voice commands, such as performing Tai Chi. Alpha Mini rolls its eyes and starts Tai Chi actions. All children are in awe that robots listen to voice commands. Niya expressed that her robot has ears too and listens. After the play session, the children were asked to draw their own robot and what they would like it to do. Children made posters of their robot drawings and presented their robot features as an oral presentation over Zoom. Below is the set of conversations about children's robot creations.

NIYA: Today I programmed a robot. I learnt how to code a robot. I built one too last time using Lego. My designed robot can make drawings. Some things that Mini can't do. And some other things that mini can – actions like dance. Mine can dance too. My robot has a sensor that senses light so it doesn't get scared.

R: So what is it your robot called

NIYA: It is an artificial intelligent smart robot.

R: How come it is intelligent?

Figure 7.4 Myra as a digital tactician while coding of spy bot

NIYA: Because it always knows and listens to our command. So it is intelligent.
R: Do you enjoy the programming?
NIYA: Yes.

Riya shares her robotic creation with her peers.

R: Today I learnt how to code a smart robot. And how to make it dance and do yoga.
R: How did you make it talk.
RIYA: We did some actions using the iPad.
R: What can your designed robot do?

RIYA: I have a robot. My robot can colour using a pen.
R: What's is the difference between your robot and Mini
RIYA: Mine sings, dances.
R: How does it do all those actions? Why does it happen?
RIYA: Because it is intelligent. I like coding, when a robot records the sound and
     does action. And also listens and speaks.
R: What is the best part you like about this mini robot
RIYA: That it can fart.
R: What else?
RIYA: It can dance, yoga and I enjoyed coding it

Designing is considered a main feature of cognitive activities because it is a process of child's critical reasoning related to knowledge construction (Erduran, Simon, & Osborne, 2004). This relation is very strong according to Osborne (2010): "critique is not, therefore, some peripheral feature of design thinking, but rather it is core to its practice, and without evaluation of what we learn and design or create, the construction of reliable knowledge would be impossible" (p. 464). In Riya-Niya's perceptions, we see how the child's interactions with the AI robotic toys led to hyperreality perspectives becoming real when the child acted as the controller of robot actions, which informs their own embodiment, actions and mental thinking. The robotic toys allowed for free flow play without getting "stuck" in a game or a story that needed to have a specific outcome. As such, Riya and Niya's interactions with the robot were not being caught in a game or story loop, allowing the two girls to ask questions and design stories based whenever they liked (see Figure 7.5). To support Riya-Niya with such flexible interactions and responses to non-predetermined questions, the toy was required to enable free flow play that included socio-dramatic elements of children's storytelling. This enabled Riya to use the coding platform that also had visually appealing integrated instructions. Through trial and error, the girls naturally learnt how robots work and what they can do. This then sparked their creativity to become digital designers and adaptors, thus needing no explicit advance demonstration of robotic features that can colour using a pen or perform yoga poses, thus providing a continuum for children to become a digital designer and adaptor.

It must be noted, however, that Riya's perceptions of AI robots were shaped by her previous encounters with the technology such as Scratch Jr App. Riya's previous interactions and learning about intelligent technologies included coding using animations and creating animated stories, watching robots from television, movies and conversations with parents. All these help children to develop an opinion of the nature of these devices. Their personal interactions with the devices, apps and coding platforms also shape their opinions. However, Riya's perception of what AI features could support her understanding of using the coding app safely and keeping privacy information safe was yet to come. Through robot and coding interactions and related AI platforms, children learn about rule-based systems, but to a lesser extent about how to use it safely and keep their data safe. We know that robotic platforms give continuous feedback on a child's actions and reasoning

Figure 7.5 Riya-Niya's coding with AI robot, Alpha Mini

through movement, voice including voice recognition, and sound. However, there is a need to devise a curriculum and related strategies to help adults to reinforce the AI concepts presented in such IoToys/robotic toys and lead to children's comprehension of them (McReynolds et al., 2017).

The ways in which the child perceives the game/app/robot as an interesting object of investigation is an area under-addressed in the research literature. For this reason, we suggest that playing and communicating with robots indicate most of the digital design schemes, and dispositions happen through firstly making predictions, which is child's hypothetical reasoning. This then allows the child to understand the concept of "from cause to effect." The fact that Mini performed songs, danced and did Tai Chi hooked children's hypothetical reasoning that acts as a stepping stone to designing their own robotic creations. Reclaiming early problem-solving dispositional learning includes offering children opportunities to learn digital technologies. As an early digital designer and adaptor, Riya embodied different positions of literacy as she encountered each new digital experience of interpreting the visuals, giving codes and commands within varied social contexts. She actively participated, first as an observer of a demonstration on the iPad app and the robot and again through independent discovery and exploration. Finally, in their role as a digital adaptor and their perceptions of what robots can do and how, Riya and Niya demonstrate to us that young children's meaningful digital experiences are important additions to their learning dispositions and the development of educational repertoires.

Theme 4: Child as a digital play explorer

Two children (Thea, 5.8, and Johan, 5.3) are on the table with Osmo Awbie. The educators have given the children the opportunity to play alone with Osmo Awbie (the children had participated before in a planned activity by the educators where Osmo Awbie was introduced). The researcher is sitting next to the children observing (Figure 7.6).

Figure 7.6 Children as digital explorers

THEA: Let's start Awbie! I can click on the start button.

JOHAN: Can we continue from where we stopped last time Thea?

THEA: I think so!

THEA: (to the researcher): Can you come and help us to continue the last game?

RESEARCHER: Yes, of course. You know, Osmo saves your previous games.

JOHAN: Really?? I like that! I don't have to start from the beginning.

THEA: There, there it is! (points at the picture)

RESEARCHER: Yes, it is that.

JOHAN: I like Awbie. He is fun.

RESEARCHER: Thea, what do you think about Awbie?

THEA: I think he is sweet! He eats a lot of strawberries.

RESEARCHER: Yes, you are right. He loves strawberries it seems like.

THEA: That's why he is running after them.

RESEARCHER: Johan, you like Awbie you said. Why?

JOHAN: Last time we played with Awbie, I helped him eat many strawberries and I got many points.

RESEARCHER: So both happy!

THEA: Today it is my turn. He will have a big belly (points at her belly).

RESEARCHER: Would you like to play more often with Awbie?

JOHAN: Yes! but then he will be so fat that he will not fit in the screen!

RESEARCHER: Do you really think so?

THEA: And his belly will explode!

The story from this conversation between the researcher and the children showed that children seem to be engaged in playing with Awbie. They mention that they like to feed Awbie with strawberries and would like to play more often with him. Children reflect that if they played more often with Awbie, it would mean that he might become fat from all the strawberries. For children, Awbie is a part of a play scenario in a multimodal learning context (Yelland & Gilbert, 2017) and is being explored as a real partner in this play context. Awbie represents a character that can be "really fat if you feed him many strawberries."

IoToys thus provide children an opportunity to explore the possibilities of a variety of dimensions of play (Kewalramani et al., 2020). Children's play can be inspired by IoToys and can be expanded in different contexts. Children's voices related to how IoToys can be an exploration aspect in new play scenarios, and new opportunities are important in order for children to experience engagement, excitement and joy (Letnes, 2016).

Conclusions and limitations

The types of robotic toys/apps/games employed in our study had a diverse range of features. This study provides a robust foundation for how IoToys, for example, robotic toys and the play interactions occur in ECE classrooms/home settings in Australia, England and Norway. We provide evidence as to how IoToys offer a symbiosis of different roles that children embody that spur creativity, design and tactful thinking and communication. Integrating IoToys play acts as a conduit for children's digital learning repertoires and activates design thinking through visualising and adapting the interactions encountered during IoToys play. This creates a culture for children to become multiple digital experts to guide and support the future design of technologies. Policymakers should be aware, however, that all of these connected devices, such the AI robots, may share issues when children interact with them, including privacy concerns and the appropriateness of content. For instance, while Alpha Mini was designed to have child-safe answers and actions, not all toys or devices may be designed to take the same precautions (McReynolds et al., 2017).

Thus, we argue that we should seek an understanding of children's digital lives and the roles they hold during play with IoToys, in the context they occur ("what-is"), if we want to capture children's realities, agency and voice/s. We propose that creating technologies that allow spaces for children should position themselves within the lived digital era. For this to happen, there is a need for an epistemological discussion on how we can achieve a creation of play which bridges commercially driven IoToys and children's agency. It is important that any discussion on the use of IoToys, to entail the sensitisation of children's play habits and lives and focus on fostering of children's agency and voice/s, focuses on *how* children play with IoToys.

Finally, we reflect on the limitations of this study which was conducted with a relatively small sample size, with limited demographic diversity. Because the observations and consultation sessions were conducted via Zoom and some in person, our data collection relied on parents' discretion of sending the data they wished to include in the study. The fact that we did not randomise the order in which children played with the toys may have affected their impressions and interactions. There may also have existed potential priming effects in the initial questions from the parents that could have led children to share their ideas that were only fruitful and positive interactions with the IoToys, and as such we do not have data of children discussing privacy concerns. We also recognise that privacy decisions in a home setting may be different from those that children follow in an ECE setting. Despite these limitations, however, we consider this work represents an important first look at child interactions and voices and choices made while interacting with these AI toys, particularly from a children's perspective of the types of roles they embody and adapt, and we hope that it will inspire future and ongoing work in this space. Our findings also bear implications on developing robust theoretical perspectives to understand factors around children's AI-related technology perceptions and put measurable solutions in place using rigorous methodological innovations.

Recommendations: Elephants in the "AI room" and implications on AI/IoToys-producing industry

As intelligent machines become more social and more informative, it is important that children develop both an understanding of how machines work and a sense that they can build their own "artificially intelligent" machines (Williams,

2018). Our hope is that this work is useful to educators and parents, as well as for companies building AI-interfaced toys for children's use. Using the findings of this study, we pose the following recommendations:

1 Capacity building in the AI ecosystem that involves child's perceptions and voice:

There is a need to educate a range of stakeholders in the AI ecosystem on child rights. UNICEF (2019) suggests that urgent attention should be paid to developing training materials, ensuring effective delivery and offering continued support for capacity building of children, parents/caregivers and teachers to have a basic understanding of AI systems and how they affect people. People, including young children, need to be taught how to be conscientious users of technology. Various strategies to educate the direct users and affected communities of AI should be provided in preschools/schools or in out-of-school programmes by developing partnerships with popular television shows and campaigns by social media influencers to build awareness of AI issues. Some populations, such as those living in rural areas, are hard to reach through conventional channels. Engaging with the local officials and community figures of those populations can spark creative communication tactics.

2 Prioritise research and knowledge so that policies, guidelines and implementation are informed by evidence:

UNICEF (2019) has identified that any research must be based on child participation wherever possible. Participants agreed that research and findings from applying principles in practice should be shared as widely as possible to help us all make sense of emergent AI issues. Such knowledge sharing could be in the form of case studies, lessons learned and policy briefs which impact on children's dispositional learning and digital competencies when planning and deploying AI systems.

3 Including diversity for children and developmentally appropriate practice with children when designing, developing, deploying and using AI systems:

When creating AI systems for children, we need to consider including perceptions of paediatricians, educational specialists and child psychologists. We must also include child voice, views and experiences of child as co-researcher when developing a child's understandings around data privacy protection while using "household" robots. With the relatively recent appearance of IoToys in homes, relevant research on listening devices in the home can be found in studies of household robots such as Alexa and Siri, which may share interaction and privacy characteristics with devices. Communicating with parents about the privacy and security properties of these toys may also increase their willingness to allow their children to play with them (Williams, 2018).

Another important aspect that AI technology toy creators should keep in mind is the activity design in keeping the activities hands-on and personable to the child (Holloway et al., 2021; Molenaar, 2021). Children may or may not need hands-on and/or multisensory learning (Good, 2021); hence, technologies should cater for all abilities; whether it incorporates sound, movement or touch, children of all abilities should have the opportunity to become digital designers, explorers, adaptors and tacticians. Therefore, an AI curriculum for these children should be more like building with blocks than playing with a computer. The IoToys and robots should be able to either blend or make real-world concepts and ideologies visible for children of all abilities to be able to adapt to their physical world. Although the children in this study wanted to use the robots for coding and some entertainment such as music and dance, they saw many more areas where robots could be applied. Children were able to give real-world examples of their designed AI robots. In essence, these perceptions came from their past knowledge and interactions and children could see that intelligent technology was all around them and that it manifested itself in many ways (functional, entertaining, creative and assistive). It is important that children not only see these examples but also have an opportunity to interact and tinker with them as well (OECD, 2019). In the future, AI devices should be more transparent and trainable so that children are more able to relate their own cognition to them. For example, toys such as Alpha Mini should try to explain to children why they could not help (e.g. did not hear them perform the song/dance) and have the ability for children to create a feedback loop for the children to teach each other. These kinds of changes will give children more agency when interacting with AI technologies.

References

Bailey, C. (2016). Free the sheep: Improvised song and performance in and around a Minecraft community. *Literacy, 50*(2), 62–71.

Chaudron, S., Gioia, R., Gemo, M., & Holloway, D. (2017). *Kaleidoscope on the Internet of Toys: Safety, security, privacy and societal insights.* Retrieved from file:///C:/Users/skewalramani/Downloads/Kaleidoscope_on_the_Internet_of_Toys_Saf.pdf.

Clandinin, D. J. (Ed.). (2007). *Handbook of narrative inquiry: Mapping a methodology.* Thousand Oaks, CA: Sage Publications. DOI: 10.4135/9781452226552.

Czeskis, A., Dermendjieva, I., Yapit, H., Borning, A., Friedman, B., Gill, B., & Kohno, T. (2010). *Parenting from the pocket: Value tensions and technical directions for secure and private parent-teen mobile safety.* In *Symposium on Usable Privacy and Security (SOUPS).* Retrieved from https://cups.cs.cmu.edu/soups/2010/proceedings/a15_czeskis.pdf.

D'Mello, S. (2021). Improving student engagement in and with digital learning technologies. In *OECD education outlook: Pushing the frontiers with AI, blockchain, and robots.* Paris: OECD. Retrieved from https://www.oecd-ilibrary.org/sites/8a451974-en/index.html?itemId=/content/component/8a451974-en.

Erduran, S., Simon, S., & Osborne, J. (2004). Tapping into argumentation: Developments in the application of Toulmin's argument pattern for studying science discourse. *Science Education, 88*(6), 915–933.

Glaser, B. G., & Strauss, A. L. (1967). *The discovery of grounded theory: Strategies for qualitative research.* London: Aldine Transaction.

Good, J. (2021). Serving students with special needs better: How digital technology can help. In *OECD digital education outlook 2021: Pushing the frontiers with AI, blockchain, and robots*. Paris: OECD. Retrieved from https://www.oecd-ilibrary.org/sites/40fa80d3-en/index.html?itemId=/content/component/40fa80d3-en.

Holloway, D., Green, L., & Livingstone, S. (2013). *Zero to eight: Young children and their internet use*. London: LSE and EU Kids Online.

Holloway, D., Willson, M., Murcia, K., Archer, C., & Stocco, F. (Eds.). (2021). Young children's rights in a digital world, children's well-being: Indicators and research. DOI: 10.1007/978-3-030-65916-5_15.

Ihamäki, P., & Heljakka, K. (2021). Internet of Toys and forms of play in early education: A longitudinal study of preschoolers' toy-based learning experiences. In D. Holloway, M. Willson, K. Murcia, C. Archer, & F. Stocco (Eds.), *Young children's rights in a digital world. Children's well-being: Indicators and research*, Cham: Springer. DOI: 10.1007/978-3-030-65916-5_15.

Kewalramani, S., Palaiologou, I., Arnott, L., & Dardanou, M. (2020). The integration of the internet of toys in early childhood education: A platform for multilayered interactions. *European Early Childhood Education Research Journal*, 28(2). DOI: 10.1080/1350293X.2020.1735738.

Letnes, M.-A. (2016). *Barns møter med digital teknologi. Digital teknologi som pedagogisk ressurs i barnehagenbarns lek, opplevelse og læring* [Children's encounters with digital technology. Digital technology as an educational resource in kindergarten children's play, experience and learning]. Oslo: Universitetsforlaget.

Mascheroni, G., & Holloway, D. J. (2017). *The Internet of Toys: A report on media and social discourses around young children and IoToys*. Retrieved from https://leibniz-hbi.de/en/publications/the-internet-of-toys-a-report-on-media-and-social-discourses-around-young-children-and-iotoys.

McReynolds, E., Hubbard, S., Lau, T., Saraf, A., Cakmak, M., & Roesner, F. (2017). *Toys that listen: A study of parents, children, and Internet-connected Toys*. DOI: 10.1145/3025453.3025735.

Miller, J. L., Paciga, K. A., Danby, S., Beaudoin-Ryan, L., & Kaldor, T. (2017). Looking beyond swiping and tapping: Review of design and methodologies for researching young children's use of digital technologies. *Cyberpsychology: Journal of Psychosocial Research on Cyberspace*, 11(3), article 6.

Molenaar, I. (2021). Personalisation of learning: Towards hybrid human-AI learning technologies. In *OECD digital education outlook 2021: Pushing the frontiers with AI, blockchain, and robots*. Paris: OECD. DOI: 10.1787/2cc25e37-en.

Nathanson, A. L. (2015). Media and the family: Reflections and future directions. *Journal of Children and Media*, 9, 133–139.

Nikolopoulou, A. (1993). Play, cognitive development, and the social world: Piaget, Vygotsky and beyond. *Human Development*, 36, 1–23.

Organisation for Economic and Collaboration Development. (2019). *Artificial intelligence in society*. Paris: OECD.

Organisation for Economic and Collaboration Development. (2021). *OECD digital education outlook 2021: Pushing the frontiers with artificial intelligence, blockchain and robots*. Paris: OECD.

Osborne, J. (2010). Arguing to learn in science: The role of collaborative, critical discourse. *Science*, 328(5977), 463–466.

Palmér, H. (2015). Using tablet computers in preschool: How does the design of applications influence participation, interaction and dialogues? *International Journal of Early Years Education*, 23(4), 365–381.

Preissler, M. A. (2006). Play and autism: Facilitating symbolic understanding. In D. Singer, K. Golninkoff, & K. Hirsh-Pasek (Eds.), *Play=learning: How play motivates and enhances children's cognitive and social–emotional growth* (pp. 231–250). Oxford: Oxford University Press.

Radesky, J. S., Kistin, C., Eisenberg, S., Zuckerman, B., & Silverstein, M. (2015). *Parent views about mobile device use around and by young children: Implications for anticipatory guidance.* In Abstract presented at the Pediatric Academic Societies, San Diego, CA. Retrieved from http://www.abstracts2view.com/pas/view.php?nu=PAS15L1_2195.2.

UNICEF Office of Research – Innocenti. (2019). Growing up in a connected world: Global Kids online project. Retrieved from https://www.unicef-irc.org/publications/1060-growing-up-in-a-connected-world.html.

Williams, R. (2018). *PopBots: Leveraging social robots to aid preschool children's artificial Intelligence education.* [Masters thesis]. Massachusetts Institute of Technology.

Wohlwend, K. (2016). Toddlers, touchscreens, and tablet technologies learning "concepts beyond print. In R. J. Meyer & K. F. Whitmore (Eds.), *Reclaiming early childhood literacies: Narratives of hope, power, and vision* (pp. 64–74). London: Routledge.

Yasmeen, H., Bunt, A., & Young, J. E. (2014). *Involving children in content control: A collaborative and education-oriented content filtering approach.* In *Conference on Human Factors in Computing Systems 2014 (CHI).*

Yelland, N., & Gilbert, C. (2017). Re-imagining play with new technologies. In L. Arnott (Ed.), *Digital technologies and learning in the early years* (pp. 32–43). London: Sage. DOI: 10.4135/9781526414502.

8 Conclusions

The changing playscapes of early childhood education

The changing playscapes

This chapter aims to summarise the key findings and discuss them in line with the axiological lenses that underpinned this research. It will then reflect on these lenses and examine the importance of a home-grown theory to conclude that the transfunctionality of IoToys is already changing the playscapes of young children. As technologies continue to develop, these playscapes will continue to evolve.

To begin, in Chapter 2 there was a comparative analysis of the curricula in the three countries where, in contrast to Norway, it was demonstrated that for Australia and England the inclusion of technology into the curriculum has not yet been fully implemented. Our conclusion (and concern) is that in a digitalised world, we cannot afford anymore to exclude technology from ECE and especially haptic technology such as IoToys and AI. As emphasised in the book, the importance of technology became even more apparent during the lockdowns caused by the Covid pandemic as it enabled us to stay connected and continue the education of young children via technology integration as an instructional practice even for young children.

What became evident, however, was the notion of a digital divide as households did not have the technology to support their children. This is a continuing concern for policymakers and educators, for as we have demonstrated in this book, access to appropriate technologies is central to children's learning in the future. As shown in Chapter 3, most young children use a repertoire of IoToys and other technologies at home, but their use in their educational settings is limited or none. That creates a divide between home and ECE which, we argue, establishes an urgent need at policy and practice level to examine the role of the technology and how it can effectively be integrated in ECE. Such ambitions do not come without certain implications, and it is recognised, firstly, that resources need to be available. The technology, especially IoToys and AI, is not coming without a cost, so financial investment in ECE needs to be prioritised. Secondly, the pre-service and in-service training of early childhood educators needs to be reviewed to include digital competencies. As technologies are developing, and we cannot predict the directions and functionalities that technology will take,

DOI: 10.4324/9781003185840-8

it is important to prepare educators for the unknown by paying attention to the quality of the training that is based on research evidence.

As shown in Chapters 4 and 5 when technology is integrated and the educators are confident about its uses or are not afraid to use it to scaffold children's learning, then the creation of a learning environment becomes creative, imaginative, supportive, interesting, stimulating and facilitating playful learning, such as STREAM-based play. Thus, we propose that emphasis should be placed on digital competencies on the training for educators that are appropriate for ECE. The European Framework for the Digital Competence of Educators defines this in broad terms and focuses on educators being "confident, critical and creative [in the] use of ICT to achieve goals related to work, employability, learning, leisure, inclusion and/or participation in society" (Redecker & Punie, 2017, p. 90).

The framework proposes six areas that focus on different aspects of educators' professional activities:

1 "Area 1: Professional Engagement: Using digital technologies for communication, collaboration and professional development.
2 Area 2: Digital Resources Sourcing: Creating and sharing digital resources.
3 Area 3: Teaching and learning: Managing and orchestrating the use of digital technologies in teaching and learning.
4 Area 4: Assessment: Using digital technologies and strategies to enhance assessment.
5 Area 5: Empowering Learners: Using digital technologies to enhance inclusion, personalisation and learners' active engagement.
6 Area 6: Facilitating Learners' Digital Competence: Enabling learners to creatively and responsibly use digital technologies for information, communication, content creation, wellbeing and problem-solving" (pp. 15–16).

Such universal frameworks, however, do not come without critique and especially that the terms are used in a narrow way, either, for example, referring only to internet skills, touchscreen technology or media literacy not taking into account the haptic technologies (e.g. Ala-Mutka, Punie, & Redecker, 2008; Ilomäki, Kantosalo, & Lakkala, 2011) or ignoring the cultural differences that shape ECE curricula approaches in different countries. Hence, we propose that any discussions about the digital competencies of early childhood educators need to be rooted in the peculiarities of ECE, as was shown in Chapter 2, and be home-grown to meet the requirements of the ECE setting.

While the research-based evidence in this book acknowledges how ECE is recognised as having an essential role in children's everyday life, we are yet to meet the opportunities and challenges of new contexts and landscapes of play and learning. As demonstrated throughout the book, this is caused by an important challenge that is related to teachers' and parents' views, attitudes and practices of new technologies in ECE. Having a pedagogical vision and competence to identify the dilemmas, potentials and opportunities is an important condition to meet children's perspectives in the use of IoToys, both in preschool and in home settings. Children's own experiences with IoToys are where everything starts with developing the understanding of how children use and make meaning of IoToys. Thus, research should explore children's interactions with IoToys, with each other and their teachers in order to investigate the role of each one of them in a holistic approach to learning, play, development and technological formation in terms of critical thinking and reflection.

Chapter 6 discussed how technology and especially robotic one can help children with diverse needs with their emotional literacies. The research discussed from Australia and England showed that the integration of robotic technology can act as a therapeutic tool that not only supports but also meets children's needs as children feel in control despite their diverse needs. Although both projects discussed were small scale and more research is needed in this field, we suggest that further implications lie in upscaling and upskilling early childhood (EC) educators and providers who work with young children with diverse needs. Our research showed that if we provide opportunities for children to interact with AI robotic toys in play-based programmes, it fosters social-emotional competencies. As it has been shown elsewhere in this book, EC educators and other providers need to capitalise on children's intentional emotional practices, including facial expressions, gestures and vocalisations evoked through play with robotic toys, that actively contribute to the dynamics of children and this needs to be extended to children with diverse needs. Children co-develop with adults and peers in EC contexts, and through transfunctional play, social-emotional interactions are fostered by IoToys.

The discussion in Chapter 7 revealed that when children engage in technological play, they hold several roles and are in control due to the nature of the haptic technology. As this technology is transfunctional, children have greater agency than with touch screen technology which can be static, not multifunctioning and having a need for the children to stay within the perimeters of the application in use. Based on the analysis of observations when children are using IoToys we show that children can be digital observers and motivators and these roles are interchangeable, even within the same play episode. Contrary to some views that have been discussed in this book that children have very limited control when using technology, our research showed that children are skilful tacticians, explorers and designers. Such a finding enables us to suggest that technology designers need to "hear" the voice/s of children and work in collaboration with children, rather than designing technology that has adult-oriented views of children's needs and interests. We have demonstrated through our transnational research findings that child-oriented learning is more likely to happen when the children are given opportunities to design their own technologies, with designers facilitating those needs and interests more fully.

As stated elsewhere in this book, the aim of this study was not to be a cross-cultural comparative study, but to examine ways of how IoToys and AI are integrated at home and ECE. Consequently, as explained in Chapter 1, we positioned IoToys as polypronged, transfunctional toys that enable children to engage in playful learning that moves beyond multimodal playscapes to transplayscapes. Examining the evidence of our research in the three countries, this initial theoretical conceptualisation at an abstract level is now supported by our findings. For example, in the observation of Harry (see Chapter 7), when engaging with IoToys, he transcended his house to make it a battlefield, with the stairs becoming a mountain, a box of cereals becoming his armour and the IoToy either his enemy or his co-soldier. Similar examples have been presented in the Australian (Chapter 4) and Norwegian data (Chapter 5), where children when given the space (physical and digital) they became interwoven and transcended into imaginative spaces that served their development of STREAM-based play fostering, for example, literacy, numeracy and spatial reasoning skills.

Such findings suggest that as adults while we still make the division of playscapes, children do not differentiate between them. Although as adults we may be under the impression that we know what children think, act and want, this cannot fully be achieved as our understanding is removed from a child's cognisance. We propose, therefore, that we as adults in a child's learning environment should start examining children's engagement with technology beyond any division of playscapes and acknowledge that as adults we will not be able to fully understand children's playscapes. Instead, if we locate children's play and learning in transplayscapes, it should allow us to create environments that can cultivate children's play and learning.

A major feature of this book is the recognition that haptic technology, because of its transfunctionality, offers opportunities to afford trans- and polymodes of tactile, visual, virtual and physical engagement and has much potential to design play-based pedagogy that synchronises and synergises the digital eco-communities in which we now live by exploring the nature of translearning spaces afforded by IoToys play.

To conclude, we propose that if we are to achieve such synchronised and synergised eco-communities, the digital lives of children should be situated in the landscapes that children are creating where "persons" and "things" are not only interconnected but are also transcended to transform children's experiences, play and learning. As adults we need to be alert to the notion of continuous changing playscapes, with such thinking urging us to challenge a "static" approach to our pedagogy that is not only a *how* to do approach but one that is also a *why, what* and for *whom* pedagogy that understands the transplayscapes of children in the 21st century.

Feed forward: Next steps for researching children's transplayscapes

Pedagogues in children's everyday learning environments should understand and recognise that technological "affordance" is not a property of the environment (or any part of it) – nor a psychological property of an individual (or cultural group). So, affordance should be understood consistently as children always create, recreate and expand affordances available to them in the interaction of both the individual and the environment (and its components/artefacts). The digital landscape is given, but the change in the lives of our young generation will be rapid, so before seeking for new forms of play (digitally), why not continue examining whether children exhibit developmental characteristics of play when interacting and engaging with digital devices, IoToys and robotic toys. Researchers should continue the debate and further explore children's characteristics of emergent learning such as patterns of behaviours that are associated with transplayscapes when children are engaged with IoToys. Feeding forward from the findings discussed in this book, we suggest researchers use the following questions as a descriptive analysis for understanding children's transplayscapes afforded by IoToys.

- Type of activity (e.g. gross, motor, construction, games, fantasy and imagination)?
- Who initiates (e.g. child and adult)?
- Who facilitates (e.g. child, adult and IoToy)?
- Who inhibits/ends the activity?
- What are the affective components?
- What are the social components?
- What are the cognitive components?
- What are the narrative components?

References

Ala-Mutka, K., Punie, Y., & Redecker, C. (2008). *Digital competence for life-long learning*. Luxemburg: Office for Official Publications of the European Communities. Retrieved from http://ftp.jrc.es/EURdoc/JRC48708.TN.pd.

Ilomäki, L., Kantosalo, A., & Lakkala, M. (2011). What is digital competence? *European Schoolnet (EUN)* (pp. 1–12), Brussels. Retrieved from https://helda.helsinki.fi/handle/10138/154423.

Redecker, C., & Punie, Y. (2017). *European framework for the digital competence of educators: DigCompEdu*. Luxembourg: Publications Office of the European Union.

Index

Note: Locators in *italics* represent figures and **bold** indicate tables in the text

ABER *see* Arts-Based Educational
  Research
adaptive play styles **42**
ADHD *see* attention deficit
  hyperactivity disorder
AI *see* artificial intelligence
Alexa 4, 143
all-inclusive teaching and learning
  framework **105**
Alpha Mini **128**, 136, 139, 142;
  robot **8**
Anzalone, S. M. 5
Arendt, H. 83–84
Aristotle 84
artificial intelligence (AI) 4, 22, 52,
  125; ecosystem 143; family 5;
  interfaced technologies 23; robotics
  101; robotic toys 4, 106, 142–143;
  virtual worlds 116
Arts-Based Educational Research
  (ABER) 103–104
attention deficit hyperactivity disorder
  (ADHD) 99
audio-video link 101
Australia: Australian digital technology
  curriculum 26–27; Australian early
  childhood (EC) sector 99; Australian
  EYLF 56, 119; data analysis and
  findings from 107–108; ECE
  curriculum in 26–27
autism spectrum disorder (ASD) 100
AV1 internet-connected robot 114

Bachelor of Early Childhood
  qualification 57
Beast of Balance **11**
Bednet project in Belgium 101
BERA codes 38

Bers, M. U. 55
binary digital–non-digital debate 41
block-based programming 63
Blue-Bot 87, *88*, 89; robot **10**
Bluetooth 88–89
Bøe, M. 82
Botley the Coding robot activity set **10**
brain development 102
Braun, V. 40, 87
Bsiri-Moghaddam, K. 98
Butterfield 1 131

Chaudron, S. 127
child-centred-initiated pedagogy 1–2
children and IoToys at home 37–38;
  characteristics **43–45**; context
  38–40; data analysis 40; digital
  landscapes 41–46; findings 40–41;
  numeracy skills development *68*
children's agency 125–126; children's
  voices in ECE settings 129; children's
  voices of play with IoToys in home
  setting 129–130; children's voices
  of play with robotic toys 127–128;
  data analysis 130; digital designer
  136–140; digital motivator 132–134;
  digital observer 131–132; digital
  play explorer 140–141; digital
  tactician 132–134; ethics 127;
  finding 130; international research
  context 127; state of the art about AI
  technologies 126
Children's Developmental Play
  Instrument (CDPI) 40
children's digital learning 24–25, 37
children's emotional inquiry and
  problem-solving skills 108–110
children's free play 54

children's social-emotional development 13
children's use of digital technology 12
children's voices: in ECE settings 129; of play with IoToys in home setting 129–130; of play with robotic toys 127–128
child–sibling dyad 107
chronic illnesses 98
Clarke, V. 87
coding exercises 72
cognitive and creative function, robots 53
COJI **128**
Coji robot **8**
collaboration literacy development 72
computational thinking skills 134
computer-aided design (CAD) 100
computer simulation 4
conflicted play styles **42**
COSMO **10, 128**
COVID-19 pandemic 7, 31, 38, 57, 61, 66, 112, 129, 136, 147; lockdown 106, 127; sanitation and quarantining procedures 106
Cowan, K. 54
creative inquiry literacy 63–65
creative learning spiral *80*
creative thinking 79
critical reasoning 138
critical thinking 30, 84, 89
4Cs (children's communication, creativity, critical thinking and collaboration) 23
6Cs (communication, collaboration, community building, content creation, creativity and conduct) 55
culturally and linguistically diverse (CALD) 98
curriculum 22–24; Australia, ECE curriculum in 26–27; balanced/blended way 25; children's digital learning 24–25; component **26**; developmental goals driven 25; development for young children 31; documents 23; England, ECE curriculum in 27–29; framework 28–29; learning goals driven 25; methods and curricula contexts 25–26; Norway, ECE curriculum in 29–30; play-based approach 25
cyber-bullying 78

Dash–Coding Robot **9**
degree of wholeness 41
design-based research (DBR) 56
developmental learning process 24
digital cameras 4
digital competency (DC) frameworks 6, 25, 30, 53
digital designer 136–140
digital devices 2, 12
digital disconnect 37
digital environments 14, 27
digital games 4; design 126
digitalisation 78
digital judgement 83, 93
digital literacy 23
digital motivator 132–134
digital observer 131–132
digital play 79; explorer 140–141
digital tactician 132–134
digital technologies 4, 80; and children's learning and development 25, 31; as third teacher in child's learning environment 15
disorganised play styles **42**
3D printers 100
drones 5
Dýrfjörð, K. 55

early childhood early intervention (ECEI) community service 99
early childhood (EC) educators 149
early childhood education (ECE) 1, 13, 61, 101; Australia, curriculum in 26–27; curricula and instructional practices 25; England, curriculum in 27–29; home, digital disconnect 37; ideology of play 13; inter-multi-disciplinary field 1; Norway, curriculum in 29–30; and pedagogical landscape 24
Early Learning Centres (ELC) 56
Early Years Foundation Stage (EYFS) curriculum 27–28; learning requirements 28
Early Years Learning Framework (EYLF) 26–27
ECE *see* early childhood education
Edwards, S. 13
EECERA: codes 38; Ethical Code of Practice 87
Effective Early Education Experiences for Kids (E4Kids) study 57
E4Kids 57
emotional competencies 99–100

England, ECE curriculum in 27–29
English as an additional language
   (EAL) 57, 98–99
EUKids Online report 78
evaluative function, robots 53
expression of emotions 102

face/voice recognition 5
formation 82
framework plan 83
free play 54

game-based apps 3
game consoles 4
Google Assistant 22
Google search 4

handheld computers 4
hands-on robotic activities 55
haptic technology 4
Havu-Nuutinen, S. 57
Hedegaard, M. 61
Hedegaard's wholeness approach 61
Hello Barbie 5
Hjorth, L. 100
holistic development and learning
   81–82
Holloway, D. 53, 127
home and hospital education
   (HHE) 101
Hreiðarsdóttir, A. E. 55
hubs of techno-learning 6
Huijnen, C. A. G. J. 100
human activity 14
human intelligence 4
humanoid robot Nao 5
hybrid design 3
hybrid learning spaces 1
hypothetical reasoning 139

imaginative play 119
in-car *sat-nav* 4
information communication technology
   (ICT) 27, 102
information security 84
inhibited play styles **42**
interaction analysis 3
interactive AI robotic toys 100
interactive projects 5
internet 14, 87–89
Internet of Toys (IoToys) 1, 4–5, 55,
   125; children played with **128**;
   children's engagement during play 22;
   and children's social and emotional

literacies 7; daily life, integration in
   40; in ECE classrooms 26; ECG
   settings 6; at home 1, 6–7, 38–40;
   permanent connectivity 46; play 100;
   play-type situations 87; play with 1, 7;
   semantic analysis 40; social practice
   78; technology 47; transfunctionality
   of 46, 147; used in households, participants and **39**; *see also* robots
interpersonal relationships 83
IoToys *see* Internet of Toys
IoToys and social-emotional literacies
   98–99; Australia, data analysis and
   findings from 107–108; Australia,
   research from 103–106; children's
   emotional inquiry and problem-
   solving skills 108–110; children's
   social communication and social
   collaboration 110–111; children
   with diverse needs 99–102; England,
   data analysis and findings 113–115;
   England, research from 112–113;
   ethics 107; participants and methods
   106–107; theoretical underpinnings
   102–103
IoToys in early childhood education in
   Norway 78–79; children's meaning
   making 85; children's participation
   in kindergarten's everyday activities
   81; children's play 79–80; critical
   thinking 83–84; digital judgement
   83; digital judgement in children's
   play 93–94; ethical reflections 83–84;
   findings and analysis 86; forms of
   play 80–81; holistic development
   and learning 81–82; internet 87–90;
   method and ethics 85–86; purpose 85
iPad 61, 87

Johnson, M. 100
judgement 83

Kalogiannakis, M. 55
Keeping Connected in Australia 101
Kewalramani, S. 57
Kim, M. 3
Kindergarten Act 81–82
kindergarten children, EAL needs 63
Krüger, T. 82
Kucirkova, N. 80

Lahiri, U. 100
Learning at Home and in the Hospital
   (LeHo) project 101

Learning Resources Zoomy Handheld Digital Microscope **12**
LegoBoost Bot **8**
Lego Wedo 2.0 **128**, 134
Lehesvuori, S. 23
LeHo 102
limbic mammalian system 102
lockdowns 12
Lombaert, E. 102

makerspace learning 1
Markauskaite, L. 3
Mascheroni, G. 127
media players 4
Minecraft 100–101, 108, 116
mobile technology 78
Monster Mo 90–93
motivating function, robots 53
multiliteracies 53
multimodality 1–4, 116, 126; children's engagement in science learning practices 3; interactions 3; learning 2–3, 80; of Robots 67
multimodal play 2, 4, 15, 65, 74, 119, 149

Nao robot 5
national educational policies 25
neurodiverse children 98
Nikolopoulou, A. 134
Norway 29–30; ECE curriculum in 29–30; kindergartens, framework plan for 29–30
Norway, IoToys in early childhood education in 78–79; children's meaning making 85; children's participation in kindergarten's everyday activities 81; children's play 79–80; critical thinking 83–84; digital judgement 83; digital judgement in children's play 93–94; ethical reflections 83–84; findings and analysis 86; forms of play 80–81; holistic development and learning 81–82; internet 87–90; method and ethics 85–86; purpose 85
Norwegian Centre for Research Data (NSD) 87
Norwegian DigiCompEdu framework 119
Norwegian Directorate for Education and Training 84
Norwegian Framework: for Kindergartens 81; Plan for Kindergartens 84

not-for-profit (NFP) organisation 106
number-based concepts 72
Ødegaard, E. E. 82

Organisation for Economic and Collaboration Development (OECD) 23; Health 117
Osborne, J. 138
OSMO **128**, 131; Awbie 140; Coding Awbie 9, **128**, 129; Coding Jam **128**, 129; Monster **128**, 129, 132, *132*; Monster Mo 9; Newton **128**; Words **128**

Palaiologou, I. 38, 103
Papadakis, S. 55
parent–child dyad 107–108
pedagogical directions for technology 27
pedagogical function, robots 53
pedagogy of education system 127
phishing 78
phronesis 84
planning cycle structure 26
play: culture 80; forms of 80–81; psychological functions 46; styles **42**
play-based pedagogy 2, 22
PlayStation 131
Plowman, L. 24
policymakers 117
pornography 78
problem-solving and communication literacy 68–72
problem-solving literacy 23
programming-related concepts 23
psychological dimensions of learning 38

Qobo (snail-looking robot) **8**, 68–72, *71*

Ramnarain, U. 23
real-life social interpersonal interactions 3
remote-controlled toys 4
resilience-building event 116
Resnick, M. 79
revising function, robots 53
r-learning 6
Roblin, N. J. 23
robot-assisted intervention 100
robot-child interactions 100
robot-child play 117
robotics 23, 52; education 53; play 23; reasons for 53–54; STREAM-based play 72; toys 103, 128, 138

robotic technologies in ECE classrooms 51, 57, 61, 99, 101, 104; children's STREAM literacy 55–56; COVID-19 pandemic 61; data analysis 61–63; educational content 72; findings 63; participants and data collection 57–61; research design and context 56; STEM-based play 51–52; STREAM-based play 53–55; STREAM-based play practices associated with creative inquiry literacy 63–65; STREAM-based play practices associated with empathy literacy 65–68; STREAM-based play practices associated with problem-solving and communication literacy 68–72; synergies between robotic integration and STEM-based play 52–53
robotic user interface (RUI) 4
Robot Mouse **11**
robots 4–5, 52, **111–112**, 115; artificially intelligent behaviours 5; coding process 65; digital play 61; family 68; functions 53; storytelling functions 52; toys 55; virtual interactions with 63; *see also* Internet of Toys
robot therapy 100
role-play scenarios 54

sandbox play 80–81
school readiness 28
Scratch Jr **128**
self-reflexivity 84
self-taught learning opportunities 126
Settings Safe Internet Use Policy 127
Shapiro, J. 80
Siri 4, 22, 143
Siry, C. 3
(Smart)phones 4
smart technologies 126
Smart Toy Bear 5
social communication 72
social emotions: behavioural characteristics 103; competencies 100, 106; development 53, 102, 104; health 99; learning 104; well-being 99
social interaction 82; and learning 80
socialisation skills 23–24
social robotic toys 3
sociocultural familial values 126
spatial reasoning 72
Sphero Edu app 64
Sphero robot 63–65, *65–67*

Spin Master Code-A-Pillar **11**
spy bot 135–137
state of the art about AI technologies 126
STEAM education 51
STEM-based play 51–52; defined 51; education 51, 62; synergies between robotic integration and 52–53
Stephen, C. 24
storytelling 54, 61; functions 52
STREAM-based play 51, 53–55, 73–74, 148; children's STREAM literacy 55–56; creative inquiry literacy 63–65; empathy literacy 65–68; literacy opportunities 53; observational protocol and pedagogical steps for robotic integration **58–60**; practices associated with creative inquiry literacy 63–65; practices associated with empathy literacy 65–68; practices associated with problem-solving and communication literacy 68–72; problem-solving and communication literacy 68–72; and robotic technologies 52, 72
STREAM-based practices 62
STREAM (Science Technology Robotics Engineering Arts Mathematics) literacy 52, 55, 62–63; development *56*
synchronous internet education (SIE) 101

talk back 5
teacher-directed learning environments 54
teacher professional learning 16, 73, 116
technology-based gaming platforms 100
therapeutic function, robots 53
third-party services 78
Tielen, L. 102
touchscreens 4, 24, 37; navigational practices 126
toy cars and robots 5
toys-to-life 5
transplay learningscapes 7–15
transplayscapes 150–151
TTS wireless Digiscope **10**

UN Convention on the Rights of the Child 81
UNICEF 143

University Human Ethics Committee 107
unsafe material, accessing 78

Vai Kai **11**
6 values (caring, connection, contribution, competence, confidence and character) 55
Van den Akker, J. 26
Viiri, J. 23
virtual assistants 22
virtual multimodal environments 116
Voogt, J. 23
Vygotsky, L. S. 82

web mapping 13
WhatsApp 128
Willson, K. 53
Wilmes, S. 3
Wu, L. 3

Yelland, N. 2
YouTube 88

Zoom 7; based instructional support 66–67; based storytelling 127–128; video workshops 106